MW00811231

Mattie

Wyatt Earp's
Secret Second Wife

E. C. (TED) MEYERS

hancock
house

ISBN 978-0-88839-628-0
Copyright © 2010 E.C. (Ted) Meyers

Cataloging in Publication Data

Meyers, Edward C.
  Mattie : Wyatt Earp's secret second wife / E.C. (Ted) Meyers.

Includes bibliographical references and index.
Issued also in electronic format.
ISBN 978-0-88839-628-0

  1. Blaylock, Mattie, 1850–1888. 2. Earp, Wyatt, 1848–1929
—Marriage. 3. Prostitutes—United States—Biography. I. Title.

F786.B585M49 2009   306.74092   C2009-906854-0

Printed in Indonesia — TK PRINTING

Editor: Theresa Laviolette
Production: Ingrid Luters
Cover Design: Mia Hancock

*We acknowledge the financial support of the Government of Canada through the
Book Publishing Industry Development Program (BPIDP) for our publishing activities.*

Published simultaneously in Canada and the United States by

HANCOCK HOUSE PUBLISHERS LTD.
19313 Zero Avenue, Surrey, BC Canada V3S 9R9
(604) 538-1114 Fax (604) 538-2262

HANCOCK HOUSE PUBLISHERS
1431 Harrison Avenue, Blaine, WA, USA 98230-5005
(604) 538-1114 Fax (604) 538-2262

Website: **www.hancockhouse.com**
Email: **sales@hancockhouse.com**

Contents

This book is dedicated to my sons,
Scott and Craig

Pale death, the grand physician, cures all pain;
The dead rest well who lived for joys in vain.
— John Clare (1793–1864)

My husband, Wyatt Earp, ruined my life.
— Celia Ann Blaylock Earp

Supposing…supposing…Oh, well!
— Among Wyatt Earp's last words, according to Josephine Earp

The <u>trouble</u> that woman could get herself into!
— T.G. Vynsand, Mattie's great-niece

Author's Note

A history writer's important duty is to present his findings so those who know little, perhaps nothing, of the subject will be able to understand why and how certain things came to pass. Because of this requirement, a history sometimes contains material and comments that may appear alien to the overall theme. Those familiar with the subject tend to look upon these additions as unnecessary. However, to those unfamiliar with the topic such comments and endnotes bring the subject into better focus, making the subject era a little more understandable. For that reason I have included endnotes and five appendices.

    This book is not for those familiar with the darker side of the Earp saga. It is for those unfamiliar with it. It should probably not be read by those who refuse to believe Wyatt Earp had a dark side because their minds are made up and they will not wish to be confused with facts.

Acknowledgments

This book was made possible through the cooperation of many people. I am deeply indebted to Glenn G. Boyer for sharing with me his vast expertise on the Earp clan. Without his generosity, encouragement, assistance, constructive criticism, and his openness with his records, letters and files pertaining to Wyatt Earp that he let me read at leisure, plus photos he loaned me, I would still be stumbling about in the maze of Earp fact and fiction. Mr. Boyer, to my mind, is the definitive authority on Wyatt Earp and his brothers.

I also wish to thank the following people who aided my research:

Roger Myers of Kansas, an astute writer of Old West history, mined Dodge City files (1876–79) for me and emerged with interesting data. He also discovered some exciting things from the Rice County files. His website, www.larned.net/rogmyers/rogmyers.htm, is highly recommended. His periodic articles appearing in *True West* and other magazines are also highly recommended as reading for students of Old West history.

Steve Gatto of Michigan, also a *bonafide* Earp expert, for his help in uncovering the *Root's Peoria City Directory* for the years 1870, '71 and '72. They indicate, with no room for doubt, that Wyatt Earp was in that city during 1872. Mr. Gatto also sent me a list of Peoria's night ladies who graced the courts that year. Several names on the list were Mattie's co-workers.

Ms. Sokolowski of the Peoria Library Research Dept. helped me locate records that reinforced the City Directory information. She was also helpful in assisting me with the city's newspapers.

The Peoria Historical Society for additional information pertaining to life in 1872 Peoria.

Karen Deller and Sherri Schneider of the Special Collections Unit at Bradley University in Peoria who uncovered documents that showed ownership of Haspel House and the roles played by the Earp brothers in its operation.

Susan Sheehan of the Arizona Historical Society in Tucson. Her patience in answering innumerable questions is greatly appreciated. Thanks also to the other staff members. All were helpful.

Nancy Sawyer, archivist at the Arizona State Library, Archives and Public Records, who sent me copies of the inquest into Mattie's demise and the notice of her death from the *Globe* newspaper.

The Kansas Historical Society for assistance with Kansas Census records and descriptions of Wichita in the years from 1870 to 1876.

Vicki Goacher, Records Clerk at the Rice County Court House, sent me a certificate certifying the 1873 marriage of Celia Blaylock to Ed Davis. The certificate proves *conclusively* that there was another Celia Blaylock in Rice County, Kansas and lays to its final rest an erroneous belief that Mattie had left Wyatt Earp to marry a local man named Ed Davis. Celia Ann "Mattie" Blaylock Earp had absolutely no connection with Ed Davis. Besides, the future Mrs. Davis was only sixteen on her nuptial day of January 1.

Kathy L., a Wichita researcher, wants no recognition but deserves some anyway. Kathy dug up some interesting files on the Earps' stay in Wichita — among which was the certainty that Bessie Earp and Mattie Earp were partners in the infamous house at 12 Douglas Avenue. Thank you, Kathy!

Jack Lowell of Tempe, Arizona, over a course of several years, sent me articles from local newspapers that helped me understand the present-day Earp controversy a little better. Thanks, Jack.

Special thanks to Mrs. Tony Gene Heim Vynsand of Humboldt, Iowa. Mrs. Vinsand is the great-granddaughter and direct descendant of Tony May Blaylock DeGroote Heim, Mattie's youngest sister. Thus Mrs. Vynsand is Mattie's great-niece, one of three. Mrs. Vynsand told me of Mattie's (and Sarah's) life and childhood, information she had learned from Tony May. That information shed light on Mattie's reasons for leaving home.

Thanks to Karma Heim Lanning of Reedsville, Wisconsin, also directly descended from Tony May. She told me much about her great-aunt Mattie, put me on the right track to Mattie's grave and was extremely helpful in other phases of the research. She also put me in contact with another of Mattie's great-nieces, Sandy Anderson of Missouri, who in turn put me in touch with the family that has tended Mattie's grave for many, many decades.

I must mention the assistance received from Michael Collett of Globe, Arizona. One morning in 2004 we had a lengthy conversation concerning The St. Elmo Hotel and its probable connection with "Big Nose Kate" Elder. Where Kate was, so was Mattie.

Thanks to Dr. William Urban of Monmouth, Illinois. Dr. Urban gave me valuable information about the infamous gunboats that plied the Illinois River as floating brothels — including the one in which Mattie and Wyatt were arrested in September 1872.

A very special thanks to Mrs. Maria Guzman of Superior, Arizona. She told me where to find, and how to recognize, Mattie's grave. She told me many things not generally known about Mattie's final months. She related particulars of Mattie's life in Pinal handed down over the years through family members. Mrs. Guzman's late husband's great-grandparents, who lived in Pinal, were among those who befriended Mattie. The family has known since 1887 that Mattie Blaylock Earp was Wyatt Earp's wife. Mattie is well known to the Guzman family.

Special thanks also to Ms. Rita Wentzel, Superior's Town Clerk. Ms. Wentzel gave me copies of documents concerning Mattie. Early researchers thought the Pinal documents were lost. Because their attention was concentrated on Florence, the county seat, they missed finding them. Florence officials had, years before, sent the Pinal files to Superior.

Thanks also to Superior's public works director who accompanied me to the old graveyard where Mattie lies at rest. He pointed out places of interest along the way and included a short history of the Silver King Mine.

I also want to thank several persons (who prefer anonymity) of the same area, descendants of original miners who had lived in Pinal. They talked to me about Pinal and, somewhat guardedly, of Mattie through stories told them by family members. Mattie Earp is considered a member of Superior's greater family and, as such, is considered a local treasure.

Thanks also to Hancock House Publishers and the always-helpful Hancock staff. My gratitude is extended to publisher David Hancock who suggested the History Detective Series, of which this book is the first. Many thanks to Theresa Laviolette whose expert editing of the manuscript made it more readable.

I also thank the many persons who over the years replied to my questions placed on various Old West discussion boards on the Internet.

— ECM

Introduction

The search for the woman who had been Celia Ann Blaylock and became Mattie Earp, Wyatt Earp's second wife, was not easy. Her trail, variegated and erratic, led from Iowa, where it started, to Kansas, Illinois, back to Kansas, to Texas, New Mexico, Arizona and California before doubling back to Arizona, where it ended. Finding the trail took many years and uncovered some interesting facts. In Mattie's case trail's end necessarily became the starting point.

Where, why and how the trail ended was known. Not known was the in-between. Where had she been during her disappearance from Iowa in 1868 and her rediscovery in Arizona in 1888? When and where had she met Wyatt Earp? When did she marry him? For that matter, *did* she marry him? The major problem was the almost seventy years that elapsed before her association with Earp was revealed. Seventy years. Plenty of time for the trail to go cold.

If her mystery was to be solved the trail had to be retraced. That meant trying to locate every place she had been, determine how long she had stayed, what she had done and with whom she had been. Much was revealed but Mattie had covered her tracks well. Still missing are several months between 1868 and 1871.

The task forced this researcher to become a history detective, prepared to enter areas researchers often fear to tread. The Old West of the late 1800s can still be a dangerous place and the history detective's task is never easy. Clues are few, original witnesses are long gone and trails are cold. More often than not towns — and the trails that led to them — no longer exist. Sometimes a dusty file hidden in a half-forgotten archive, a family bible or a trunk in an attic is discovered to cast new ideas on an old subject. Mattie's case uncovered several dusty files, nearly all connected with one of the Old West's greatest legends — Wyatt Earp — and therein lay the trouble.

When searching for clues to any Old West character the most contentious issues are the legends and myths that created heroes from outlaws, gunfighters and lawmen. Sometimes the hero was all three at the same time — or is alleged to have been.[1] The legends are often fiercely protected. Descendants and relatives are usually reluctant to discuss their ancestor's misdeeds and some even refuse to discuss the good deeds. But relatives pale beside the legend's loyal devotees. Old West characters have aficionados who object to seeing their heroes dissected, deflated, debunked or diluted. Few are willing to accept new facts. Covering their eyes and ears they staunchly deny that those they have placed on the pedestal had imperfections of character. They pout and attempt to execute the messenger. Researching the Old West is not a task to undertake if one hopes to avoid offending anyone.

Many of the admiration groups have struggled for years to suppress any mention of Mattie Blaylock as part of Wyatt Earp's life. Earp, they insist, had only two wives. Mattie was merely an acquaintance, a saloon girl he tried to reform.

"Do not confuse us with facts," they bluster, "our minds are made up."

Despite such difficulties there were new clues here and there to be unearthed. Mattie left several. One was her long-forgotten grave. Sometimes the history detective stumbles across a ghost town's graveyard and discovers the clue that supplies an answer. In the case of Mattie's mystery the clue was not a headstone, but a family who had tended the grave for decades. They shed light on darkness as it were.

Once the history detective has all available information the task turns to sorting and three files emerge — the "F" files —

Factual, Feasible and Fictional. Fictional is always the thickest. Mattie Earp's case was no exception.

Factual evidence is gleaned from census forms, newspapers, court and police records; and even these are often suspect. Citizens of that era were not always truthful with census takers. Some fudged ages or past history, many avoided the census, and those who could not often gave false names, ages, places of birth and occupations.

Newspapers printed what reporters perceived as facts. Editors, swayed by reputation, political affiliation or membership in a lodge or a church, printed nonsense to make a likeable rogue appear innocent or a charismatic crook seem a good choice for public office. Rival newspapers printed accounts contradictory and confusing. For example, in 1881 *The Epitaph* and the *Daily Nugget*, both Tombstone newspapers, printed accounts of the gunfight at the OK Corral. A reader could easily wonder if the participants had perhaps staged two gunfights that day so divergent were accounts. Court records and police files contain more aliases than correct names. Court reporters spelled names phonetically, which causes problems for researchers.

Feasible items mean just that: an item sounds true — but… If information might be true then further study is warranted, sometimes leading to facts. More often it ends in supposition. Presenting fiction as fact remains the greatest flaw in many who write of the Old West. Failure to identify a feasible item as speculative is no less fraudulent. A feasible item, unproven, must remain speculative regardless of how much sense it makes.

Fictional items abound in matters of the Old West. Many a "true story" shows only misplaced hero worship. Fiction permeates the era, particularly in illustrations of the gunfighter/ lawman.

James Butler Hickok (1837–76), better known as "Wild Bill" Hickok,[2] is a case in point. For decades he was acclaimed as a two-gun marshal. In reality his tenure as a lawman was limited to a few months as city marshal of Abilene, Kansas. Mostly he was a failed gambler, a drifter and a sullen, paranoid killer who shot first and explained later. The reason for his shoot-first policy proved to have been a degenerative eye disease that was bringing on blindness. Hickok knew if his condition became known others would be encouraged in attempts to kill him to make names for themselves.

Bat Masterson (1853–1921)[3] also became a legend during his lifetime. Actually, he wrote much of it himself. He was indeed a lawman, but first and foremost he was a gambler and saloonkeeper. He did not slay dozens of bad men as early biographers claimed. His only recorded victim was Sgt. Melvin A. King,[4] whom he shot in a Sweetwater, Texas saloon. King discovered Molly Brennan, a saloon girl he considered his woman, partying with Masterson. Enraged, he stormed into the saloon and began shooting. His shots all went wild except one, which killed Molly. Masterson returned fire.[5] King died. No one, his fellow troopers included, mourned his death.[6]

Fiction writers, in particular those who wrote during the 1930s, created the legends of the two-gun, fast-draw lawmen. In fact the fast draw was generally unknown to Old West gunfighters. Aim well and shoot once was the rule. Few put faith in pistols. Most preferred a shotgun as their weapon of choice.

The legend of Wyatt Earp is an example of fiction run amok. Earp was brave, cool, dauntless and a competent lawman.[7] However, his champions, in their haste to create, improve and perpetuate his legend, ignore his knaveries going to great lengths to hide them. One of those knaveries was his contemptible treatment of Mattie Blaylock, his second wife and his darkest secret.

Mattie's story is bitter. It is not one of a determined pioneer woman helping her husband scratch a living from the hard earth. Neither is it of a fearless woman raising her children in a sod hut on the unrelenting prairie. It is quite the contrary. She and Wyatt had no children and farmed only one season. She hated farm life as much as he did. It was one of the few things they had in common.

Mattie was a woman who ran away from her farm home as a teenager and embraced the sporting life.[8] During her twenty years in the west she sought happiness, but attained sorrow.

Her final act was to ring down the curtain on her personal tragedy.

Mattie was also a woman of several identities. She was christened Celia Ann but her family called her Celie. The Earps knew her as Celie and Mattie. Court and police records list her as Sally and Sarah. She was calling herself Mattie when she met Wyatt Earp.

For four of her first five years with Wyatt she was a brothel resident. During their remaining six years she spent three working the saloons whenever their fortunes took a downswing. Earp was beginning to enjoy success as a gambler from 1874 but no "man of the green cloth,"[9] regardless of skill, wins every hand every time.

It would be nice to think Mattie's almost eleven years with Wyatt Earp was a great romance but it was not. It would also be nice to think that he, following the sad, untimely death of his first wife, had found comfort with Mattie and had fallen in love with her. That was not the case either.

Their association originated when their tryst gave rise to a straightforward business proposition. Wyatt, at least primarily, considered Mattie a business partner. Their marriage followed but holds uncertain status. It remains unknown if they wed formally or by common-law union. Mattie adamantly insisted they had formally married and Wyatt's post-desertion behavior supports her averment. The only proof lacking is a marriage record. It may be eventually found in some forgotten file of some forgotten Justice of the Peace or within some long-lost church book. If Mattie ever told anyone the place or date of their marriage the confidant apparently never mentioned it to anyone.

That Mattie was a "soiled dove[10]" was no impediment to marriage with Wyatt. In the Old West men often selected wives from brothels or saloons. Bat Masterson's marriage to a Dodge City saloon girl lasted many years.[11] Neither was it uncommon for wives, sisters and daughters of gamblers — and lawmen — to augment the family income working in saloons and houses of ill fame. James Earp, Wyatt's eldest brother, married Nellie Bartlett Ketchum, a well-known madam. After they married she continued in the trade. There are those who think Morgan

Earp's wife, Louisa "Lou" Houston, may also have dabbled in the business. Alvira "Allie" Sullivan, Virgil Earp's third and final wife, has gaps in her history that might produce interesting details. It is not without reason that in Kansas the Earp boys were referred to as "the fighting pimps." The epithet, incidentally, was contemporary and not coined after the Earps left the state.

Mattie was not blameless in her tragedy. In many ways she was its genesis and her behavior accelerated its conclusion. She could be a terrible nag and a splenetic shrew; one or both of these traits, plus her addiction to whiskey and opium, certainly factored into Wyatt's decision to desert her.

Mattie's later use of laudanum[12] was caused by her quest for relief from intense pain. It was long thought her pain was caused by cancer or the final, fatal phase of a sexually transmitted disease.[13] In an ironic twist, her worst pain came from a more prosaic source, which is more thoroughly covered in chapters 23 and 24.

Mrs. Wyatt Earp, by and large, led a lonely life. From 1876, her husband, absorbed in gambling and other pursuits, had little time for her. When they moved to Tombstone in 1879 Mattie took up domesticity in a small house they co-owned and hoped for better days. In 1881 a dark-eyed beauty of questionable morals, named Josephine "Sadie" Marcus, set her sights on Wyatt and Mattie became a hindrance. Though they continued to live in their little adobe hacienda, Wyatt's departure was but a matter of time.

After Wyatt abandoned Mattie he never once mentioned having a second wife. All memory of her was drowned in a sort of convenient Lethe.[14] So far as Wyatt (and the third Mrs. Earp) was concerned Mattie did not exist. Both took such extraordinary pains to erase her memory that she remained a secret for years.

Mattie was not the only person victimized by Wyatt's memory lapses. When Earp met author Stuart N. Lake about 1927, and his biography became a possibility, he developed convenient amnesia. Entire periods of his life suddenly became blurred, especially those from 1870 to 1874. He declined to discuss those years at any length citing the fog of old age. Lake never knew Wyatt had been in Illinois for most of 1872. That period in Wyatt's life remained so well hidden full details did not emerge until 2003.

Lake's knowledge of Earp's life prior to 1874 was so exiguous he could not properly account for his hero's activities. He wrote the missing years ad lib until he could safely have Wyatt resurface as a lawman in Wichita — and then he got the particulars wrong. Relying on stories Wyatt told him — and Wyatt told some whoppers[15] — Lake embellished the stories and invented some of his own.[16]

Mattie received no commentary in Wyatt's biography because he never mentioned her and Lake apparently did not interview pioneer residents of Wichita; Fort Griffin, Texas; Las Vegas, New Mexico; Dodge City or Tombstone. In 1928–30 there were still a considerable number of people who had known Mattie Earp. Lake may have avoided such interviews on purpose. He would not have wanted to know about her. He was creating a nonpareil, squeaky-clean hero, a champion for the ages. Such a paragon cannot have a woman like Mattie as his wife. How to deal with her would have been a daunting challenge.

Lake would have been tempted to suppress Mattie. The first Mrs. Earp, a respectable woman, could be mentioned. The current Mrs. Earp, despite youthful notoriety, but alive and acknowledged as Wyatt's wife, had to be considered. Mattie on the other hand was unknown, lacked respectability and could be safely suppressed. Withholding Mattie to accommodate his legend-in-the-making may have been the course he chose. It is not outside the realm of possibility.

Earp died before the book, titled *Wyatt Earp, Frontier Marshal,* could be scheduled for publication. Josephine, fearing Mattie might yet be discovered, attempted to stop the book's publication with the same zeal she had mustered all along to discourage Wyatt from having the book written.[17] She twice applied for court injunctions against Lake and his publisher. For two years she fought hard but, in 1931, her final suit was dismissed. *Frontier Marshal* was off and running.

In fact, Earp's life would likely have raised little interest had he and Lake not found each other. In a case of a writer seeking publishable stories narrated by a real-life gambler/ lawman, Earp, an elderly man craving fame, filled the bill. Neither was concerned that the stories were not absolutely true, only that they were publishable. If heroes are made, not born, so also are legends. Earp became a legend only because Stuart Lake made him so.

The legend that Lake created enjoyed immediate popularity, perhaps because Wyatt had died. Americans have always preferred dead heroes.[18] Living heroes are usually ignored, often shamefully, until after the funeral. Once *Frontier Marshal* made the bestseller list the legend took hold and prospered. Other writers quickly discovered Wyatt Earp and they fictionalized his adventures even further. Eventually Hollywood and television advanced his reputation as a straight arrow, two-gun, quick-draw, law-and-order peace officer. He was converted to a paragon of virtue and defender of American values. He was elevated to US Marshal to enhance the legend.

If Lake portrayed Earp as a latter-day knight, Hollywood and TV canonized him. Like a western Saint George, slayer of dragons and protector of pilgrims, Earp roamed dusty trails smiting lawless men who terrorized towns and tormented honest folk. Garbed in the black suit of the professional gambler, hat shielding his ice-blue eyes from the high noon sun, his marshal's badge glinting with reflected sunlight, right hand hovering lightly above the butt of his Colt Peacemaker, Marshal Wyatt Earp tamed the west. It was no problem that Hollywood and TV lacked the facts. These were easily replaced with exciting fictions. When legend clashed with truth, Hollywood extolled the legend.

Earp's fame grew but still there was no mention of Mattie. Those who had known both Wyatt and Mattie, and knew the role she had played in his life, said nothing.[19] Even those who would have welcomed a chance to unhorse a popular knight breathed not a word. The result of this bewildering silence was that Mattie remained completely forgotten. Not until 1953 did her tragedy begin to slowly unfold.

The intent of this book was originally to portray Mattie and investigate the tragedy of her life. Earp was cast only as a bit player in Mattie's greater drama. However, the deeper her troubled life was mined, many disturbing facts emerged. Original casting became impossible to follow; and when a visit to Peoria divulged some long forgotten files, the picture changed completely. Those files revealed Wyatt and Mattie had, to borrow an old vaudeville phrase, foolishly decided to "play Peoria." Their act bombed, but the files meant Wyatt could no longer remain hidden in the chorus line. Had they stayed away from Peoria Wyatt's function in Mattie's story might have remained essentially short paragraphs and footnotes.

Having gotten to know Mattie over several years of research I am in many respects sympathetic to her. She made no lasting mark on history. Her claim to fame is that she was both Wyatt Earp's second wife and his darkest secret. Nonetheless, she was a real person with real dreams who chose first the wrong path and then the wrong man. It happens in life. The final result was that her life, her husband and history all treated her shabbily. That she knew the inner sanctums of brothels is never in doubt, but we must not judge her by present-day standards, a fault far too prevalent nowadays. Mattie lived in a different time. In the Old West there were no social programs, no welfare, no food stamps, no shelters for women in need. There were no safety nets for a woman like Mattie. Abandoned, alone with no place to turn, she saw no choice but to resume the life she thought she had escaped.

In 1887 her downward spiral dropped her into a doomed mining town called Pinal and within six months she was dead. During the official enquiry into her demise witnesses told of the intense pain she suffered during her final months. She died broken-hearted, lonely, forlorn, unloved and unwanted in a grubby little house in a grimy, dying town. Having descended to the bottom rung of the social ladder, her very survival depended on men who knocked on her door in the night.

Mattie deserved better. Perhaps this book and what it reveals will counter some of the misinformation and malicious fiction that has been written against her. Perhaps a few followers of Old West history will reflect and say to themselves, "Mattie Earp was doomed by circumstance. Seeking happiness and decent treatment from the man she loved she got neither. Put simply, she fell for a bounder."

— E.C. MEYERS, Victoria, BC, 2007

Prologue

He is always included when mention is made of famed lawmen such as Ed, Jim and Bat Masterson, George Scarborough and Thomas J. "Bear River" Smith. He is mentioned when gamblers such as Luke Short and "Canada Bill" Jones are discussed. He was eighty-one when he died in bed in Los Angeles on January 13, 1929. He was afforded a deluxe funeral with many in attendance. There was an eloquent eulogy. Tom Mix, Hollywood's reigning cowboy star, was one of six pallbearers.

His name was Wyatt Earp.

Her husband became a legend but for over sixty years she remained a dark secret. For her seventeen years of married life, the final six as a deserted wife, she led a vagabond existence traveling with him from town to town and state to state. With one exception, she never lived three complete years in one town. She did not live into old age. She departed this world on July 3, 1888 an embittered, ailing, alcoholic prostitute addicted to opium. She was afforded only a pauper's grave with few in attendance at the interment. There was no funeral service. There was no eulogy. There were no pallbearers. She was thirty-eight years old.

Her name was Mattie Earp.

CHAPTER 1

The Road to Fort Scott

I owa was in winter's icy grip when Celia Ann Blaylock entered this world in January 1850,[1] the third child and second
daughter of Henry Blaylock (1817–1877) and Elizabeth "Betsy" Vance Blaylock (1825–1899). Henry and Betsy had come
to Iowa from Indiana about 1846, had obtained a farm eight
miles south of Fairfax, and through hard work and no small
sacrifice were developing it into a paying proposition. For the
next eighteen years Celia, called Celie by family and friends,
called the farm home until one fateful day in 1868 when she
and her younger sister Sarah[2] (1853–1906) ran away to discover the world.[3] What they ultimately discovered was likely not
what either had expected.

Family sources indicate Celia's reason for running away
was to escape strict parental discipline. Henry and Betsy subscribed to the fundamentalist concept that children be allowed
little leeway. Timeworn adages "spare the rod and spoil the
child" and "children should be seen and not heard" were
taken literally. Such discipline was not at all out of line in the
1860s. Indeed, it was advocated — and practiced — by religious leaders and school authorities. At Sunday school she
was instructed in Biblical parables and taught that the Ten
Commandments must be her guide.

Celia was schooled to the standards of the era. She attended
the local schoolhouse where she learned to read and write. She
read books about large towns and great cities and she wanted
to live the adventures such places provided. She dreamed of

stylish clothes and of dwelling in a large house. For Celia a little education would prove dangerous.

The Blaylock farm was in no way isolated. Located near a main wagon road passing strangers often stopped to ask for directions and a cup of cool water. If they seemed hungry food was offered, for it was an age when strangers were not turned away.

It was also an age when neighbors helped each other and were cordial. Several farms approximated the Blaylock acreage, and social gatherings, community picnics and barn dances were held from time to time. The Blaylock girls enjoyed dancing, so when the fiddles struck the first notes they joined the squares. Celia's early teen years were not devoid of social contact.

Henry's canvas-topped buggy and sturdy horses eased the burden of travel. From spring to autumn the family made regular trips to Fairfax to purchase supplies and renew acquaintances. The family was not unknown in Fairfax.

It was also an age of early marriage. Females married, on average, at seventeen; males a few years older. The eldest Blaylock daughter, Martha Jane, followed the trend. When she was seventeen she married Charles Probst. The wedding ceremony was performed on July 01, 1860. Ten-year-old Celia and eight-year-old Sarah were both in attendance.

Both Celia and Sarah inevitably attracted the attentions of young farm lads. By age fifteen Celia had become an attractive girl of medium complexion with auburn tresses that were usually kept in long ringlets. Sarah was prettier than Celia. Of a fairer complexion her long, sandy-blond hair was usually in braids. Both girls were of average height, about five feet, three inches. Both could turn on the charms if they wished, but there is no indication either was overly flirtatious. In fact family sources suggest Celia generally ignored her would-be suitors for, according to them, she considered farm life so boring she harbored no desire whatever to become a farmer's wife. She foresaw little joy in a lifetime spent toiling in the fields, tending snorting hogs and milking cows. Producing a child every two or three years was not on her agenda either.

Sarah apparently shared her sister's loathing of farm life. There seems little doubt that neither intended to marry into a farm family, regardless of wealth or acreage owned, although Sarah eventually did. Life, the girls decided at an early age, had more to offer. Meanwhile, they did their chores, attended the social events, teased the boys, and dreamed of the day they would escape. Such dreams, however, were one thing and reality quite another, so as time passed the dream remained only in their minds.

Then one day in 1868 the opportunity to bolt hearth and home presented itself and the two threw their destinies to the fickle winds of fate and were gone. Celia's baby sister, Tony May, who passed down the family history to her children and grandchildren, indicated that her sisters left very suddenly. Because she was only two years old at the time, her details are sketchy[4] and the month of their departure remains unknown. Tony May probably learned a certain amount from Sarah, whose memory of the events would naturally be selective; and she would also glean details from her parents who would also censor forbidden information. It seems unlikely the girls left prior to March or as late as October. Even in 1868 teenage girls were not inclined to leave home with winter's grip still on the land or the north wind readying once again to drive autumn into exile.

As in many cases of this sort the decision to flee may have been little more than two girls balking at the idea of spending another humid summer amidst corn rows while fighting off wasps, gnats, hornets, mosquitoes and voracious horseflies. That they left without financial help or parental approval seems unquestionable, especially the latter, considering the bitter reception Sarah received when, months later, she presented herself at the farmhouse door, thoroughly chastened, deeply remorseful and begging forgiveness.

While the circumstances of departure are not fully known it is certain they had run away knowingly trading the security of home for uncertain futures. The road they chose led them to different ends. Mattie's road, however circuitous, led to an early grave while Sarah's path made a U-turn. After about a year Sarah became disillusioned and returned in cheerless homecoming to her outraged parents, shocked relatives and tongue-wagging neighbors.[5] Henry and Betsy took Sarah back, but held her in disgrace. For all concerned she was "spoiled goods."[6]

Whether the girls had given any thought to destination or employment is also unknown. Destination may not have been a high priority, but they had little time to decide their means of support. By virtue of experience in household chores they may have sought work as seamstresses or laundry workers. It is known that Mattie was a reasonably skilled seamstress, but whether she was skilled enough for employment is not known. They might also have sought work as cooks, perhaps in a camp setting as many buffalo hunters and woodcutters worked from camps. Perhaps they sought work as maids in some town's hotel. They may have enquired about employment in cafes. Whatever they may have applied for, they quickly discovered their chances of finding worthwhile employment was poor. The labor pool for women in the west of 1868 was neither wide nor deep. A dollar for a ten-hour workday was a normal wage and the workweek was six days. They would have quickly discovered the west was not a worker's paradise.

Logic suggests they proceeded west immediately. Horace Greeley's oft-misquoted advice to the nation's youth, "Go west young man and grow with the country"[7] also held appeal for young women. Both girls knew their choices of destination were hardly narrow. Five large centers, strung north to south along the Kansas/Iowa/Missouri boundaries gave them a deal of latitude. Kansas towns of Atchison, Lawrence, Fort Scott and Leavenworth, Iowa's Ohio City and Missouri's Kansas City and Lamar[8] were all bustling with post-war activity, but offered little work for women.

Fort Scott may have originally figured in their plans. An essential stop on the trail west, and the chief commercial center for nearby Lamar, the town was booming with westbound pilgrims. It would hold attractions for two young women seeking their fortunes. That, added to other clues available, makes it a very logical destination. There is, however, no indication that Fort Scott was an immediate choice.

In fact, there is nothing suggesting Sarah was ever there at all; and no local records indicate Mattie's presence until 1871 when her residency is established because she attended a photographer's studio to pose for a photo. In fact there are no records to indicate where the pair had been during their months together. Wherever they ventured in 1868 and 1869, they traveled quietly and stayed out of trouble. What had the girls been up to and where had Mattie been between the day she said goodbye to Sarah and the day she posed for her photo? No one has yet determined the definitive answer to either question.[9] For Mattie the months between 1868 and 1871 form a black hole into which she slipped to remain completely out of sight in the silence of time.

Celia may have already begun calling herself Mattie, but it appears throughout her life to have had little more than occasional use. Court records, always a good yardstick, indicate that for the most part she continued to call herself by her childhood name. However, her Iowan enunciation caused Celie to sound like Sally and court clerks who listened and wrote at the same time were disposed towards phonetic spelling. Spelling was secondary so they wrote what they heard and, as a result, police and court records list her as Sally.

She never once appears in court records as Mattie.

Her use of an alias was undoubtedly for one or more of the same reasons that most sporting women used them: they were necessary in order to remain as unknown as possible, to hinder searches by concerned family members, to avoid lawmen with outstanding warrants, or even to spare bringing shame to the family name. Why she chose Mattie remains unknown, but it suggests she determined her means of making a living soon after she left home.[10] It is her proven means of livelihood from 1872 to 1876 and from 1883 to 1888 plus the other twists and turns in her life that have more than just coincidental significance.

CHAPTER 2

The Silence
of Time

M attie and Sarah no sooner shook the farm's loamy soil
from their high-buttoned shoes than they became what
is commonly referred to as "lost to history." Sarah never told
anyone the details of her actual adventures, or if she did her
confidant was sworn to secrecy and never betrayed the trust.
Wherever they had been, Sarah's unhappy homecoming and
Mattie's eventual destiny suggest they had embraced the
sporting life. If they did, the "why" of the matter presents no
great mystery.

Women who journeyed west during that era were of four
categories. In the first were those who accompanied husbands
or families to locate farmland or find employment in other
fields of honest endeavor.

The second was comprised of unattached women with
money to invest in remunerative ventures. These included cafes, boarding houses, stores and laundries. This category also
included dressmakers, tailors and milliners, all occupations
requiring skill and business experience. There are also a few
instances where women made names for themselves as professional gamblers.[1]

Women of the third classification sought work in education or commerce, both extremely difficult fields in which to
obtain positions. The west was so much a man's world that
males were preferred as schoolteachers. Women who applied
could receive consideration, usually reluctant, only if no man,
even one with less credentials, was unavailable. In rare cases

a woman might be considered for work in a bank, but tellers were usually male. When a woman was part of a financial institution it was generally because it was a family business. Women were not hired as accountants, secretaries or stenographers. Court clerks were always male. Female doctors, lawyers, ministers and police officers were still many years into the future. The world of commerce was mostly a closed shop to the feminine gender.

The fourth faction accommodated unskilled, uneducated, often unattached women. For them little legitimate work was available.[2] Hotels hired chambermaids and cleaners as openings came available. A general merchandise store from time to time hired a female clerk. A café sometimes needed a waitress. In large cities domestic work in private homes on occasion became available. In all cases wages were low, the competition inordinate.

Conversely, there was no lack of work available for young ladies not encumbered by a strict morals code — and experience was not a prerequisite.[3] As a result, once the desire for regular meals overrode moral issues, many women gravitated to saloons and brothels. Mattie — and of this there is no doubt — was no stranger to brothels.[4]

One can only muse over what Mattie thought her rewards would be. Unless she was extremely naive she would have quickly realized prairie bordellos were not often opulent houses providing carefree lifestyles awash in easy money. The elegance found in San Francisco, New Orleans and St. Louis houses of ill fame was not the norm in frontier towns. It is unfortunate the role of these houses has been so often fictionalized. They were not joyful places and the women within were rarely, if ever, good-natured, laughing sprites.[5]

When Sarah turned towards home Mattie continued alone, but where did she go? Her name appears nowhere in any state, town, city or county record during 1868 to 1871.[6] Neither are any of her known aliases in surviving newspapers of the day. Her trail from Fairfax, Iowa remains a mystery from 1868 until 1871 when she resurfaced in Fort Scott, Kansas to pose for a photo.[7] That she was well settled in that town appears emphasized by her photo. The fashionable dress she wears indicates she was doing quite well from a financial standpoint. She was obviously indulging her fondness for finery.

Mattie's Fort Scott photo is one of two extant portraits. The other, also studio posed, was taken at Globe, Arizona in 1885. The fourteen-year time gap shows marked differences in Mattie's appearance that go beyond the intrusions of normal aging. The first shows a young, vibrant Mattie while the second depicts a careworn Mattie, greatly aged beyond her thirty-five years.

She was calling herself Mattie in Fort Scott when she picked up her photo from J.T. Parker Ltd. Palace of Fine Arts. On the back of the photo is listed the studio's address: "#1 on the corner of Wall & Main Street."[8] The back also bears the company stamp, but no date is shown.

Mattie is posed before the standard backdrop of a curtain with pseudo-marble columns on each side. Her left arm rests lightly against a stele, also pseudo-marble.[9] Her left hand is visible. Her hair appears brunette, but as one of her relatives observed, it was auburn. Two tresses of semi-tight ringlets fall across her right shoulder to rest upon an ample bosom. Her face is softly attractive. Her mouth, set in a straight line, indicates a determined personality. The photo shows no sadness. Quite the contrary, there is an aura of serenity, indicating her life was reasonably happy. It also indicates she was beginning to appreciate the fashions of the day. In fact, Mattie came to like finery and developed a taste for silver jewelry.

Mattie's floor length, high-necked, pleated dress of checked material is obviously of higher quality than inexpensive gingham. It has a fashionably wide furbelow, perhaps silk, satin or taffeta that embellishes the hem. It is probably her best "Sunday-go-to-meetings dress" to use the colloquial slang of the day. Neither flowers nor jewelry decorate it, but there is a clasp of some sort on the white collar at the throat. She does not yet wear the silver bracelets that in later years became her trademark.

Mattie's eyes, seemingly focused on someone to her right, show a misty, far-away look, possibly the dreamy gaze common to any young lady who has recently discovered the love of her life. There is also an almost imperceptible smile indicating she is with someone she cares for. It is possible that Wyatt Earp had already become the object of her affection.

As Mattie does not appear in any Fort Scott census or other records it cannot be known with certainty how she was supporting herself in that tough frontier town. Neither is she mentioned in the town's newspaper within its court reporter's column. So, what was she doing in Fort Scott? All factors considered, plus recently acquired knowledge of what her immediate future held in store for her, the line of work she had chosen for herself indicates prostitution. Work was no more abundant in Fort Scott than elsewhere, but in its prominent sporting area a personable and reasonably pretty girl (many a plain one for that matter) could earn serious coin.[10]

Secondly, and equally important, is that Mattie and Wyatt definitely met in 1871 and it seems unlikely they met anyplace but in the sporting area. If Mattie was engaged in respectable work her chances of meeting Wyatt would have been greatly reduced, as their areas of social interest would have been too dissimilar. Of greatest importance, though, is this: Had Wyatt suggested to a woman of "respectable" status that she accompany him to Illinois she would have insisted on some details — and would likely have been aghast at what was on his mind. Given the circumstances of the next phase in Mattie's life, it is more than certain she was already engaged in the one occupation that could have exposed her to a meeting with Wyatt Earp.

CHAPTER 3

Enter Wyatt Earp

Contrary to fictions written about Mattie Blaylock over the decades, Wyatt did not rescue her from an evil madam in a Kansas City brothel. Neither did he liberate her from the licentious clutches of a Dodge City saloon owner. He definitely did *not* win her in a high-stakes poker game. Neither was she a whiskey soaked, opium ingesting, cigarillo-smoking streetwalker when they first met. When Mattie Blaylock met Wyatt Earp she was a garden-variety prostitute quietly residing in a pleasure palace operating just off the main street of Fort Scott, Kansas.

During late summer in 1871, while living at Newton's farm, Wyatt paid a visit to town. A virile young man with an eye for women, he sought female companionship. Because fate works in curious ways, the house he selected happened to be the one Mattie was calling home. They were attracted to each other and the meeting appears to have produced love at first sight — albeit strictly on Mattie's part. Wyatt, unlikely to have been harboring thoughts of everlasting love, decided Mattie could be his favorite whore and left it at that.

Mattie's attraction to Wyatt Earp should surprise no one. Tall, slim, with blond hair and neatly trimmed mustache, he was very handsome. (The full, bushy mustache that became his trademark was not cultivated until several years later.) She could not have helped but to also notice his blue eyes and how ice cold they were. She would have also eventually seen how they could so quickly turn even colder when fixed on anyone who displeased him. She would not have failed to notice his self-confidence as being the quiescent arrogance that underscores the aura of a quietly dangerous man. She would also sense that, despite his slender build, he was ox-strong and in any situation, win or lose, those long arms and big hands were capable of inflicting a fearsome beating on anyone who went against him.

Mattie of course had no idea her new acquaintance would someday become a legend. Indeed, she would never know, as fame, save to a very minor degree, eluded Wyatt Earp until he was well into middle age. Not until 1931, when he was already two years beyond the pale and forty-three years after Mattie had been lowered into her own cold pauper's grave, would her new friend become acclaimed and admired by so many as the greatest gunfighter/lawman of the 1870s and 1880s.[1]

It is beyond doubt that Mattie ever learned much of Wyatt's life prior to their meeting in Fort Scott. Already guarding dark secrets this very private man would have told Mattie few details of his life. He obviously mentioned his marriage[2] and that his wife, Urilla, had died. Perhaps he mentioned she died with their newborn child during, or shortly after, childbirth.[3] An admission of a previous marriage seems certain, as Mattie would not have married him had he not been legally available. Because Mattie was also secretive, Wyatt probably learned little of her past.

It did not take Mattie long to realize Wyatt's principal ambition was to obtain well paying, easy employment.[4] She would not have been surprised to learn that his quest had motivated him to run for the elected position of Lamar, Missouri's town constable, which he had won. She would eventually learn his main opponent had been none other than his half-brother, Newton Earp.[5] Whether Wyatt would have done an admirable job as Lamar's lawman will never be known for his term of office proved short.

Wyatt would not likely have told Mattie the circumstances of his departure from Lamar. Stories of an inter-family dispute has long been thought the cause,[6] but this is not so. An equally erroneous second reason is attributed to Fred and Bert Sutherland, Urilla's brothers, who had long run a still in partnership with three friends, Lloyd, Jordan and Granville Brummet.

One night Wyatt, as town constable, assisted the county sheriff in a raid on the Sutherland still. Fred, Bert and partners became convinced his participation had been solely a desire to eliminate a major competitor. They thought Wyatt perceived that their still was draining profits from the one operated by his father, Nicholas Earp. They need not have worried. Both stills, competition notwithstanding, were active, profitable concerns.[7] Nonetheless, they took umbrage,[8] engaged Earp in a street fight and ran headlong into the Earp family's celebrated loyalty.[9] It was long thought that the Lamar Town Council had looked upon the brawl with such displeasure that Wyatt's resignation had been demanded, but this was not the reason Wyatt resigned so hastily either.

The real reason for the hasty departure was because, on March 14, 1871, Barton County filed a lawsuit against Wyatt charging he had collected business license fees in the sum of $200 but had failed to submit them. Wyatt heard of the impending suit and before the summons could be processed and served he was gone.[10] It was never served. Other circumstances[11] involving Nicholas Earp soured the family on Lamar and the decision to leave was made. In what was rapidly becoming a family trademark, the Earps left Lamar quietly, without fanfare literally overnight and vanished. Some went into the vast outreaches of the Great Plains while others deployed to points east.[12]

Wyatt joined his father at Pineville, a small settlement in southwestern Missouri near the Arkansas boundary where Nicholas had located a farm, obtained a mortgage and moved onto the acreage. James, having also decided to remain in Missouri, moved to Aulville where he found work as a bartender. Virgil and Morgan left the state for unknown destinations. (Virgil appears again in Iowa in 1873 while Morgan resurfaced in Peoria in 1872 when he joined Mattie and Wyatt.) Newton moved his family to Kansas where he leased a farm a couple of miles from Fort Scott.

Possibly because Nicholas's farm required horses Wyatt

ventured southwest to obtain some. He obviously had no intention of buying them because he rode directly to The Indian Nations,[13] a sparsely populated area that saw much rustling during that period. Somewhere along the way he met Edward Kennedy and John Shown, two men on a similar mission. Had Wyatt been older or more experienced in tossing a long rope he would likely have shunned their company.

On or about March 26, near Van Buren, Arkansas a Deputy US Marshal apprehended the trio with a number of horses for which they could produce neither bills of sale nor proof of ownership.[14] They were taken to Fort Smith and lodged in the jail. In retrospect, considering horse theft was then a hanging offence, the three were fortunate a lawman happened upon them before the horses' owners found them. Owners of purloined livestock very often meted out spontaneous justice, a stout tree being usually closer than the courthouse in the nearest town.[15]

Earp, Kennedy and Shown were arraigned on March 28 with bail set at five hundred dollars[16] each. Wyatt contacted Nicholas who produced the necessary funds.[17] Wyatt was released. Shown also produced bail money and vanished. Kennedy, with no one to turn to, remained in custody.

On May 8, at Fort Smith, the Grand Jury for the Western District Court of Arkansas returned a true bill of grand larceny against Wyatt B. Earp, John Shown and Edward Kennedy for "horse stealing in the Indian Nations." Trial was set for June 28.

On that date Kennedy was escorted to court, but Earp and Shown failed to appear. Kennedy entered a plea of not guilty. The jurist, identified only as Judge Story, noting the absence of Kennedy's co-accused, may have viewed Kennedy as the fall guy. He accepted the plea and Kennedy was freed. Judge Story then issued bench arrest warrants for Shown and Earp and ordered their bail forfeit.

(In November, Marshal Logan Root returned the warrants to the court. An attached note states in part that "Wyatt B. Earp...can not [sic] be found in this District." Root also wrote "no further action would be taken as Earp has left the area.")

Earp had indeed left the area. The court clerk was still counting the bail money as Wyatt was hightailing it out of that inhospitable town. He cut a direct line either northwest to Kansas[18] or northeast to Pineville. If he returned to the farm he did not stay long because within a few weeks Nicholas was himself again on the move. Unable to pay the mortgage or forestall foreclosure he went to Aulville to stay with James. Wyatt journeyed to Kansas for a stay with Newton.

It is unlikely Mattie knew that her new husband had been in such trouble in Arkansas, nor would she have been all that curious. Wyatt would have considered it none of her business and she probably felt the same way. In fact Wyatt never mentioned Fort Smith or Fort Scott to anyone. To do so would have meant admitting to horse theft charges and jumping bail, as well as acknowledging Mattie as the wife he deserted. None of these events was he prepared to reveal. Even Josephine Marcus, the third Mrs. Earp, apparently knew nothing of the 1871–1874 chapters in Wyatt's life. If she did she never mentioned them, even obliquely.

Wyatt spent the remainder of 1871 with Newton and his family,[19] and when he introduced Mattie to them they accepted her as his wife. For some time it was thought Newton's daughter, Alice Earp Wells, had, years later, made that disclosure to her daughters, but a letter she wrote to Arizona writer John Gilchriese negates this. In that letter she wrote:

"No, I did not know that Wyatt was married in Tombstone, Ariz. Are you sure that he was?"[20]

Obviously, Alice was not the source. She would not have known Mattie, anyway, as she was not born until 1878. Information about Mattie from Newton's family possibly would have come through daughter Effie Mae, as she was two when Mattie first stayed with the family and nearly four the second time. Effie Mae would likely have remembered Mattie, but was not very old when Mattie died, so may not have told her children much about the early years.

Earp told his biographer he had worked from 1871 to 1874 first on a railway survey crew in Oklahoma and then as a buffalo hunter in Kansas venturing far and wide from camp to camp. When asked for names of fellow hunters his memory took one of its several failures. He replied of having met many hunters but he could remember few names. Earp explained his extreme difficulty recalling fellow hunters because, he said, everyone was so transient[21] that lasting friendships were not formed. He must have been convincing, because after *Frontier Marshal* appeared Lake did not seem at all perplexed when men who had been active buffalo hunters could not recall a fellow named Wyatt Earp being amongst them. They wondered about this man with a name not easily forgotten who had allegedly been so prominent within their burly fraternity.

In fact many of the adventures Wyatt narrated had not happened. What transpired is an entirely different story, one that reveals Wyatt Earp as a very different young man from the hero created by Lake, and later exalted by others.

CHAPTER 4

Mattie, Take Thee, Wyatt...

M attie Blaylock may have thought herself the luckiest of women the day she met Wyatt Earp. In retrospect she might have fared better by walking away instead of tying her wagon to his erratic star. From that day and for the next eleven years, she went where he went, stayed where he stayed and did his bidding. Once her fateful decision had been made she tied herself into the transient life of the Earps. It was a life never settled but always unsettling.

Still, Mattie should not be too harshly judged for exercising poor judgment. She was young, only twenty-one, in love, and her time with Wyatt started out well enough. She had no way of foreseeing she had set herself on a path leading to tragedy. She certainly had no way of foreseeing how their years together would crumble to dust. That she made a disastrous decision is without question, but for a time she was happy in her blissful ignorance.

They were not long together before she began calling herself Mrs. Wyatt Earp and to her final day identified herself as such. While this suggests the two had married legally, the uncertainty is whether the marriage was formal or common-law. Thus, questions arise. If Mattie and Wyatt had in fact married with solemn vows in a civil ceremony, where and when did the ceremony take place? Who officiated? To date those questions remain unanswered. The most likely time for a marriage to have taken place was late 1871 or early 1872.[1]

Mattie first began referring to herself as Mrs. Wyatt Earp in her sporadic letters to Sarah[2] that continued over the next fifteen years. All bore the several return addresses of Mrs. Wyatt Earp[3] and Sarah addressed her replies to Mrs. Wyatt Earp. Most researchers now agree Mattie and Wyatt were legally married but few, if any, believe it had ecclesiastic blessing. Opinion is almost evenly split between civil law sanction and common-law union. Despite the absence of records there are some indications they had wed formally, the most solid being the degree of uncharacteristic behavior Wyatt exhibited between 1882 through 1888. His actions indicate he acknowledged Mattie as his legal wife. For her part, Mattie firmly maintained they were married and she never wavered in that insistence. It is unfortunate she failed to leave any indication of where and when they had wed. This, of course, all points towards common-law status. Regardless of status, provisions required by the various jurisdictions in which the two had lived over the years were sufficiently met to legalize a common-law marriage.

By Old West standards marriage was often subject to vague and ambiguous interpretation, with legal status dependent upon where the parties resided. All the territories recognized marriage certificates issued by recognized religious bodies and most civil authorities, but few had hard and fast laws defining marriage. Until well into the early 1900s some regarded common-law unions as legal and binding while others viewed unwed co-habitation as unlawful. Jurisdictions that recognized common-law marriage included the states of Kansas and Texas and the territories of New Mexico and Arizona, all places where Mattie and Wyatt lived during their time together.[4] However, all insisted certain benchmarks be met.

One such standard was a time period of continuous co-habitation that ranged, depending on the jurisdiction, from three to seven years. Another was a public acknowledgment by the parties involved. Mattie and Wyatt met both conditions. They had lived together continuously for ten years and both had made public acknowledgment through legal documents where both had signed in their married names. There were other references as well. In of these documents witnesses refer

41

to Mattie as being known to them as Mrs. Wyatt Earp.[5] One such witness was a Justice of the Peace for the Territory of Arizona.

It is also worth noting that Mattie's status as Mrs. Wyatt Earp carried no value in notoriety or fame. During their years together Earp was virtually an unknown transient, a gambler, an impermanent lawman, and a sometimes farmer. He lacked prominence and had no distinct reputation — except in Arkansas where he was considered an indicted horse thief, bail jumper and fugitive. Until October 1881, when a gunfight in Tombstone brought his name to limited public attention, Wyatt Earp was about as obscure as any man can possibly be. Mattie had certainly not latched onto him in order to be married to, or even be associated with, a renowned celebrity.

CHAPTER 5

Mattie Meets Her In-laws

Mattie did not meet all her in-laws during her first years with Wyatt. She met Newton (1837–1928) and his wife, Nancy Jane (1847–98) at Fort Scott in 1871. Morgan (1852–82), probably her favorite, entered her life in Peoria in 1872. She met her parents-in-law, Nicholas Porter (1813–1907) and Virginia Ann (1821–93) in 1873 in Rice County, Kansas. In December 1873, when she arrived in Wichita, she met James (1841–1926) and his wife Bessie (1845–87). Introductions to Virgil (1843–1905) and Alvira (1849–1947) were made at Prescott in 1879. Louisa Houston (1857–94), Morgan's wife, appeared in Tombstone in 1880. She met the youngest Earp brother, Baxter Warren (1855–1900), in Tombstone in 1881. She might have met Adelia, Wyatt's youngest sister,[1] in 1873. She definitely met her again her in California in 1882. Adelia was then Mrs. Adelia Edwards.

That Wyatt had taken up with Mattie caused nary a ripple amongst the Earp clan. Neither her past nor her present was cause for concern. Mattie settled into the family as comfortably as a foot fits into a warm woolen sock. Wyatt's parents accepted her and treated her very kindly, proving their concern when they opened their home to her in 1882. At that time she stayed with them several months. Virgil, Morgan and James all liked her, although Virgil lost patience for her in Tombstone when her drinking got out of hand (see appendix 5). She got along with her sisters-in-law. Alvira, better known as Allie, not only liked Mattie she became her good friend. The two shared many a bottle during the almost four years they were together.

Allie became a ready shoulder to cry on when Mattie's troubles with Wyatt finally became overwhelming.

Mattie and Bessie got along so well they became business partners in Wichita, and perhaps worked together in Fort Worth where Bessie is known to have been managing a bawdyhouse.

Newton and Nancy Jane, Wyatt's straight-laced half-brother and sister-in-law, also had her live with them on two occasions. Newton was a gentle, hard-working man devoted to his family. She could not have helped but notice the differences between Newton and his brothers.

During the years Mattie lived with Wyatt she worked with and shared the lives of all his family. That she got along well with them is apparent as Allie and Adelia kept in touch with her after she moved to Globe.

As Mattie began meeting her in-laws she can be excused if at first she was overawed. She quickly discerned the diversity of these unusual people and by the time she had met them all her curiosity may have run the gamut from bewilderment to befuddlement to bemusement. She learned the brothers, aside from Newton, chose their wives, friends, associates and business partners from within the sporting fraternity. She also discovered they were all well acquainted with killers, ruffians, outlaws, grifters and other misfits who circulated around and below the "deadline" (the separation between the respectable areas and the red light district; see appendix 5). The Earps presented a certain, if uneasy, tolerance for even the most disagreeable of this group because their work and lifestyle forced them to dwell among such people. By allowing them a wide enough berth, clashes were infrequent. Even in Tombstone a final, fatal encounter with the Clantons was avoided until even a small degree of tolerance was no longer possible.

Mattie came to understand that Wyatt was no stranger to the left hand of free enterprise, so it came as no surprise to discover his brothers would also sidestep the law when the need arose. In several instances, as in Tombstone, they were a distance to the left of the law they had sworn to uphold. Hard cases all, the Earps made their money by whatever means were available to them. Business being business, they showed no reluctance to own shares in brothels and some saloons that had small back rooms.[2]

The Earp brothers, proficient gunfighters all, would — and did — kill when they deemed it necessary. Though not run-of-the-mill hired guns, they ventured into that category in their capacity as Tombstone lawmen. In that deadly town they were well-paid employees of a cabal of politicians and merchants directly opposed to Newman Clanton and his allies. Old-timers, when asked to comment on the brothers, would quote a saying of the era: "They saw life through the gun smoke," an expression that sums up the Earp brothers very accurately.

Mattie was not slow in realizing the brothers wore the lawman's badge not so much through dedication to law and order, but as a convenient method of protecting their interests or advancing personal agendas. The badge meant authority and he who wore it gained advantages. Sheriffs, marshals and their deputies were free to come and go where and as they pleased. They were not bound by the town's ordinance against wearing guns within jurisdictional limits. There was one other — a very important — advantage. A lawman could openly carry a shotgun without invoking undue comment or criticism.

Even while serving as lawmen the brothers maintained their fundamental pursuits, be they faro banks, brothels or saloon operations. Those pursuits, however, are never mentioned in federal or state and territorial census in which the Earps appear. Only one census (Wichita 1875) lists the occupations of both Wyatt and James as "sporting," and this was during the time when Wyatt was an official member of the police force. Interestingly, none of the brothers, not even Virgil, the only brother to hold a position of Deputy US Marshal,[3] is ever listed in a census as "officer of the law."

With the exception of James (who is mostly listed as either "sporting" or bartender) the brothers are invariably listed in city, state or territorial census occupation columns as "farmer" though none farmed to any extent except Newton, the only Earp who farmed throughout his entire working life. He steadfastly remained aloof from his siblings' escapades and political games. The late Ed Bartholomew, an unabashed anti-Earp author, labeled him "Newton the Good," a sobriquet not without some justification. Newton would ride with sheriffs' posses when called upon and served as town marshal in Garden City, Kansas for several years.[4]

James (the most itinerant of the group) lived in a succession of towns and cities. His tracks are not difficult to trace as his various addresses are on record with the Civil War Pensions Board in Washington. Federal census records list him as "saloon manager." He worked mainly in saloons, but was also capable of earning a good living as a gambler. James claimed he wed Nellie Bartlett Ketchum in Illinois, according to his Union Army pension record.[5] It was in 1872 that she began calling herself Bessie Earp.

Virgil, the second eldest of the famed quartet, is listed as "bartender" in Peoria during 1869 and 1870[6] and a "grocer" in Lamar, Missouri.[7] Other records have him listed as a farmer, but he spent little time tilling the soil. During his sixty-two years he was a Union soldier, bartender, freight wagon driver, Deputy US Marshal, city marshal, private detective, a city policeman, and finally a prospector.

While Virgil has been mentioned as having held an appointment as a US Marshal at Prescott, Arizona Territory there is much doubt of this. No record exists supporting the claim but, it should be stated, the Department of Justice was very slipshod in its early record keeping. However, at the time period in question the US Marshal for the Prescott area was Crawley Dake, a solid indication the claim is untrue. It seems more likely that Virgil was a deputy serving under Dake.

Virgil was wed three times, his last wife being Alvira Sullivan Packingham (c1849–1947). His first marriage to a young lady who did not have her parents' consent (they disapproved of the Earp family) was annulled by the court.

His second wife, a seventeen-year-old named Rosilla Dragoo (more likely Drageau) was also known as Rose. They married in Lamar on May 30, 1870.[8] The marriage certificate, on record in Lamar, is dated and signed by Nicholas Earp, who was Justice of the Peace at the time. They appear in the county census later that year, but when Virgil left Lamar in 1871 Rosilla did not go with him. No trace of her has yet been found.[9]

Morgan never pushed a plow or hoed a cornrow once he grew to manhood. His was also a variegated career. He had connections with two Peoria brothels where he was arrested and, in 1872, served a jail term on charges of "Keeping a house of ill-fame." He lived briefly in Wichita early in 1876 before moving on to Dodge City. From there he went to Butte, Montana and from there to Tombstone where he consistently worked for Wells Fargo as a stagecoach messenger (familiarly known as "riding shotgun"). His connections with the law were service as a police officer in Dodge City and in Butte, Montana, and as deputy city marshal under Virgil in Tombstone. He took part in the famed shootout. Morgan's only known wife was Louisa Houston, also known as Lou.

Baxter Warren, called Warren, was the youngest brother. He became a surly man, mean-tempered when drunk, which was often. He was generally disliked, even within his own family. He was never a bonafide lawman, but may at one time have been a range detective although nothing substantiates the claim.[10] Too young to share in his brothers' fame Warren spent his adult years as a drifting ranch hand and freight wagon driver. Occasional efforts are made by Earp aficionados to implant Warren's biography into the overall Earp legend. The efforts beg the question: To what point? His only claim to fame is having been gunned down in a Willcox, Arizona saloon by an inoffensive ranch hand named John Boyett. Warren, for some reason, had taken a great dislike to Boyett and one night challenged Boyett and advanced toward him, a knife in hand. Boyett shot him. The jury decided it was self-defense. Warren neither earned nor deserves recognition as part of the Earp legend.[11]

As Mattie came to know and understand her in-laws, she realized they were a unique breed of restless souls. Fully cognizant of their endeavors and schemes, she did not follow blindly in blissful ignorance of what was happening. She pursued life as Wyatt's wife and companion, not only in full knowledge of "what was what," but anxious to share in the spoils. A willing and integral part of the group, she eagerly shared and assisted in their adventures. That she failed to attain her dreams was not through lack of endeavor. Had she been able to avoid the heartache of Tombstone, in all probability she would have succeeded.

CHAPTER 6

Haspel House, Peoria, 1872

On page 81 of its 1872 issue, *Root's Peoria City Directory*, an annual publication, shows the name Wyatt S. Earp. It is followed by his place of residence. The address was that of The Haspel House, a notorious brothel well known to the police.[1]

Mattie may have had no burning desire to go to Peoria but did so in acquiescence to Wyatt's desire to leave Fort Scott. There was nothing keeping her there as she had no firm ties to Fort Scott, and with her sights firmly set on her handsome drifter she would have accompanied him anywhere he wished. At that moment he wished to go to Peoria.

Peoria was not unknown to Wyatt. In 1867 he had worked a short distance north hauling logs from a logging camp to a mill in the village of Slabtown. He was aware that some friends and acquaintances from his youthful days in Monmouth, Illinois had recently moved to Peoria, so he may have seen opportunity in renewing contacts. His main reasons for returning to Illinois however were more pragmatic. One, possibly the most important, was a wish to increase the distance separating him from the Arkansas court. Because marshals were known to occasionally pursue fugitives, Fort Scott was too close to Fort Smith to allow him an absolute feeling of safety. Departure made perfect sense. He also had a second reason. Virgil had told him of his Peoria adventures during 1869[2] and undoubtedly had mentioned the easy money available in Peoria's sporting district. The prospect of easy money always held appeal to Wyatt so he had deposited Virgil's information in the back of his mind for future reference. Virgil, as events transpired, had perhaps painted a rosier picture than warranted.

Wyatt informed Morgan, whom he knew was at loose ends, of his plans and when he and Mattie arrived in Peoria they found Morgan waiting for them. Thus three Earp brothers, and perhaps all four,[3] had been drawn to Peoria's red light district at varying times between 1869 and 1872. Though Morgan does not appear in the city directory, police arrest and court appearance records prove his presence.[4] He was likely also a resident of Haspel House.

Exactly when Mrs. Wyatt Earp and her new husband arrived in Peoria is not clear, but the directory entry indicates their arrival as having been in late December 1871 or early January 1872. It is also obvious Mattie was again calling herself Celie but, as mentioned above, her Iowan twang caused police and reporters to think she was saying Sally and apparently she never bothered to correct them. Instead she adopted Sally as an alias, although she used Sarah as a convenient alias in a September court appearance.[5] During her stay in Peoria Mattie managed to remain so anonymous that, had it not been for the September court appearance, in which she identified herself as the wife of co-accused Wyatt Earp, her presence in Peoria might have gone undetected.

The city of Peoria spread northeast to southwest along the western shore of Peoria Lake. Mattie quickly became oriented to the sporting district,[6] a narrow urban ghetto of irregular shape that was wide at its north end and narrow at the south end. The eastern boundary, twenty-two blocks of lakefront, began at the northeastern point of Peoria Lake where the Illinois River enters into the lake. It extended southwest to Caroline Street, the district's three-block-long southern boundary. The western boundary, the east side of Adams Street, stretched eighteen blocks from Caroline to Edmond Street which, only two short blocks in length, served as the northern boundary. Washington Street, the district's main thoroughfare, ran almost dead center through the area, parallel to the railroad yards that took up the entire space between Washington and the lakeshore. The entire vermin-infested precinct encompassed an area of some eighty-four square blocks. Its inhabitants resided in small shacks, large wooden houses and rundown tenements. They earned their money in brick commercial buildings, brothels, saloons, card rooms, dance halls and several seedy hotels. Peorians of moral bent objurgated the residents, and one preacher condemned the entire zone in a particularly fiery Sunday sermon he delivered under the title "Sodom by the River."

Mr. and Mrs. Earp, with Morgan in tow, took what may have been pre-arranged lodgings in a two-story brothel known to the police, the public, and the press as Haspel House.[7] It was operated by an aspiring madam named Jane Haspel, who harbored a burning ambition to become a madam of stature,[8] perhaps even to outdo Mrs. Thankful Sears, Peoria's most infamous madam.

Jane Haspel, who had deserted her Civil War veteran husband and their young son,[9] had arrived in Peoria from nearby Bloomingdale in 1868 with her daughters, sixteen-year-old Sarah and Mary, age seven. She immediately apprenticed Sarah to Thankful Sears (who also took in Mary as a personal servant)[10] and then set about establishing herself in her own house. For two years, operating on her own, she changed locations regularly until finally settling in a small house on Maple Street. She enlisted two young women willing to tolerate her mercurial temperament, twenty-year-old Minnie Randall (real name Abbie Soder) and Carrie Crow, twenty-three.[11] Sarah rejoined her mother and, with three girls now on staff, Jane ran her house successfully until, in 1871, she felt the time was ripe to improve her social position. In August of that year she signed a lease on the Washington Street house that became known as Haspel House. Jane was harboring lofty ambitions when she moved uptown.

Haspel House was a two-story wooden structure about twenty-five feet wide by forty feet on a lot not much larger than the house. A photo of Washington Street in the Bradley University Collection reveals a corner of the house peeking from the protecting shadow of its looming neighbor, the Cooper Institute. The photo partially reveals steps from the sidewalk and a narrow porch. A tree grows near the corner.[12]

Though sizeable enough to accommodate a large staff, lack of working capital kept Madam Jane from making the needed improvements that would attract other women. Lack of capital was not her only problem, either. An implacable drunk of troublesome disposition, Jane had trouble attracting women who would consider working for her.

There was nothing extravagant about Haspel House; in fact, it was spartan. No entertainment was provided for, and the parlor did not boast a piano played by a man in a striped jacket and boater hat and referred to as "the perfessor." At Haspel House entertainment might suggest itself if one of the girls, should the mood strike, get up to sing a song or do a little high-kicking dance. There was a bar well stocked with liquor bottles bearing labels of popular brands. The contents all came from a singular barrel kept in the kitchen, but it is unlikely anyone ever raised questions. The clientele attracted to Haspel House would not likely notice that such a variety of brands all had the same coloring and flavor. Despite reaping an enormous net profit on each bottle, Jane could not alleviate her financial woes to the point where she could ameliorate the parlor's ambience.

Neither did Haspel House operate a gambling room. Wyatt, when he moved in, might have considered such an enterprise, but if he did he never followed through. Not yet a full-time gambler, he had neither the capital nor the time to indulge in it. Drumming up adequate business to keep Mattie and himself financially buoyant kept him busy. Madam Haspel would likely have gladly accepted the idea of a gambling room, as she naturally would consider any idea that provided clients the opportunity to spend every dollar in their pockets. Several plans might have easily come to pass had the vice squad, under the resolute command of Captain Samuel Gill, not kept interrupting her expansion agenda.

All things considered, the move to the big house looked promising. The main door of Haspel House fronted on the busy street. The back door, an exceptional escape route in case

52

of a raid, opened to a large commons, a square block in area. It was a warren of escape routes through the narrow spaces between the dozen or more shacks, all bawdy houses, within the garbage-littered, rat-infested square. With her house tucked within the looming shadow cast by the Cooper Institute on one side, rows of saloons and card rooms along the other, and the maze of shacks behind, Jane felt secure in her belief that she had established her enterprise in a choice location. Alas, she quickly learned her move had caused her to become too visible.

Madam Haspel was no stranger to the police, but when she was in the back streets she was not bothered beyond the two raids staged annually against all such houses. They were token raids, fully expected and provided for in the operating budget. Thus, under the protocol of the system, Haspel's latest raid, in June 1871, should have exempted her until December. Unfortunately her high-profile ambition did her in.

Anticipating an untroubled adjustment period, Haspel and her three girls moved to Washington Street during the final week of August. They were barely settled when the vice squad crashed through the front door. Not six weeks had passed. In October, Jane, her girls and three clients were hailed into court. Jane was shocked and dismayed. The unexpected raid upset everything. There had been no time to generate business back to full tilt.

In court she pleaded her case before the stern but fair judge, Magistrate James Cunningham. He might have been surprised as well to see her and her women again so soon but nonetheless he fined the girls and their clients the customary $20 and Jane $30.[13] However, he graciously allowed the women four days to pay. They respected his kindness by paying within the allotted time.

The fines,[14] however, forced Jane to sell several items of her parlor furniture to cover expenses. For their part Minnie, Sarah and Carrie pawned personal belongings to help settle their obligations. Now forced to continue on the small scale she so badly wanted to escape, Jane saw her dreams rapidly fading.

Madam Jane was, therefore, pleased to welcome Wyatt, Mattie and Morgan for she saw in the men producers of fresh cash and in Mattie another — and new — attraction. She introduced them to Sarah, Minnie and Carrie and also to George Randall, twenty-two, a well-known pimp, street brawler and police blotter veteran. They also met Randall's mentor, James Dougherty, the city's most notorious pimp and chief procurer for Mother Sears.[15] Their meeting with George Randall set into motion the first thoughts of a partnership with Jane Haspel. The three men thought they could turn Haspel House into a thriving endeavor.

Even before discussing a financial merger with Randall events had moved quickly, if not altogether smoothly, for Mattie, Wyatt and Morgan. Mattie joined the staff while the two men assumed a variety of tasks and responsibilities within and outside the house. In fact they functioned as pimps and when they and Randall formed their partnership and became shareholders they became "keepers," a term of reference used to denote brothel owners or managers. Wyatt and Morgan obviously considered the partnership good for the long term. The Earps had decided to settle in Peoria.

CHAPTER 7

attie's Peoria

If Mattie explored Peoria to any degree during her residency it was probably limited simply because her interest in the city would, by inclination, be restrained. The center of her little universe was the west side of Washington Street three doors south of Hamilton Avenue, and it is unlikely she traveled far afield. Women in Mattie's profession tended not to venture far from home. However, had she gone for a walk beyond Adams Street she would have liked what she saw.

In 1872 Peoria, the area west of Adams was essentially residential. Here were the schools and churches. There were also large houses of fieldstone or red brick nestled amidst the scenic beauty of natural woodland growth. Within those stately homes the wealthy, genteel families of commercial, judicial and political influence resided in unconditional comfort. The houses, with green lawns and privacy hedges, stood along both sides of wide, tree-lined streets. The citizens who lived within may have been insulated from the squalor of the waterfront, but they were certainly not unaware of the blight on their fair city. Though these citizens of prestige, influence and respect railed against the lakeshore area, they ventured east of Adams Street only during daylight.[1]

Peoria below Adams Street may have been dangerous by night, but during the day it was busy and scurrying with commerce and industry. Its hustle and flurry alone would have awed a farm girl like Mattie. If she had thought Fort Scott was astir with activity, Peoria would have truly astounded her. Never in her twenty-two years had she seen a city whose industrial engine was driven by such numbers of distilleries, breweries, factories, railroads and slaughterhouses. Besides the dozen companies that dealt in beef products, there were also three pork and two poultry packers. All were doing business at a steady pace.

Six railroad depots served the ten railways (with more expected) that rumbled in and out of the city, some on a daily basis. Long lines of passenger and freight cars arrived and departed on regular schedules. Locomotives trailing long lines of cattle cars crowded with western steers were daily arrivals. The Chicago, Burlington & Quincy Railroad and Chicago, Rock Island & Pacific Railroad shared tracks with smaller lines that included the local Peoria & Bureau Valley Railroad and Peoria, Pekin & Jacksonville Railroad.

Because of its booming post-war economy Peoria had attracted job seekers in unprecedented numbers. Slaughterhouses provided steady employment to butchers, meat cutters and others in related occupations. Distilleries advertised as far afield as Canada and Britain for experts in the distillation of whiskey. Coopers, skilled tradesmen who constructed the oak barrels needed for the trade, were in short supply. Many were migrants from Scotland and England and, realizing the continuing shortage gave them an advantage, they were advocating a union. They were also fully aware of the inherent dangers in promoting unionism so they registered their membership as a social club. They took a long-term lease on the four-story building that completely dominated the northwest corner of the Hamilton and Washington intersection. They re-named it "The Cooper Institute" and quietly promoted unionism under the cover of gaming and sporting events. Jane Haspel's house of ill fame quietly rested in its massive shadow.

Peoria boasted six cemeteries, two of which were for the general public with one incorporating space for non-whites, paupers and indigents. Three religious groups maintained their own burial grounds. The sixth was for the exclusive use of the Freemasons.

The city maintained ten public recreation areas and parks

of varying sizes throughout the city, plus a large exhibition and fair grounds in a northwest district called Bluffside. There were also two public squares adjacent to the town center. Peoria was already a well-appointed city.

In the bustling downtown area along both sides of Adams Street many large stores and emporiums competed. One of the largest, Hartz & Company, had originated as hatters and furriers but had expanded to the wholesaling and retailing of blankets, dresses and robes. Its major competitors, Anderson, Gilbert & Rice and The G.W. Gilbert Co., conducted thriving businesses off Adams Street on Wellington. All three stores were but a short walk from Haspel House.

The downtown area had produce markets, law and accounting firms, dentists, doctors, oculists, public stenographers and banks, all bustling and busy. A short distance from the commercial district, were factories ranging from knitting mills (hosiery, suits, woolen sweaters, socks and mittens) to manufacturers of leather goods including horse collars and harnesses. Three paper-box factories hummed with the sounds of industry. Horse-drawn carriages met each train to whisk disembarking passengers to the city's eighteen hotels. It is small wonder that Wyatt and Mattie saw Peoria as their chance to make a quick and easy fortune.

Also close to Haspel House stood buildings housing the energy of civic interest. City Hall, centrally located on Main Street, was less than two blocks distant. Nearby were two courthouses,[2] one of which became all too well known to Mattie, Wyatt and Morgan. This court, three short blocks from the house the Earps called home, was presided over by Justice James Cunningham, Peoria's chief magistrate and author of the city's by-laws. Wyatt, Morgan and Mattie would all have dealings with this learned jurist.

Peoria also featured a wonderful thing Mattie had never seen — a street railway. Horse-drawn trams of The Central City Horse Railway proceeded back and forth along Adams Street on a more or less steady schedule. For five cents Mattie could ride in comfort across town from Garden Street in the southwest to Grant Street in the northeast. Neither Fort Scott, nor certainly not Fairfax, had known such a wondrous form of transportation.

Each day Peoria's busy downtown was crowded with women of various social standing busy with their diverse errands, meeting for gossip or just wandering about. Mattie certainly ventured out to shop and browse in the manner of women of all ages and status. She loved fine clothes and would have admired the dresses and bonnets on the store racks. She would spend an occasional dollar on a pretty bonnet or perhaps $3 on a nice dress.

Though many Peorians lamented the lackadaisical attitude shown toward waterfront vice by a series of city councils, they grudgingly admitted those same councils had achieved progress in other areas of civic improvement. Long before 1872 Peorians could boast of their streetlights and efficient water works. The police force was as reliable as its political masters would allow and the city's fire department was dedicated and efficient. In 1872 two-dozen fire alarms, called Fire Telegraph Stations, stood in readiness throughout the city, with as many more planned.

Large enough to justify a ward system, Peoria was already divided into seven such zones. Mattie resided in the smallest, Ward Four. If she was aware of this it is doubtful she had any interest.

Of Peoria's five newspapers two were dailies. The most popular, the Republican-leaning *Peoria Daily Transcript,* was available every morning (except Sundays and holidays) at newsstands for two cents a copy. Its publisher had also thoughtfully inaugurated a convenient home delivery service for a weekly cost of twenty-five cents. Its editor was George V. Kent, a cynical man who hired astute reporters capable of writing with a biting wittiness. Kent, who held no respect whatever for those on the wrong side of the law, eventually aimed his barbed witticisms directly at Wyatt Earp. The *Daily Transcript* and George V. Kent became Wyatt Earp's nemesis.

The *Daily National Democrat* was the city's largest paper. Well written but lacking its rival's humor, the paper's editorial mandate was seemingly to attack all things Republican.

Its editor also came to direct some harsh words against Wyatt Earp.

Still, despite the abundance of good fortune, the city had civic troubles. Its prosperity attracted newcomers hoping to find work, and many of the newcomers arrived in Peoria with larceny aforethought. A large segment of this latter group, many of whom were rogue war veterans, footloose, rough-hewn and brutalized by four years of conflict, had come to Peoria between 1865 and 1870. Unable, or unwilling, to adjust to civilian life, they had quickly wrested control of the water-front saloons, dance halls, card rooms and brothels from local thugs.

Worse was to come. In 1871 Chicago was almost destroyed by a massive fire[3] that produced adverse affects on Peoria. Within days hundreds of homeless and unemployed men left Chicago to seek work elsewhere. Many arrived in Peoria only to find no work available. Most moved on but some, for their own reasons, remained. Within a few weeks Peoria had become an unwilling hostess to large numbers of homeless men who drifted aimlessly about the streets and alleys.

It was inevitable that some turned to crime while others became beggars, but all became tagged with the single soubriquet: Peoria bummers. That was the label the editor of the *Daily National Democrat* later saw fit to attach to Wyatt Earp. The editor of the *Daily Transcript* was no less scathing and both editors, while poles apart on politics, fully agreed the Earp presence was highly undesirable. Mattie's husband had quickly become well known, not only to police officers and magistrates but also to police-blotter reporters and their crabby editors.

Peoria, however, was not without civic blemish of its own genesis, one of the worst being its jail, commonly known as the calaboose. Old, bleak and decrepit, it was a crumbling edifice whose conditions within were so depressing and appalling that the *Daily National Democrat* launched a scathing attack aimed directly at city hall. On January 6, 1872 an editorial pointed out the conditions thus:

The calaboose is in wretched condition, and it is absolutely

cruel to confine prisoners in it. In corners of the men's and
women's departments are vaults [latrines and open sewers],
which are left uncovered and the stench arising from them
is horrible.[4]

Mattie was fortunate enough to be spared the ordeal of
confinement within its fetid cells, but Wyatt and Morgan both
spent a full month behind its forbidding, gritty walls. They
could have avoided the ordeal by paying the imposed fines or
agreeing to work on civic tasks but, unwisely, both opted for
confinement. When they emerged their moods had altered.

Chapter 8

Masters of the House

In January 1872, Wyatt and Morgan entered into partnership with George Randall and invested in the Haspel House. It is not known who approached whom, but it seems likely that Randall instigated the merger. That the three young men formed a partnership is not in question.[1]

Randall was a thug, tough and surly. He was so much a hoodlum the *Peoria Daily Transcript* had once described him as "a hard one." He had left his job as a cooper in a distillery when he discovered managing bawds meant more, and easier, money than making whiskey barrels. Within a year he had become well established amongst the red-light denizens. He also, as his lengthy police record attests, was equally well known to the courts. Before teaming up with Jane Haspel he had worked for Thankful Sears[2] who, in order to keep her twelve to fifteen women busy, relied on four full-time pimps plus several part-timers, one being George Randall. Because he was part-time he was free to work anywhere, so he also worked for Jane Haspel from time to time. For the last few months he had been attached full time to Haspel House.

The details of the Earps' agreement with Randall are not fully known, but the decision to buy a share of Madam Jane's pleasure palace was neither sudden nor made at a chance encounter. The new partners offered Mrs. Haspel a deal, the terms of which were simple: Wyatt, Morgan and George would provide some working capital, solicit clients and provide the muscle whenever needed. She was overjoyed for she saw that perhaps now her dream of expansion could be realized. When the Earps appeared she had seen them as helpful additions, but in this new offer she saw salvation. She welcomed her new partners with open arms.

Her plans moved quickly ahead. First was an improvement in ambience, a necessity in such a house. As atmosphere was primary, she began with furniture to replace that which she had sold just weeks before. She bought sofas and overstuffed chairs in which the clients could enjoy comfort. The girls were now able to lounge comfortably in their diaphanous gowns displaying enough of their seductive, come-hither charms to capture clients' interest. She also sent word to the street that Haspel House wished to increase staff. The acquisition of new furniture was no problem, but a staff increase was another matter; finding women who would work for Mother Haspel would require her to severely moderate her mercurial disposition. Another problem would be for her to remain sober enough to deal with day-to-day matters. Both proved difficult. For Madam Haspel her reputation proved her undoing. No new women were lured to the house.

For a time, though, all other matters went well. Business improved. The house gained popularity, especially during weekends when the partying was non-stop. Jane slowly began to recover from the effects of the October convictions. Then the police struck again. On January 12, Jane, Minnie, Carrie and Sarah were nabbed along with two clients and two pimps.[3] Jane saw her dreams of fame and fortune take yet another backward step.

The raid should also have involved the Earps but it did not. For some reason none of them, Mattie, Morgan or Wyatt, was home at the time of the raid. Neither was George Randall. Wherever they were, all were spared a court appearance and the usual financial reversal. Nevertheless, they were likely made a little nervous considering the call had been so close.

Even after discovery of the Earps' presence in Peoria it has been thought by some that neither of the Haspel House raids of October 11, 1871 and January 12, 1872, had involved them in any way. Those who thought thus believed the trio had not arrived in Illinois until February. The October raid certainly did not involve them, but by good luck alone they were spared arrest during the January raid. Nonetheless, it did have an impact on them.

Details of the Earps' Peoria adventures were slow to emerge — 117 years to be exact — and then they came piecemeal. The first disclosure came in 1989.[4] Then, two years later during early research for this book, it was discovered Wyatt had indeed been in Peoria with an unknown man and woman in early January 1872. Interest increased when shortly after that discovery it was learned Wyatt had met Mattie at Fort Scott in 1871 and that she had accompanied him to Peoria. The new information forced a shift in thought and warranted further searching for Peoria files. Ultimately Morgan's presence was disclosed. The three peas were now in the same pod and much of the Earps' missing history was suddenly thrust from the dark into the light.

CHAPTER 9

Taking Care
of Business

B ecause when they first bought into Haspel House it was
basically such a penny-ante operation, the Earp brothers
and George Randall assumed the responsibility of improving it. They tended bar, pimped, procured and were capable
bouncers ever watchful for trouble. Despite outraged denials
from Earp apologists there is no longer any doubt that Wyatt
and Morgan were indeed pimps. Intense competition dictated
that sporting houses employ such agents, many of which were
in permanent residence.

Randall, well established with many clients, was also a
procurer who had found girls for various madams. When he
found Abbie Soder, however, he kept her for himself, changed
her name to Minnie Randall and became her protector. Wyatt,
whether he realized it or not, had followed the same procedure when he took up with Mattie. Morgan was not in league
with a specific woman so far as is known. Neither is it known
if the Earps attempted to recruit women in Peoria, but if they
tried they were not successful as the Haspel House staff never
increased. Neither were they ever charged as procurers.

That in itself means nothing. "Keeping a house of ill-fame,"
so far as Peoria's prosecuting attorney was concerned, was the
more serious charge and lesser charges were only rarely included in arrest warrants. Nonetheless, it was necessary for
"keepers" to promote business any way they could and to
keep the place staffed, so it cannot be said with any certainty

that Wyatt and Morgan did not engage in procurement just as it cannot be said they did.

A settled time followed the January 12 raid. The remainder of the month went smoothly for the inhabitants of Haspel House. Operating unmolested by the law, Mattie and the other girls were in demand and the bar did a steady business. Life was akin to holding three aces and two kings in draw poker, not a sure thing but, considering the circumstances, a "full house" was about as good as it could get. The remainder of January allowed everyone a reasonable net profit.

It was the Earps' misfortune to have arrived in Peoria just as the city was experiencing both an oversupply of soiled doves *and* the emergence of dedicated reformers to city council. Had they sought work in industry perhaps Mattie might have happily settled into a long life of domesticity. That was not to be, for in a major error in judgment she had fallen for a man whose very nature would never allow him to either embrace steady employment or remain settled for any length of time. There was also one other little problem: Wyatt Earp had an extraordinary propensity for embroiling himself in trouble.[1]

Toward the end of 1871 Peoria's sporting area had become an arena of extreme competition. Life for pimps, madams and soiled doves was not easy toil. Difficulties abounded, not the least of which was a plethora of bawds; there were too many individuals competing for the available dollars. Supply exceeded demand, always a sign of economical downturn, and business quickly became cutthroat. Even city authorities, usually the last to admit troubles, acknowledged the situation along the riverside had become acute. By November of 1871 a move to curtail the left hand of free enterprise had gained public support.

Despite a reasonable January and indications that February would be profitable, 1872 did not present a rosy picture. In a January editorial the *Daily National Democrat* calculated that sixty brothels were operating along the waterfront. Even half that number would have been too many in a city of less than 29,000 residents. Part of the problem was unknown numbers of transient sporting ladies. Brothel owners who read the editorial agreed. They resented women who worked the streets or operated from seedy hotels.[2] While most stayed in town only a short while, during their stay they could hook a sizeable share of business away from the established trollops. Thus was aggravated an already dismal situation that had come about when voters turned city hall over to a slate of determined reformers under the leadership of Mayor Peter Brotherson. The election results had not augured well for the frail denizens, their madams and their agents.

Adding to the Earps' woes was that the January raid had greatly alarmed Mattie. All indications are that she had never before been scooped up in a raid and the prospect of a court appearance depressed her. Mattie was not a happy hooker. It may be that Wyatt was also beginning to harbor second thoughts concerning their connection with Jane Haspel, whose public behavior tended to draw unfavorable attention.

During the remainder of January doubt and uncertainty nagged the rugged confines of Peoria's red zone. Captain Gill's raids during December and early January had plunged Peoria's demimonde into a state of apprehension.[3] The pressure proved too much for some, and several houses closed. The soiled doves so displaced flitted from house to house in a flurry of nervous rotation. Gill had intended to continue the raids, but the courts had become so overloaded he decided (perhaps at request of higher authority) to curb his operations temporarily. For whatever reasons, the big raids suddenly stopped allowing the sporting ladies to breathe a little easier.

Thus, in January and February, Mattie and friends saw a welcome increase in business. Life returned to normal as the weekend parties reignited the whirlwind existence Mattie had come to enjoy. Money began to flow in amounts sufficient to keep the proverbial wolf from the door. January had not started well, but the remainder of the month had been profitable. Better yet, February had gotten off to a good start. It was beginning to appear that Haspel House just might accommodate the financial desires of Mr. and Mrs. Earp when Mayor Brotherson informed Captain Gill that his "flying squad" could resume the raids.

Saturday, February 26 was one of merriment within Haspel House, but since the last raid Jane and her merry men had kept a tight lid on noise because it attracted unwanted attention. The bar was busy while Mattie, Minnie, Sarah and Carrie kept the clients happy and laughing with ribald songs and jokes. Madam Haspel sipped whiskey while happily anticipating the evening's receipts would be higher than usual. The night was progressing well. Wyatt, Morgan and George were efficiently going about their duties. Life was good.

A few minutes before midnight the night's placidity was shattered by ear splitting shrills of police whistles as Gill's spoilers burst through both doors. The frightened women dispersed, screaming, in all directions while clients sought refuge behind sofas, in closets and under beds. The raid was over in minutes. The entire household and their guests found themselves hustled away to police cells, the night definitely ruined.

Had the Earps been able to read signs they would have seen in the raid an omen of forthcoming disaster. The next few months were going to be tough. One cannot help but feel sorry for Mattie who, having eluded the January raid, had every reason to believe there would be no other until well into summer. Now, suddenly, she found herself arrested. Worse, Wyatt and Morgan were being led away in handcuffs and that meant she would have to spend the night in jail. Worse still, their names would be in the papers. She need not have worried. A deal and a span of a hundred years would forestall anyone's notice.

When someone did notice it was like a bomb exploding. The sound and fury fell directly into the midst of the Wyatt Earp aficionados and so disrupted their tight little world that most were reduced almost to the point of apoplexy. Wyatt Earp, the sterling marshal and all-American hero, had been arrested as a resident of a brothel. It was difficult to take. His supporters, following the initial shock, rallied to support their hero. Earp, they insisted, had been a visitor, not a resident. His fine had been that of a "found-in." Residents, pimps and keepers were always fined in excess of $40. It was actually a reasonable assumption when one considers the light fine, that he, a virile young man, was quite liable to be merely a client of one of the girls. The matter eventually subsided to rest on that point until 2003 when the real reason for his presence in Jane Haspel's infamous house of whores was discovered. No visitor he; quite the contrary. Wyatt Earp had not only been a resident, he had been "a keeper of a house of ill-fame." He shared ownership in the place.

As noted above, when Wyatt and Morgan invested in Haspel House it seemed a good idea at the time. Wyatt was already living there with Mattie, who had become one of the girls. That the brothers Earp had indeed become "keepers of a house of ill-fame"[4] is proven by the charges read against them on Monday, February 26.

Mattie and Wyatt might have enjoyed a lengthy connection with Haspel House had it not been for that fateful Saturday evening when the local police swooped down on their *maison d'amour*. Wyatt, Morgan and George Randall were all charged equally as "keepers," Jane was charged as the madam and Sarah, Minnie, Carrie and Mattie faced charges of being common bawds. Things were looking bleak when the prosecuting attorney suggested to Jane a way out. She was willing to listen to his offer.

Madam Jane listened as the prosecuting attorney outlined his offer. He explained to her the targets in his sights were not Jane and her girls. He wanted "keeper" convictions against Randall and the Earp brothers. He suggested the women could go free, and their names not made public,[5] providing Minnie Randall would testify against the three men. Jane bought the deal.

That Jane Haspel was able to deal her way out of her predicament is no indication she enjoyed favor with the legal authorities. Her numerous charges of being drunk and disorderly in public places point out she enjoyed no such privileges.

Why did the prosecutor choose Minnie when he also had Mattie, Sarah and Carrie Crow? Because Randall was Minnie's pimp, her testimony would carry added weight with the magistrate. He would not have considered Mattie, who even then was regarded as Wyatt's wife, to testify. Her testimony would have involved Wyatt and the law expressly excused a spouse from unwillingly testifying against the other. Neither Jane's daughter nor Crow's testimony would carry much weight, so Minnie was chosen. The offer was one that Jane and the others, all mentally calculating their financial losses, could not reject. They took the offer and Minnie, perhaps reluctantly, agreed to testify.

Poor Minnie! It frightened her to think of the reaction Randall might show. Although ostensibly her boyfriend he was every inch a thug, not likely to let endearments cloud his views of retaliation. The situation had to be a terrible quandary for the poor girl, faced with yet another hefty fine and an overwhelming aversion to spending a month in Peoria's pestilent prison.

Except for the fact that Wyatt would be charged, Mattie welcomed the deal also because she would emerge free and clear. She hoped Minnie would not change her mind. Mattie did not want to face the judge.

The prosecutor was pleased as he felt it worthwhile to trade five small convictions for three big ones. He could have introduced all eight, presented his case and gained convictions on all counts; but the higher goal clouded his judgment. He wanted convictions against the three men, but in particular he wanted Randall who was facing his third charge. The prosecutor felt Minnie's testimony and Randall's record would convince the judge to levy a fine heftier than the usual $45 and impose jail time as well. Three "keepers" were far better trophies than a bevy of bawds. As events transpired, he would have been wiser to stay on his original course.

Wyatt, Morgan and Randall were brought before Magistrate Cunningham and the charges were duly entered into Docket Book "E"[6] which recorded all cases brought before him from January 27, 1871 until March 26, 1872. The hand-written notations allow no doubt that the charges against the men were as "keepers."

Docket Book"E" records the following charges:

Page 256.

City of Peoria vs George Randall Feb 26 1872.

Complaint by Policeman McWhirter for Keeping and being found at a house of ill-fame. A Warrant issued to Policeman McWhirter and returned served with the deft. in court.

Deft. files an affidavit for a change of venue and the same was granted and the papers sent to Wm. Rounseville, Esq. P.M. Police Magistrate

(Signed) James Cunningham

Page 256

City of Peoria vs Wyatt Earp

Feb. 26, 1872. Complaint by Policeman McWhirter for Keeping and being found at a house of ill-fame. A Warrant issued to Policeman McWhirter and returned Served with the deft. in court.

Deft. files an affidavit for a change of venue and the same was granted and the papers sent to Wm. Rounseville, Esq. P.M.

(Signed) James W. Cunningham
Police Magistrate

Page 257

City of Peoria vs Morgan Earp

Feb 26 1872,

Complaint by Policeman McWhirter for Keeping and being found at a house of ill-fame. Warrant returned served with the deft. in court.

Deft files an affidavit for a change of venue and the papers sent to Wm. Rounseville, Esq. P.M.

(Signed) James W. Cunningham
Police Magistrate

At that point the case took the first of two unexpected turns. Each defendant had presented a written request for change of venue and in a decision that surprised everyone — and dismayed the prosecutor — Judge Cunningham granted the requests. He reassigned the cases to Magistrate William Rounseville. The Court Daybook gives no reasons for his approval, but it was almost certainly because Cunningham's caseload was greatly overloaded. At the other end of the building Justice Rounseville, having just been elevated to Criminal Division, had such a light caseload that at the moment he was doing absolutely nothing at all.

The three men were escorted down the hallway to face the novice magistrate and the trial got underway without delay. The judge called the court to order, charges were read and the accused entered pleas of not guilty. Minnie was called. Her testimony was convincing enough for the judge who pronounced all three guilty as charged. He then levied their penalties.

The case now took its second unexpected twist. Justice Rounseville had no hesitation in finding the three guilty of running a brothel, but the fines he imposed were incorrect. He assessed each man $20, the amount customarily levied against a brothel's client. Fines for keepers, procurers and pimps ranged from a minimum $40 to a maximum $100 and/or jail time as an added option.

The imposition of the incorrect fines caused puzzled comments the following day in both newspapers. As this was Randall's third offence on the same charge it was expected he would be fined in excess of the average and perhaps draw jail time as well. This was not overlooked in the write-up appearing in the *Peoria Daily Transcript* the following day. In his account of the assessment, editor Kent added his usual sardonic comments concerning George Randall and his previous convictions. Obviously everyone was surprised at the naivety shown by the novice judge.[7]

The misplaced clemency was emphasized 120 years later when full details of Wyatt's arrest became known. His apologists were no longer able to deny his status within the brothel's hierarchy. They had long insisted he should never have been referred to in the newspapers as a "resident." The $20 fine, they insisted, clearly indicated he had been a client. The court documents prove otherwise, fully justifying the reference as resident. The entry on page eighty-one of *Root's (1872) Peoria City Directory* distinctly shows Wyatt S. Earp as living in Haspel House[8] and Docket Book "E" showing his conviction for "keeping a house of ill-fame" indicates clearly he was involved in its management.

In Justice Rounseville's defense it should be noted he had long been a civil law magistrate accustomed to mediating complaints of neighbor against neighbor or determining if a tradesman actually intended to defraud a homeowner. Having never presided over a case concerned with indictable felony, he was unfamiliar with the penalty structure. That became apparent when he fined the men only $20 each.

Perhaps there is something to the story that Wyatt had studied law for a brief period in his youth. He may have been acting as the trio's lawyer and may have sensed they might fare better before an inexperienced magistrate rather than the no-nonsense Cunningham. Requesting a change of venue proved a prudent step.

It is unfortunate that Justice Rounseville's Docket Book for February 1872 is lost or misplaced because until it is located transcripts of the proceedings, including Minnie's testimony, will remain unknown. The fines and some details, fortunately for latter-day researchers, were reported the following day in the *Peoria Daily Transcript*.

CHAPTER 10

From the Frying Pan to the Fire

F ollowing her release Mattie apparently decided enough was enough. Taking a cue from Wyatt's strategy she also demanded a change of venue and must have been persuasive because Wyatt listened to her. They left Haspel House within days, severing ties with Jane Haspel and taking up with Jennie Green, an equally notorious madam, but better established. As events unfolded, the move was a matter of leaving one calamitous situation only to become embroiled in another that proved even worse.

Mattie wanted to leave Jane Haspel for her own reasons, but Wyatt's reason was possibly the deal Jane had made with the prosecuting attorney. Though Mattie had been spared, and Wyatt himself had gotten off lightly, he may have viewed her deal as a betrayal of trust.[1] That Minnie's testimony had also gone against Wyatt and Morgan seems not to have turned them against her, because they remained on friendly terms; and Randall, also, obviously had forgiven her. Mattie certainly bore no rancor because the two women remained good friends. The same lack of concern may not have salved Minnie's conscience, however. With her subsequent actions, one wonders if perhaps she had felt that she had betrayed her friends.

Though Mattie and company signed on with Jenny Green, George Randall and Minnie remained with Jane Haspel.[2] Randall may have bought the shares held by Wyatt and Morgan, but the partnership did not fully dissolve. They remained friends and that summer Randall, Wyatt and Mattie reunited for a new, albeit short-lived, venture that lasted until late August.

The move to Jennie Green's bagnio may have been nothing more than being lured by a better offer. Both Wyatt and Mattie were always on the lookout for an easier dollar, so if Green had offered more for less they would have taken it. Morgan needed no reasons and would have gone wherever the other two went. Whatever the rationale, the Earps moved into Jennie's house, and by that costly mistake doomed their futures in Peoria.

Jennie Green had long operated from a grubby shack in the court behind Haspel House, but she and her sporting ladies had recently moved into a suite of several rooms in the McClellan Institute, a large building on Main Street. The *Daily Transcript* usually referred to the building as "That hotbed of iniquity" while musing that it "does seem strange that the owner of the Institute cannot find a more respectable lot of tenants than he usually has there."[3] Located one block north of Haspel House and a half block west, Mattie, Wyatt and Morgan did not have far to go. They moved in with Jennie Green and for a while fared rather well financially, all things considered.

However, if Mattie thought she and Wyatt had found their Utopia she was due for a shock. Whatever serenity Mattie may have found in Green's second floor pleasure palace was short-lived. One Sunday afternoon everything changed and her world began to crumble around her. On April 23 Green's bordello crashed into the news with an impact heard throughout the city. Few would have noticed if it had it been raided three nights in a row, but a single incident gained the rapt attention of police, local newspapers, city hall, the mayor's office and, worst of all, the general public. For Mattie it was a tragedy on a personal level.

Throughout Peoria citizens were enjoying the first truly warm and sunny weekend of spring. West of Adams Avenue, in the respectable part of town, parks were filled with happy picnic-goers while within private yards garden parties were in full swing. The waterfront denizens were also enjoying the weekend. Taverns and saloons were in full bloom and the streets were filled with people. Jennie's place had been in the midst of revolving-door-style revelry since Friday evening. Merriment continued unabated as participants came and went non-stop. The liquor flowed, gaiety was in full swing and the girls were popular.

Minnie Randall had come to the festivities and was having a good time. In fact, from Friday evening until Sunday noon, she was the life and soul of the party. Why Minnie was there has never been known, but it was probably because Haspel House had been closed since Friday. Jane Haspel had been arrested while staggering about the streets in a drunken state so she was spending the weekend in jail. George Randall was also in jail. He had been arrested for fighting in a saloon and was denied bail. Thus, with no one to tend to the business, the door remained locked and Minnie had joined the party at Green's, showing up with ten grains of opium she had bought.

Throughout Friday and Saturday she was having a good time drinking, laughing, dancing, singing and making an occasional trip to one of the small rooms. Sometime during Sunday morning she decided to use her opium. She grew careless however and either measured incorrectly or took it too often. Within a short time she had ingested six grains — far too much by any standards — and her gaiety quickly disappeared. She began staggering about in what everyone thought was advanced inebriation. It soon became clear to others that she was not drunk but in deep distress. By then Minnie was almost totally incoherent, but just prior to passing out she managed to tell someone she had swallowed too much opium. When black splotches — the tell-tale sign of an opium overdose — began to appear on her face and arms a frantic message was sent to the home of Dr. Lucas, a nearby physician. He came as quickly as he could but Minnie had already begun to slip away.

The physician administered antidotes to the stricken girl as her friends stood by silently watching. The party broke up as clients furtively slipped away to disappear into the crowded streets.

The Monday morning issue of the *Peoria Transcript* notes:

"Minnie Randall, about 21 years of age, and who has been many times among the inmates of certain bagnios 'pulled' by the police, attempted suicide by taking morphine [while staying] in McClellan's building on Main Street. At first Minnie attempted to make it appear that she was drunk, but after a while the strangeness of her conduct aroused suspicion and, we believe, she confessed to what she had done. It appears she had purchased some ten grains of morphine, six of which she had swallowed. Medical aid was summoned and reached her about three hours after she had taken the poison. She was then quite black in the face and insensible. Dr Lucas was the physician called. He administered the proper antidotes and up to ten o'clock the girl was alive, with a prospect that she would be saved."[4]

Shortly before midnight, the paper already typeset, with presses ready to roll, the editor inserted the following addendum:

"Later - The girl Minnie Randall still sleeps. Her funeral will take place this evening [Monday]."

While Minnie fought for her life George Randall sat in a cell. By the time word reached him of the situation Minnie was already comatose and near death. He begged the watch sergeant to release him so he could go to her. His request was granted after he paid a security and promised to appear in court the next morning. Tuesday's *Daily Transcript*, in a follow-up to Minnie's demise, reported how Randall had stayed with Minnie throughout Sunday night "rubbing her hands and bathing her forehead with cool water." The paper noted that "he performed good service and for awhile it appeared he was being successful in winning her back to life."[5]

Not many attended Minnie's funeral, but in all likelihood Mattie was there as she was one of Minnie's few friends. It is unknown where she was buried but unless her remains were returned to her family, she lies in an unmarked grave in the paupers' section of the public cemetery. None of the newspapers mentioned the funeral itself nor was an obituary printed. A coroner's inquest, mandatory in such cases, was held several days later. Witnesses were called to answer questions asked by the coroner. The jury returned the verdict the death was caused from opium poisoning. The complete story may never be known because the transcript has been lost or incorrectly filed. Hopefully, it is not irretrievably lost but lies hidden somewhere in a misplaced file. All the transcripts of inquests held from 1870 to 1900 had been held in storage at the Peoria Coroner's Office until 1924. That year they were sent to City Hall for storage in the basement, and in 1945 or 1946 (the year is uncertain) they were sorted and assigned to various archives.[6] Sadly, either City Hall failed to record which archives received the records or the papers have been misplaced. Bradley University received none and neither did The University of Illinois, Western Campus[7] where Peoria's old records are normally stored. Somewhere in an obscure Illinois archive, awaiting discovery, lie the transcripts of the Peoria County Coroner Inquests for 1872. Until they are found a full account of Minnie Randall's demise and the testimony of residents of Jenny Green's establishment will not be known.

If ever there is such a discovery much will be revealed, for within the pages of the transcript are recorded the testimony of Wyatt Earp, Morgan Earp and Mattie Earp. They were among those subpoenaed as witnesses with the other residents of Jenny Green's house. Their testimonies would be interesting. Mattie's would be especially worthwhile for analysis as she and Minnie had been friends.

CHAPTER 11

Peoria Pulls the Welcome Mat

The incident in the McClellan Institute was the beginning of the end for Mattie and Wyatt so far as Peoria was concerned. On May 9, a Thursday night, Captain Gill's elite force swept into the McClellan Institute and scooped up everyone within. The May 11 edition of the *Peoria Daily Transcript* notes:

> That hotbed of iniquity, the McClellan Institute, ...was pulled on Thursday night and as usual quite a number of inmates transient and otherwise were found therein. Wyat [*sic*] Earp and his brother Morgan Earp were each fined \$44.55[1] and as they had not the money and would not work they languish in the cold and silent calaboose.

Jennie Green and all her girls were found guilty and fined. Unfortunately, because the haul was so great and the column's space restricted, their names were not published. Mattie's luck with anonymity had held and once again she escaped public identification. Green and her cyprians, released following payment of their fines, returned to their home on Main Street.

Mattie went with her fallen sisters because with her husband and brother-in-law in jail she certainly could not risk being on her own. There were other houses where she could have gone, but another move would have put her at risk of again being nabbed in another flash raid. That was the last thing she needed, so common sense kept her with Jennie. Her house would now be safe from a raid for a while, at least another month, and with luck possibly longer. It was becoming obvious that Captain Gill had decided the token six-month raid had become a part of Peoria's past.

Mattie managed to get by until mid-June when Wyatt and Morgan were released from durance vile. Morgan, who had spent his time in jail deciding he wanted no more of Peoria, quickly left for points west. Wyatt and Mattie also felt the time for departure had come. They linked up with the recently bereaved George Randall and all three of them left town. However, they did not go far. Wyatt had already contacted John Walton, a boyhood friend who was nearby on his aquatic bordello, the so-called Beardstown Gunboat, one of two such vessels he owned.

These barnacled brothels, referred to as gunboats because of their previous military status, were long, wide, flat-bottomed, and steam powered. These barges, stripped of armament and declared surplus at the end of the Civil War, were tendered for sale to the general public. Though considered useless as freight carriers, men such as Walton saw their potential as mobile brothels. Walton bought two, refitting them with two-deck, flat-roofed structures that utilized almost the entire deck space.

The housing on the Beardstown Gunboat had four doors for easy entry and quick escape. The lower deck of the housing was a saloon in which patrons could play cards and drink. John Walton's wife supervised the girls as they pranced about serving drinks and entertaining patrons. At one end a small dance floor allowed merrymakers enough room to jig to music provided by fiddles plus an occasional banjo. Patrons paid $1.00 to dance for two minutes with their favorite girls. At both ends of the saloon a staircase led to the upper deck where small rooms were available for the girls to entertain their clients.[2]

There are newspaper accounts of the various boat brothels plying the Illinois River, but none are well detailed and most are ambiguous. Moreover, the reports concentrate less on arrests of individuals operating and attending the barges than on apprehension and confiscation of the crafts themselves.[3] When apprehended by law officers, the operators, residents and clients were fined. Few owners, however, ever had their boats impounded or confiscated. Apprehension by various vigilante groups was a different matter, however. When they apprehended a boat they dutifully turned the residents and clients over to local law officers, but not until after the boat had been run aground and burned. The Beardstown Gunboat escaped that fate, but its ultimate destiny remains unrecorded.

When Mattie and Wyatt signed on with John Walton it seemed a sensible move. (All the ideas Mattie and Wyatt conceived seemed good at the time.) It got them away from Peoria and ensured mobility. Certainly both hoped things might begin to work out for them. So far, nothing had gone particularly well. They and Randall moved aboard and hoped for the best. The boat then proceeded northward to Lacon, the terminal point of the northern run. It remained there a few days then headed south again. Mattie and Wyatt were apparently convinced that only constant changes of location could assure safety from the law; and nothing changed location more often than the Beardstown Gunboat. In the long term, though, they were to be greatly disappointed.

The craft's schedule and mobility was such that no further mention is made of Mattie or Wyatt until August when they and Randall again ran afoul of the law. The boat, having commenced its southern run, moored close to Henry, a small town on the west bank of the Illinois River several miles north of Peoria. Mattie, Wyatt and George ventured ashore and while in the town met two girls about sixteen years of age. The girls, who were at loose ends, had seemingly agreed to accompany their new friends to the boat, but the town's sheriff had been watching the girls. When they began talking to the three strangers, who had also caught his attention, the sheriff apprehended the group. He held them all for questioning.

Whether the sheriff knew the Earps and Randall were attached to the gunboat and had been watching them or just happened upon them is not known. Accounts differ, but he may have suspected the girls were being recruited for immoral purposes. Mattie, Wyatt and George were eventually released, but it is not known if the girls were released with them or held for further questioning. There is nothing to indicate the two may have been released only to continue to the boat. It is likewise unknown if charges were laid against Mattie, Wyatt and Randall as no arrest records or court documents have yet surfaced. Henry's records are generally incomplete or missing, and local newspaper items that covered arrests and court proceedings are sketchy at best. Several editions are missing completely.

Nonetheless, the trio experienced some sort of unpleasantness with Henry's observant sheriff. Whatever transpired convinced Mattie and Wyatt that Peoria was not the only place where lawmen harbored negative attitudes towards those in the brothel business. Small towns apparently could also embrace such dismaying sentiments. The trio quickly returned to the gunboat, which then continued its journey south.

Randall, meanwhile, had already decided against a career on the river. He remained aboard only until the boat reached Alton, the final stop of the southern run. At that point he bid Wyatt and Mattie fond farewell and journeyed to St. Louis in search of a more desirable future. Alas, he was unaware of a preordained rendezvous with the Angel of Death. Within a few days of his arrival he was stricken with smallpox.[4] During the second week of September George Randall died in an isolation ward of a St. Louis hospital. His body was returned to his family in Peoria.[5]

CHAPTER 12

$\mathscr{N}$avigational Error

When the boat slipped its lines at Alton to begin another northward run all was well aboard the Beardstown Gunboat. During that first week of September 1872 Mattie found life on the water pleasant. River travel was agreeable. She enjoyed the quiet pace of river life. As the boat glided past the river's bank she spent many pleasant moments watching thick stands of trees on the banks, their leaves slowly turning from summer green to the multi-hues of autumn. Soprano choirs of birds warbled and chirped to baritone and bass accompaniment of bullfrogs while gentle wavelets lapped against the barge's sides in quiet rhythm. The southern run had been profitable and there was no reason to believe that life would not go equally well on the return north.

John Walton and his new partner, Wyatt Earp, had discussed the course and the stops to make on their way to Lacon, including the feasibility of an extra stop to facilitate Peoria clients. Wyatt was dubious of that stop; he was concerned the recent crackdown had not yet abated. Walton assured him all would be well because he had a plan that would avoid trouble while still fully servicing the Peoria revelers he knew would come to the boat — his proposed mooring point was outside the jurisdiction of Peoria's lawmen. Agreement was thus reached and on the morning of September 4, with the skyline of Peoria barely visible on the horizon, Walton edged his barge against a wooden landing in the sheltered lee of a small cove south of Peoria. Easily accessible by road, the cove, called Wesley Bend, seemed the perfect place. According to a map Walton used it was clearly outside Peoria's city limits.

As the boat was made ready for the expected onrush of partygoers messengers were quickly dispatched to spread the news of the fun and festivity available for one and all. By mid-afternoon the word had spread throughout the city and the citizenry responded. The first evening saw a good crowd with the bar and upstairs rooms doing a land-rush business. In fact the coffers were so well filled the decision was made to extend the stopover. It was a decision that proved as unwise as the mooring point. News of the gunboat's presence had spread throughout Peoria not only quickly, but too far afield. Tidings of such promised great joy could hardly help but catch the attention of Captain Gill. A check of a map and a meeting with the mayor and his advisors determined conclusively that Wesley Bend was actually within city limits, authorities in the State capitol having recently extended the boundaries. This gave Gill authority to raid the boat with no fear of challenge on legal grounds. He sent word to his squad members to report to his office.

On September 7, Sam Gill divided his troops into two squads. At dusk they would depart, one by road with several wagons, the other by boat. Gill had the Beardstown Gunboat dead in his sights. The boatmen left first in order that Gill could arrive before the wagons. Surprise was the ace up his sleeve.

The boat squad made good time as Gill carefully navigated the craft down the river. When the barge became visible in the distance the engine was cut. The final half-mile would be by paddle power. The officers closed the distance in silence then nudged the boat against the shore a few yards upstream. Using the bush as cover they made their way to the landing. Loud fiddle music, stamping feet and gales of happy laughter emanating from within the deckhouse covered their approach. The noise allowed the squad to slip aboard without anyone noticing. Assigning officers to cover each door, Gill entered the main hall. When he blew his whistle and shouted for everyone to stay where they were the startled revelers rushed to the exits only to discover police blocking them. They were quickly herded into a corner while a team of constables rushed up-stairs where they easily cornered women and clients. Among them was Mattie.

Walton protested vociferously, claiming his mooring was outside Peoria's jurisdiction. To his disgust, he was informed that Wesley Point was indeed within the city's legal jurisdiction. He was then formally given notice that he and all within were under arrest.

Walton, Earp, the women, and patrons were led to the wagons that had just arrived. The timing had been perfect. Taken to Peoria, the prisoners were booked and lodged in holding cells. In one sense Walton, his crew and his patrons were lucky. Sufficient wagons had been brought thus allowing everyone to find room in the wagons. Had space been limited only the women would have been able to ride; the captive males would have been required to walk the five miles of rough road. On a dark night such a trek can be tiring, especially when hands are manacled.

The raid had been executed so smoothly the Peoria *Daily National Democrat*, in its September 10 edition, extended high praise, an unusual departure for that paper. Concerning the raid itself, a quote from one of the officers summed it up best: "They were the quietest set of bawds and pimps we ever handled. They felt so cheap at their unexpected capture."

Unexpected it had been. Gill's plans had been kept such a tight secret no one, not even his squad members, knew any details about the raid, including the location of the target, before they assembled for departure. The secrecy paid off, for the police netted a fairly large number of miscreants — thirteen in all including a very young female whose tender age moved George Kent, the editor of the *Daily Transcript*, to editorialize:

> Among the females is one very young and exceedingly pretty; by far too young and pretty to lead any longer the horrible life she has but just commenced. Could not some effort for her redemption from ignominy and death be made?[1]

Was this girl one of the two teenage girls with whom Mattie had been apprehended at Henry? One wonders.

The raid had surprised no one more than Wyatt and Mattie. They could not help but feel profound disappointment after having pinned their hopes on mobility and the belief that Wesley Bend was outside Peoria's jurisdiction. Peoria's Judge Cunningham was the last person either of them wanted to deal with again. Mattie was certainly worried but Wyatt, who had much more to lose, was especially concerned.

In its Tuesday, September 10 edition, the *Daily Transcript* wryly, even cheekily, remarked that "Wyatt Earp...an old offender" was among those arrested in the raid. As if that was not humiliation enough the *Daily National Democrat* also singled him out, referring to him as "the Peoria bummer..." In fact he was the only defendant given individual comment. To his deep chagrin, Wyatt had once again found his way into the newspapers, and again he was being abased by impudent, churlish editors.

Following their night in cells the defendants were led into court. One by one they were arraigned before the bench to hear the charges read. Each in turn entered a plea of guilty. When it came Mattie's turn she stood before the bench looking up at Judge Cunningham. She listened as the clerk intoned that she was being charged with "being a resident" of the bagnio. Judge Cunningham asked her to state her name.

"My name," Mattie replied, "is Sarah Earp. I am Mrs. Wyatt Earp."[2]

The women, including Mrs. Wyatt Earp and Mrs. John Walton, were fined $24 apiece. Their clients, charged as "found-ins," were assessed fines that ranged from $22 to $24.

Having dealt with those whom he considered the minor players, Judge Cunningham turned his attention to the two who had been charged with "keeping a house of ill-fame," Walton and Earp. Cunningham commented that Wyatt had appeared before the court previously, and recalled Wyatt from the McClellan Institute raid the previous May. Obviously he took the recollection into consideration when he determined the fines he would impose. Having found both men guilty, the judge fined them accordingly. John Walton was assessed a fine of $43.15 but for Wyatt the assessment was slightly higher, $44.00 or, in lieu thereof, the usual thirty days of jail time. Wyatt wanted nothing more to do with Peoria's rat-infested jail, having been there and done that. He said he would pay the fine. Escorted by the bailiff to the payment wicket he handed over cash in the amount of $68 to cover his and Mrs. Earp's fines.

Why was Wyatt's fine eighty-five cents higher than Walton's? No one knows. Obviously Judge Cunningham knew, but he never explained his reason. Editor Kent's referral to Wyatt as "an old offender" and the *Daily National Democrat's* reference to "Wyatt Earp, the Peoria bummer" might hold a clue. Was it because this was Wyatt's third charge while Walton was a newcomer to the Peoria court? Possible, but unlikely. Judge Cunningham knew Walton was the boat's owner, but Wyatt had also been charged as a keeper. To the judge this indicated a partnership so Wyatt was singled out because the judge intended to drive home a point. The point seems to have been intended to embarrass Earp. To attain this goal Cunningham made the amount such a miniscule, trifling difference it could not help but be noticed. Whatever his reasoning, it shall forever remain the judge's secret.

The reporters present appear to have guessed the reason. Their comments, and those of their editors, indicate that Wyatt was considered more notorious than just a mere brothel keeper, but in what way? Thrice convicted as a "keeper," Earp was also known as a pimp; but was he also considered a procurer who recruited unattached, lonely or lost women for the two houses with which he had been associated? The sheriff at Henry had obviously considered him a procurer. It is also possible that Earp's encounter with the law in Henry may have filtered down to interested ears in Peoria with two of those ears belonging to Judge Cunningham. Thus, the long and lingering suspicion that Earp was also a procurer as well as a pimp and a keeper remains very much alive.

Did Wyatt and Mattie hold a fiscal interest in the Beardstown Gunboat? The thought is well within the sphere of possibility. Although only three months had passed since Earp declined to pay a fine for his arrest in the McClellan Institute because he "had not the funds and would not work," it now seems probable he did have the funds but did not wish to part with them. He might have changed his mind had he known the appalling conditions within Peoria's jail, but as seems likely he wanted his money for future investment.

Earp was hardly naive and neither was Mattie. Both were too astute to have dissolved their partnership with Jane Haspel, and later Jenny Green, without selling their interests to some buyer, and the *Root's Directory,* in its 1873 edition, notes another man as being in residence at Haspel House. Perhaps he had bought out the Earps' interests as there was never a shortage of buyers and investors in Peoria's red light businesses. Also, Mattie had kept busy with Jennie Green while Wyatt was idling in jail so it is likely there were indeed sufficient funds to invest in Walton's enterprise.

Editors' comments about being "an old offender" and "the Peoria bummer" may have hurt Wyatt's feelings, but it is more likely that Judge Cunningham's eighty-five cent difference in the fines delivered the final humiliation. Wyatt and Mattie both realized they had no future in Illinois. It was time to move on. There is also the distinct possibility they were advised by the police to get out of town and not return. Whatever the reasons, he and Mattie agreed greener fields waited.

Mattie packed their belongings while Wyatt went to the depot and bought two one-way tickets. They would return to Kansas, to the tranquil serenity of Rice County where brother Newton, having grown tired of Fort Scott, had established a new farm near a small town named Peace.

A week later, when Mattie and Wyatt appeared at Newton's door seeking temporary asylum, they were made welcome. With no prospects for their immediate future there was little for Mattie to do but to hang her fancy dresses in a closet. For the foreseeable future she would don homespun clothing and once again tolerate her childhood *bete noir* — farm life. A cornfield in Kansas awaited her presence and all she could do was to hope was that it would be temporary.

CHAPTER 13

Once Again Those Fields of Corn

Mattie struggled to put the unpleasant memories of Peoria behind her as the train engine, hissing and spitting steam, spewed smoke and sparks from its smokestack. She began to feel better as the train rumbled steadily westward towards Kansas and the Great Plains. What were her thoughts as the train coursed its way through northern Missouri across open fields and between rolling hills? Did she look northward, however briefly, towards Iowa? Did her thoughts return for a few fleeting moments to Johnson County?

During the night, with a blanket to warm her, perhaps she drew closer against Wyatt and drifted away into slumber. Sleep, however, was difficult to sustain on the seats of a nineteenth century parlor car. The sparse cushioning gave little comfort. The car swayed in monotonous rhythm that from time to time was rudely broken by a jolt that apparently had no cause. Engineers plainly gained delight in rending the still night asunder with periodic blasts of the engine's shrill whistle. Cigar, cheroot and pipe smoke wafted throughout the car assailing eyes and nostrils. If someone foolishly opened a window, smoke from the engine drifted in through the screens that were effective only in keeping out insects. Overtired children, often hungry and cranky from inactivity, took turns crying. Had it not been for the hypnotic effect produced by the steel wheels playing a three-note chorus against the tracks, sleep would have been impossible.

In the early light of dawn Mattie saw wide fields of waving

grass and knew they had reached Kansas. She may have caught an occasional glimpse of a lonely farmhouse. Perhaps she saw a small straggling buffalo herd. She undoubtedly wondered what the future held. She was becoming accustomed to being uprooted and now, once again, she found herself heading down yet another road wondering what was at the other end.

Mattie's question about destination was answered when the train slowed and rumbled to a stop at the wooden platform of the railway depot at a small town. As she stepped down from the train she noticed the small sign attached to the depot's eave that informed the travelers this town was Peace, elevation 1465 ft.[1] Wyatt collected the baggage and within the hour they were proceeding the few miles to Newton's farm.

Mattie felt comfortable with Nancy and Newton and they were comfortable with her. If questions were asked they were about the train and the trip. Nancy knew her husband's brothers well enough that she never asked more than a few questions, all of the neutral variety. Life, she had found, went more smoothly that way, particularly where Wyatt was concerned. She never knew what he had been involved in and preferred not to know. Mattie was also pleased with Nancy's reticence for she had no desire to discuss Peoria. Newton, being an Earp, asked no questions of Mattie.

In the weeks that followed Mattie kept her own counsel, said little and busied herself helping with household chores. She did her best to show her gratitude to Newton and Nancy. She hoped the stay would be only long enough for Wyatt to decide their future.

What Wyatt decided was to stay in Kansas long enough to gather his thoughts. The departure from Illinois had been too sudden, not conducive to planning beyond the initial phase of shaking Peoria's memory from his mind. Time was required to formulate a plan of action. After due consideration Wyatt decided to apply one of his father's favored philosophical maxims: When life is at loose ends, lease some land and farm a spell. In this particular case farming made sense. Watching corn grow settles a man, allows him time to think.

Wyatt informed Mattie to prepare for a return to farm life.

Whether or not she was pleased is not known, but that she did not leave suggests agreement. Finding acreage to rent complete with basic equipment posed no problem. Soon Wyatt and Mattie found themselves staring out across the fields of a small farm. The purchase of a cow, a pig or two, and a horse or mule to pull a plow put them into business in time to plant corn and a few acres of sorghum. As both were excellent cash crops, a good harvest would give them money enough to move on.

Thus, Wyatt once again joined Newton in the farming community. As at Lamar, Wyatt found himself the immediate neighbor of Newton. Adelia Earp Edwards, Wyatt's sister, is alleged[2] to have said Wyatt held leases on two farms. No available records in Kansas show any leases bearing his name[3] and it was not Wyatt's nature to assume the work two farms would involve. Besides, judging from his sudden departure for Wichita in the autumn, he had no intentions of staying on the land a day longer than absolutely necessary. Nonetheless, throughout 1873 Wyatt and Mattie played the roles of the farmer and his wife, with apparent success.

That the Earps were farming in 1873 was not known until a few years ago. Stuart Lake had convinced nearly everyone that Wyatt had spent both 1872 and 1873 taming small towns such as Ellsworth or otherwise leading a lonely life hunting buffalo.[4] Lake may have been correct that Wyatt hunted buffalo in 1873, but not to the degree he aggrandized. Any buffalo Wyatt hunted that year was necessarily on a small scale. Rice County was all but bereft of the shaggy beasts, the few that remained being in small, widely scattered herds. Any hunting he might have undertaken would have meant a day or two in a wagon searching for one of the herds or picking off a stray. If Wyatt managed to kill only one adult buffalo, though, Mattie would have kept the larder sufficiently supplied for the season. She would have cooked the meat and preserved it in mason jars. Preserved meat was a staple of homestead life.

Farming allowed Mattie and Wyatt time to formulate plans for their future, but nothing was finally decided until the day a message from James arrived. He had found the ideal town, he wrote. It had a bright future and held the promise of wealth. He and Bessie were already there and he thought Wyatt should join him. The town, a short train journey from Peace, was Wichita.

It was news well received for Mattie and Wyatt had agreed farming would not be a long-term undertaking. One of the very few things they could call a common bond was their mutual dislike of farm life. For her part Mattie was grudgingly tolerating the very moil she had escaped five years before. While willing to reside on a backwoods farm in order to be with Wyatt, the length would necessarily have limits. If she found not even a modicum of contentment in the role of farm wife, Wyatt endured the life only because it was a suitable stopgap.

Mattie had known their stay would not be overly lengthy because she knew her husband had no enthusiasm for a life of years in a cornfield. He was not cut out for bib overalls and homespun shirts. He liked the feel of white shirts and was cognizant of the image created by a man in a suit of black broadcloth, the gambler's identifying vesture of the day. Wyatt Earp's idea of a ride was astride a spirited mustang, a saddle of fine leather the only thing between them. Perched on the metal seat of a sulky plow behind a plodding, often flatulent draft horse was sheer drudgery. Even worse was walking behind a balky mule while wrestling a cutting plow along uneven furrows. It was no way to live; farm life was too mundane. He needed the challenge of the card table, the ambiance of the saloon and the action found only in large towns and vibrant cities. Those were the spices of his life.

Mattie also yearned for the excitement of big towns, vibrant cities and the sporting life. She was well aware her man was intent on becoming "a man of the green cloth" and being married to a professional gambler appealed to her. A shrewd gambler usually had money, and Mattie liked what that money could buy. She wanted money in her purse. She was aware a clever woman could make money through shrewd investments, although she had not yet had the chance to apply that knowledge. Meanwhile, she would settle for stylish dresses with frills, shoes of real leather and wide-brimmed bonnets adorned with flowers and ribbons, lots of ribbons. She had also acquired partiality to whiskey's warm, tangy bite on the throat, and farm work left little time for such a pastime. She resented the exile imposed on her. Not for her was life in plain frocks and blouses made from bleached flour sacks. She found little appeal in the rows of corn she looked upon between sunrise and sunset. Consequently, both she and Wyatt tolerated the long months, and their joy knew no bounds the day in late September when they received the letter from James.

James and Nellie Bartlett, his new wife who was now calling herself Bessie Earp, had resurfaced in nearby Wichita and were singing its praises. James had moved there on the strength of rumors that it would be the next important cowtown, the natural successor to Abilene whose doom as a cowtown had been sealed by spline fever.[5] James, who knew a fledgling boomtown when he saw one, decided Wichita was about to embark upon a solid future. He easily found work in a saloon called Keno Hall, and then sent word to his brothers that Wichita held promise. To Wyatt and Mattie the message was a clarion call. The moment they had gathered the harvest, they decided, was the moment when the farm would become part of their past.

The final acre had no sooner been reduced to stubble when Wyatt announced his departure for Wichita. Wyatt promised to send for Mattie when he got settled and with barely a goodbye kiss was gone leaving her to attend to loose ends and lock the door as she left. With Newton's assistance she set about arranging for the sale of their grains and what little equipment they owned.

When Wyatt arrived in Wichita he quickly found a saloon[6] with space available for a faro bank and settled in to seek his fortune as a gambler. Wyatt and Mattie had no way of knowing it at the time, but James' letter had brought them two strokes of good fortune. The following year a severe drought — and its handmaiden the dreaded grasshopper plague — struck Rice County. John M. Muscott, centennial historian of Rice County, wrote of the disaster:

When this scourge had fairly settled down upon us, the

stoutest hearts quailed before it, and gloom was depicted on every countenance. The plow was left standing midway in the furrow, and for a while all farm labor was virtually suspended. The most gifted pen and the most eloquent tongue are inadequate for the task, for language is too poor to paint the scene of desolation wrought by the grasshoppers of 1874.[7]

The grasshoppers ate everything, including the paint from barns and wagons. Between insects and lack of rain the dried-out crops lay in ruins. Many Rice County farmers, including Newton, were driven from the land. Troubles were further compounded for countless farmers and town dwellers who had invested in the Northern Pacific Railroad. All fell victim to the national scandal that became known as "The 1873 Panic."[8]

Mattie stayed on the farm awaiting word from Wyatt. There is a lingering suspicion that Wyatt had departed hoping Mattie might decide to go in the opposite direction. Leaving their women without notice or explanation was not an uncommon Earp trait. If that had been his desire Mattie was in no mood to oblige him. By November, having settled the farm's affairs but with no word arriving from Wyatt, Mattie realized she might not hear from him. Taking matters into her own hands she made her way to Peace and boarded the train for the sixty-mile trip to Wichita. If Wyatt was pulling a fast one, she would surprise him. Mattie had not yet become a woman who could be brushed aside easily.

CHAPTER 14

𝔚ichita 1874–1876

Wichita had just begun to earn its place in the annals of western lore but was already a town rightly called a hellszapoppin' place. It had not always been thus because prior to its incorporation in 1868 the settlement had been barely large enough to be even considered a hamlet. In 1868 it had been a singlewide street with shacks and some small buildings strung out along both sides. The entire town seemed in danger of being blown away in the next major storm. A sign propped precariously on the sway-backed roof of the largest building announced in huge, black letters: GROCERIES. A few yards along stood a saloon and an unidentified shack. Wichita was merely a way station on the trail west. For about two months each spring wagon trains heading west to California[1] and Oregon stopped there. By mid-June the yearly exodus had begun to wind down, and by July Wichita returned to its normal doldrums.

The town's fortunes began an upward turn in 1869 when the Wichita and Southwestern Railroad started operations. Expansion of the town began and within a year several brick buildings had been built. Still, despite having doubled in size, the town remained small. In 1872 the Santa Fe Railroad ran a spur line into Wichita and the following year the town became a new terminus for cattle drives. By early summer the surrounding prairie had become a mass of Texas longhorn steers awaiting shipment east. They grazed peacefully on the rich prairie grass, restoring body fat lost on the rugged trail.

Those delays were deliberate because fat steers commanded high prices. Wichita would remain an important cowtown until spline fever, in its relentless spread east, ended its days as a great cattle terminal.

For five bountiful years, however, Wichita played willing host to Texan drovers eager to spend the money they had accumulated during long weeks on the trail. It did not take long for the town to swell to many times its humble beginnings. Wichita's population began to explode in 1873, but although hundreds of newcomers arrived very few intended to become permanent residents. These were the boomers,[2] so called because they followed an erratic path that took them from one town to another. Boomers were the gamblers, saloon owners, madams with women as well as various women who arrived on their own, all anxious to reap whatever rewards the new town had to offer. Lurking along the fringes of the boomer subculture were grifters eagerly promoting various get-rich-quick schemes. These were con men and scam artists, the flotsam and jetsam of every American state as well as no small number from north of the border. Many arrived as fugitives from the law, including many on the run from European courts.

Wichita expanded every which way but west, westward growth denied, not by the Arkansas River which was already bridged, but by a wretched settlement called Delano.[3] An entity unto itself with little civic structure and no law, it offered refuge to those facing excessive pressure from the Wichita lawmen. In some ways Wichita was fortunate in having Delano as its immediate neighbor because Delano absorbed the worst of the newcomers leaving the more inhibited free to occupy Wichita.

If Wichita was wild, Delano was openly lawless. The editor of the *Emporia* (Kansas) *Ledger* was moved to remark that Delano was the place where "everything originates and culminates."[4] Not strictly true, but it was a truism that Delano was decidedly no place for law-respecting, God-fearing men. Wichita lawmen did not venture across the bridge. Not because it lay beyond their jurisdiction but because, in plain truth, they were afraid to go there.

They had good reason to stay away. During the three months prior to Wyatt and Mattie arriving in Wichita there had been at least one killing each week and no less than three general gunfights. In June a soldier from a nearby cavalry base had shot and killed one of John "Red" Beard's girls in the dance house Beard owned, and the soldier was set upon and killed by a gang of ruffians. The soldier's comrades then began to shoot up the house, and several patrons, soldiers and ruffians alike, were wounded with varying degrees of severity.

In August an individual known as William Anderson shot and killed a Wichita citizen and then had fled to Delano. There he remained free until the night of October 27 when he was caught up in the well-publicized gunfight between "Red" Beard and "Rowdy Joe" Lowe in Lowe's dance hall. In the ensuing gunfight Beard shot Lowe through the neck and Lowe shot Beard twice in the chest and belly. Lowe survived, but Beard died in agony several days later.[5] There was, however, a third casualty of the shooting. William Anderson, caught in the crossfire, had both his eyes shot out by shotgun pellets. His ultimate fate was never recorded and remains unknown.

Despite the holier-than-thou attitude she exhibited towards Delano, and the verbal stones she cast, Wichita was not without sin. Buildings of brick construction were outnumbered by false fronted clapboard and canvas tents, many slated to become saloons, brothels or gaming halls. Buildings that opened for business the minute the roof was attached to the outer walls sprung up not unlike mushrooms that follow a warm spring rain on open fields; and an open field was pretty well what Wichita had been to that point. It is significant that this section of left-handed enterprise grew in close proximity to the bridge that spanned the river. It was no coincidence that the house James and Bessie Earp leased on their arrival was but a brisk sprint to the bridge.

Within the saloons herders drank and caroused while gamblers dealt cards and worked faro games amid the hubbub of carpentry that echoed around them. Saloons remained open day and night. Wichita attracted the drovers who found Delano too tough for even battle-hardened Texans. It had everything the cowboys wanted — saloons, gambling and women. Among the women were unique groups of ensemble dancers, the so-called hurdy-gurdy girls.[6]

No cowtown would be complete without brothels and Wichita was no exception. There were several, large and small, all doing brisk business. A verse in the famous folk-song, *The Streets of Laredo* contains a line in which a young cowboy laments as he lies dying: "It was first down to Rosie's and then to the card room." The cowboy's final lament applied no less equally to the streets of Wichita where there were many "Rosie's" and no shortage of card rooms.

Equally appealing to the drovers was the tolerance shown by Wichita's lawmen. Its small police force applied the law as well as it could under the direction of a series of city marshals, but the problem lay in finding a marshal with staying power. From 1868 to 1870 no less than six city marshals had worn the badge. Only one lasted more than five months. Most endured a few weeks while the others left within days and one resigned within six hours. Not until 1871 did law enforcement became consistent with the appointment of Mike Meagher,[7] who proved himself a lawman of the first order. Meagher had William "Bill" Smith to thank for the appointment.

Smith, a man of conservative politics, had been appointed to the office on April 10, 1871. Within hours he tendered his resignation in a letter in which he cited "existing emergencies"[8] without going into details. The next morning the town council hired Meagher who took over the office on April 13. He proved himself the capable man Wichita needed. So far as Wichita's citizens were concerned once Meagher had been on the job a few weeks, the badge was his for as long as he wanted to keep it.

In 1873 Wichita celebrated Meagher's recent marriage[9] by reelecting the tough, no-nonsense lawman to a further two-year term. The election was a landslide despite complaints from several citizens of having suffered beatings while in custody.[10] The charges were never proven but, interestingly, Meagher never bothered to deny them either. Heavy-handed or not he kept Wichita peaceful until he resigned in April 1874, midway through his second term, to go into the livery business.

Meagher, one of the best of the west's better lawmen, had found through trial and error during his first term the futility of too-strict imposition of law enforcement. He decided the answer lay in a fine balance of compromise and benevolent tyranny. Before the year was out he had resolved most of the town's problems.

His first victory was with the Texans. He agreed to go easy on minor infractions providing they refrained from playing a dangerous game called hurrahing.[11] Very soon, following talks with Meagher, the Texans confined the game to Delano.

Meagher also met with saloon owners and agreed to overlook certain building infractions providing honesty was ensured at the gaming tables and in the dispensing of drinks.

He then met with the madams and struck an accord with them as well. Meagher told them they would be allowed to remain in business by obeying city by-laws that had been on the books for some time. The by-laws would be strictly enforced. He then explained the terms of enforcement. Police would leave madams and their women alone and make no raids. However, each month a token arrest would be recorded against each madam and her sporting ladies. A pre-set mandatory fine[12] would be paid to the court. Comply and remain in business, he told them, or leave town. His compromise in this matter was a promise to sharply reduce the influx of newcomers. The madams listened and agreed. Overall the system worked well. The women paid their fines as required and unregistered Cyprians were escorted to the railroad depot for passage on the next train.

Unfortunately for that segment of the sporting community, early in 1874 Meagher decided to go into the livery and cartage business and resigned his office.[13] The city council rehired the mercurial Bill Smith who had apparently resolved his existing emergencies. Smith let it be known that life for the soiled doves would remain static but that madams should expect changes.

Republican Smith was no fan of Democrat Meagher's liberal views. Benevolent tyranny was all right but compromise had limits. He immediately laid plans for a crusade, the sole purpose of which was to rid the city of all sporting women. Realizing the task was easier said than done, he decided a test case in court was the way to proceed. Accordingly, he set his sights directly on 12 Douglas Avenue, the most popular bagnio in Wichita. If he could force its closure, he reasoned, the others would fall easily. His decision brought him into a head-on battle with Bessie and Mattie and, indirectly, with Wyatt Earp.

Had Meagher, a good friend of James and Wyatt, remained as city marshal, the troubles Mattie and Bessie were about to endure would never have happened. For that matter, had Wyatt been on the police force, he could easily have forestalled Smith's plans. Unfortunately Wyatt was not yet on the force, and would not be for several months. He had applied for employment in March 1874 but his application had been rejected by city hall. Not until the following year, seven months after the conflict with Smith had ended, did Wyatt find himself in a position to protect Mattie and Bessie and their girls.

CHAPTER 15

The House at 12 Douglas Avenue

When Mattie arrived in Wichita she moved into Bessie's house and quickly decided the town offered everything James had presumed. Also in residence were Bessie's nine-year-old daughter, Hattie, and thirteen-year-old son Thomas.[1] She also met a young woman named Kate Elder with whom she would have on-going dealings during her years with Wyatt. It is now generally accepted that Wyatt was engaged in an affair with Kate, and that was the reason he delayed his call to Mattie to come to Wichita. When Mattie showed up he broke off with Kate, much to her chagrin. Kate, who from that day forward hated Wyatt, was unable to understand why he would spurn her for the less attractive Mattie.

The house at 12 Douglas Avenue was a roomy one-story located near the bridge that crossed the river. Its owner was George Wood[2] who agreed to lease it to Bessie for a monthly rent plus rooms for himself, his wife, Meg, and their two women, Georgina "Georgie" Wood and Laura Smith, all of whom were registered as sporting women.[3] Bessie took the lease to a lawyer, William Baldwin, who checked the "i's" and "t's", declared the paper in order and witnessed Bessie's signature on the lease. Bessie moved in, recruited some girls and resumed her niche as a madam. The house, soon to be generally known as Bessie's Whore House, quickly became the most popular place in town. It was staffed by women of varying ages, all of whom, with one exception, used Earp as their surname.[4]

The non-Earp was a twenty-two-year-old who eventually

became famous in her own right as "Big Nose Kate." Her court record, however, identifies her as Kate Elder (except in August 1874 when she is listed as Kate Earp). Kate, ten months younger than Mattie, had also been four years in the trade. Like Mattie, she had a voracious taste for whiskey. Unlike Mattie, she was very sophisticated and well educated, spoke five and perhaps six languages, and was artistic, enjoying dramatic theater and opera. She was less emotional than Mattie and exhibited a temper only when drunk. Kate, an attractive blonde, was fun loving and vivacious and always seemed younger than her years.

Kate was born Catherine Mary[5] to an upper-middle class Hungarian family whose surname was Harony (sometimes spelled Haroney). The family left Hungary and after diverse adventures over a period of years arrived in Davenport, Iowa about 1867. Kate immediately ran away from home.[6]

Kate did not deserve the unfortunate soubriquet she had thrust upon her and it is not really known how or why she came to be called "Big Nose Kate." Photos show her nose as the type often described as aristocratic, but it was certainly neither of size or shape that merited a derogatory label. One plausible reason may have been her insatiable curiosity. Like an inquisitive cat that just has to know what is going on around her, Kate pried into activities not necessarily her concern. It is quite possible that one day an unamused co-worker took exception and accused her of being too inquisitive (as in "Kate, you have a big nose!") and, young ladies being young ladies, a nickname was born.

Kate was not just one of Bessie's girls. She enjoyed privileges as Bessie brought her along and taught her in the ways of madams. That she learned well is evidenced by her successful later years, particularly in Globe. Kate left Wichita in August 1874[7] and later went to Fort Griffin, Texas where she met a tubercular dentist, John Henry "Doc" Holliday,[8] also destined to become a western legend.

Mattie registered with the Wichita police as Sally Earp the first week in January 1874, thus negating any doubts of when she arrived in Wichita. That month she paid the first of fourteen consecutive fines as a soiled dove. The inaugural date of her partnership with Bessie is not known but it could hardly have been more than a few weeks. The partnership is proven by the warrants Marshal Smith later swore out against them. Full details of their partnership remain another of those little mysteries that cloak Mattie's history like an overlarge serape. It was a fledgling step for her, and Wyatt would have financed most, if not all, of her input to the deal. Also, there is no doubt that Bessie remained in overall charge.

It was a solid partnership according to old timers interviewed many years later. They all said the house was highly successful, always busy and never rowdy. With the highly experienced Bessie as the alpha madam it turned a profit during its thirty months of operation. Everyone connected with 12 Douglas Avenue made money. Mattie was happy. For the first time in her life she had the kind of money that could make her dreams come true.

By April 1874, 12 Douglas Avenue had become the most successful house of joy in Wichita. Each day, Sundays included, from early afternoon the girls entertained their clients with non-stop merriment while the two madams counted the profits with unbridled elation. There seemed no end to the good times. The only one who was not happy with the situation was City Marshal Bill Smith, newly appointed and, his mind on the 1875 elections, determined to impress Wichita's moral voters.

By early June the pious marshal was ready to launch his crusade. He had made Bessie's house top priority and, as a result of his fixation, Mattie and Bessie soon found themselves up to their slender necks in very deep, very hot water. During the morning of June 3, the marshal and a deputy, warrants in hand, knocked on the door of 12 Douglas Avenue. Smith personally arrested Bessie and Mattie and escorted them to the jail and into a cell.

Within the hour the women appeared together in Justice's Court[9] for a preliminary hearing, jointly charged that on June 3 they did "unlawfully and feloniously set up and keep a bawdy house or brothel." Adding to their woes, behind the bench sat D.A. Mitchell, Justice of the Peace. Justice Mitchell was a prohibitionist, a humorless moralist, and a man of strict fundamental religious convictions. When the prosecuting attorney stood to state his case Bessie and Mattie knew they were in deeper trouble than they had thought as the prosecuting attorney was none other than Sam Martin, another avowed crusader of the moral right. Mattie and Bessie stood before the judge as the bailiff read the charges. If they felt they were being conspired against they were not far off the mark.

The official complaint, docket Number 157, recorded in longhand by the court clerk, began as follows:

> State of Kansas, County of Sedgwick: In Justice's Court, Before D.A. Mitchell, a Justice of the Peace in and for Wichita City Township.

The Bailiff read the charges of keeping a bawdy house. The charges appear in the report dictated to the clerk by Justice of the Peace Mitchell:

> State of Kansas, Plft. Vs: Sallie and Bettsey Erp, defts.
>
> Saml. A. Martin, Prosecutor, Personally appeared before me.
>
> Samuel A. Martin who being duly sworn deposes and says; that on the 3rd day of June 1874 at the County of Sedgwick and State of Kansas, one Sallie Erp and Betsey Erp did then and there unlawfully and feloniously set up and keep a bawdy house or brothel and did appear to act as mistress and have care and management of a certain one story frame building situated and located North [side] of Douglas Avenue[10] near the bridge leading across the Arkansas River used and kept by said parties as a house of prostitution in this city of Wichita, County and State aforesaid contrary to the Statutes of Kansas made and provided, and deponent prays that process may be issued against the Said Sallie Erp and Betsey Erp and that they be dealt with according to law.[11][sic]
>
> (Signed) D.A. Mitchell, Justice of the Peace.

The women, anticipating the usual fines both pleaded guilty. To their dismay Justice Mitchell refused to accept the pleas. Instead, he directed a plea of not guilty be entered by the court on behalf of both women. He then remanded them in custody pending trial. A warrant to this effect was drawn up on the spot and handed to Constable J.W. McCartney for immediate serving. McCartney dutifully served the warrant then escorted the women to a cell in the police station. It was (so far as is known) the only time Bessie was ever in jail. Mattie, of course, had spent a couple of nights in Peoria's police cells.

Bessie immediately contacted William Baldwin and a couple of hours later the two again stood before Judge Mitchell, this time for a bail hearing. Judge Mitchell set bail at a hefty five hundred dollars each, in cash.[12] This was another blow. Neither woman had that amount of cash at hand and Mitchell refused them time to raise it. He ordered them returned to custody until the money could be presented. While Mattie and Bessie sat in their cell Baldwin contacted Wyatt and James. It would be up them to produce the bail money.

Wyatt was doing well with his faro, and James had funds as well, so they posted bail. Judge Mitchell now had no choice but to release the women. After specifying the bail conditions, he set September 15, a full sixteen weeks into the future, as the trial date. He was not done yet for he then ordered the trial be moved upward to District Court to be heard before a senior judge. This dismayed Mattie, Bessie and lawyer Baldwin, but it was Wyatt who was most vexed. A large amount of his operating cash would remain tied up for weeks. Both women, free on bail, returned home to ponder the future and decide how to cope.

After due consideration and debate of the risks, both women decided to continue as normal, with certain precautions. With Bessie and Mattie on bail Marshal Smith's test case would remain at rest providing they did not contravene their bail conditions. Those terms strictly prohibited them from acting as madams, so they knew even suspicion would result in a return to jail. The judge had not, however, prohibited either from engaging as common bawds.[13] As long as they remained garden-variety harlots they would not be run in and Marshal Smith would not bother them further.

There was, however, a serious problem. A temple of tryst requires a firm-handed madam. The girls required control and their clients had to be kept on good behavior. A house without a madam was an open invitation for trouble, something Bessie and Mattie had to avoid. They needed a madam who could not be shown as being either of them. Which one thought up the solution is unknown but the idea proved ingenious.

It was at this point an unknown woman entered the picture. News quickly spread that a Mattie Bradford was the new madam at 12 Douglas Avenue. The name was duly registered in the police files and for the next three months fines of $20 to cover charges of being a madam were paid to the court in that name. For all intents and purposes she was the madam at 12 Douglas Avenue, yet she proved so elusive she seemed invisible. No one knew who she was. No one ever saw her. Not even the omnipotent Marshal Smith was able to find her.

Who was Mattie Bradford? She, in fact, never existed except within the Wichita court records. Mattie Bradford was a stalking horse, a clever stratagem conceived by Bessie and Mattie, created to outwit and confuse City Marshal Smith and his allies. For almost four months Mattie and Bessie played their game remarkably well to a successful conclusion. Together, with the help of a nonexistent madam, they outfoxed the beleaguered lawman.[14]

CHAPTER 16

The Trial of Madam Mattie

William Baldwin[1] was a very capable lawyer who later became a probate judge respected within the community his reputation for fairness impeccable. As a defense lawyer his acquittal record was above average and that may have been the reason Bessie Earp retained him to represent the residents of her bagnio. An old hand in the game, she had learned that dealing through lawyers held advantages, not the least of which was to spare her and her girls the necessity of making personal appearances in court. The lawyer, more usually his clerk, attended court on behalf of the accused, entered guilty pleas as the names were called and paid the fines. It was perfect for Wichita's system where fines for madams and bawds were pre-set and guilty pleas were expected, and it rendered unnecessary the presentation of arguments. The lawyer could, and sometimes did, request leniency on first, or dubious, charges; and the judge, should he feel magnanimous, could and sometimes did impose a lesser fine. More importantly, it meant judges, unless they frequented the brothels themselves, never saw the women whose names graced their docket books. Bessie had not thought for a moment that Baldwin would have to personally defend her on a serious charge, but now she was happy to have selected him from the onset. Equally happy was Mattie, her co-defendant in the case.

As the town hall clock struck 10:00 a.m. on Tuesday, September 15, Bessie and Mattie rose nervously and stood respectfully as District Court Judge William P. Campbell[2] entered the courtroom. The day that would decide their futures had arrived. The tone was more than just serious because, with their charges elevated to the higher court, the women now faced a jail term of six months to one year, and no one had any doubts that Prosecution Attorney Samuel A. Martin would demand the maximum sentence.

As Judge Campbell settled into the chair behind the bench, the bailiff intoned the order, "be seated," and those in attendance complied. Very few were present in the courtroom, but no one seemed to notice. The judge brought down his gavel and pronounced the court was in session. He perhaps wondered if today he might get lucky and hear some new excuses or would he have to listen to the same old, lame, tiring, familiar arguments. The bailiff rose to read the charges. The clerk picked up his pen, removed the cap from a bottle of black ink and opened the Docket Book in which he would transcribe the proceedings. Judge Campbell nodded to indicate he was ready to hear arguments.

It was at this point Campbell noticed for the first time that the table set aside for the prosecution was unoccupied. Greatly annoyed, he told the bailiff to quickly find those officers of the court. The bailiff departed only to return a few minutes later to report that no one from the prosecution team could be found — and no one seemed to know where anyone was. Only the judge, bailiff, court stenographer, Mattie, Bessie, Baldwin and his clerk plus a few spectators were in the courtroom. Wyatt and James Earp were sitting unobtrusively in the back row. One might wonder if at this point in the proceedings Wyatt was not grinning ever so slightly.

Baldwin may also have been surprised at his worthy opponent's absence but he wasted not a second in taking advantage of the situation. As quickly as a coyote can pounce upon a rabbit he stood to ask permission to address the court. Permission granted, he then submitted a Motion for Dismissal. Judge Campbell listened, pondered for a moment, nodded and with a shrug of his shoulders granted the motion by stating:

> On motion of the Defendants in said action and no one appearing to oppose, said cause is now by the court dismissed,

and it is adjudged by the court that the prosecuting witness of said cause pay the costs of such action.[3]

Both Bessie and Sally, who had both been so willing to plead guilty at the preliminary hearing, appeared momentarily stunned. Their reaction changed to elation when the judge told them the charges were dismissed and they were free to leave. The happy women fairly swaggered from the courtroom with cheerfulness neither had felt since June. They were free; their ordeal was over. They could resume their lives. Did Mattie flash a wide smile at Wyatt as she walked past him towards the door? You can bet she did.

No one was more pleased than Mattie's husband. His woman was free; business at 12 Douglas Avenue could now resume to normal status and, more importantly, the cash he had posted as bail would be quickly returned to him.

Why none of the prosecution team, including the crusading city marshal who had been the genesis of the case and the usually aggressive prosecutor, had appeared for the trial is perplexing and gives pause for some thought. No official reasons exist if in fact any were ever recorded. One suspects Wyatt Earp had a hand in it. He would naturally have wanted to protect his wife and his sister-in-law but, and more to the point, he would not want closure of the lucrative sporting house in which he held a stake. Had he somehow convinced Marshal Smith the trial was a waste of time? Was he holding a fistful of gambling markers the prosecutor had run up? One can only wonder.

What happened to Madam Bradford, the lady of the night who had appeared from nowhere and was never seen? No sooner had Mattie and Bessie emerged from the courthouse, free and clear and anxious to resume their roles as madams, than Bradford disappeared from Wichita to be heard from no more, or anywhere else for that matter. Her final mention lies in the records of the Wichita Police Court indicating a $20 fine was levied against her during the final week of September on a charge of being a madam. That was recorded during the week of September 15. The fine was paid a few days following Bessie and Mattie's final court appearance. As usual it was paid on behalf of Mattie Bradford by William Baldwin's law office.

◎h, It Was a Very Good Year

After September, with the court case behind them, Mattie and Bessie enjoyed the remainder of the year by improving business and consequently piling up greater profits. They continued paying the monthly fines as required by city law but were never again bothered by Marshal Smith or any of his minions. Wyatt had once again enquired about a position with the police force only to be informed that his previous application was being held and would not be reconsidered until spring of 1875, possibly in March. Meanwhile, he tended to his faro banks and bided his time.

For Mattie and the other women in the house, their February fines were their last. Bessie did not gain her exemption until March; that month marked her final appearance in the record, although she paid twice, both fines from charges of being a madam. Marshal Smith may have lost the prize through his never-explained absence from court, but he was also a sore loser. He gained a modicum of revenge by finally nailing Bessie on the two separate charges. However, those were the final payments ever made by any resident of 12 Douglas Avenue. With their changes in fortune Bessie and Mattie were now on the way to become the best little madams in the west as 12 Douglas Avenue increased in staff and patronage.

Bessie, Mattie et al. owed their removal from the police lists to Wyatt's impending appointment to the police force. Although his regular duties would not commence until April 21, his influence apparently began in March. Wyatt's appointment had come too late to keep Mattie and Bessie from the original clutches of Marshal Smith, but he was now enabled to protect them from further harassment.

With the court records suddenly devoid of Earps, including the several who were using the name as an alias, they might all have vanished en masse into the silence of time had it not been for an invasion of county census takers. During March a small army of agents working for the Sedgwick County Census Office, armed with pens and official forms, appeared on the streets of Wichita. Their mandate was straightforward and determined. They were to interview all of Wichita's residents, or at least as many as they could possibly find. Theirs was a difficult task because many citizens did their best to avoid answering questions.

The morning one of the agents knocked on the door of 12 Douglas Avenue the only ones at home were Bessie, Kate Elder and a domestic employee who gave her name as Mattie Blackman.[1] Each was duly listed as being female and resident. Their ages were recorded, with Bessie and Kate noted as being "white." In the occupation column beside Bessie's and Kate's names the census taker printed, "sporting." Mattie Blackman was recorded as "servant of Bessie Earp," "colored," "aged 55." He noted the house belonged to George Wood but that neither he nor his wife Meg was at home. However, Georgina Wood and Laura Smith returned before the census agent left, so they answered his questions. He listed their ages, and status and recorded their occupations as "sporting." Georgina informed the questioner that the house was valued at $350 and that was also duly noted.[2]

The census makes no mention of Bessie's children, but they were likely in attendance at a nearby school. Mattie was probably somewhere nearby but, being expert in the art of evasion, if she did not feel like talking she would not appear. None of the other assorted Earp women, all known to reside in the house, was present, either. Among the missing were two women who appear consistently in the court files under the names Minnie Earp and Eva Earp.[3] Of the known residents (generally considered to be fifteen at any given time) the census agent was able to locate only five.

Another census taker who was working the main street interviewed James and Wyatt. He listed their employment as "sporting,"[4] an indication James was then gambling rather than bartending. Because census takers filled in the address lines only when interviewing at actual residences neither man's place of residence is mentioned. Both were, however, in residence at 12 Douglas Avenue.

As mentioned above, old-timers familiar with Bessie's house, when interviewed by writers during the 1930s, all recalled James and Wyatt, all knew they were brothers, and that James was Bessie's husband. Apparently none of those interviewers asked about the connection between Wyatt and Mattie, an omission that is hardly surprising. During the 1930s no writer was aware of Wyatt's dealings in the brothel trade, and old-timers would not have volunteered such information. Westerners were, and still are, tightlipped with information concerning others. The writers learned nothing of Mattie Blaylock because none was aware Wyatt had a wife in Wichita.[5]

Mattie Blaylock Earp's census omission led several writers of the Earp saga to insist she never lived in Wichita; but police files are sufficiently detailed to reveal her presence and are proof positive that she was known to the court as Sally Earp. Adding surety is the testimony of the numerous old-timers who had easily recalled her as going by the names of Sally *and* Mattie.

Early in 1875 Wichita's councilmen, who had for the past year lamented Mike Meagher's resignation and regretted their own lack of foresight, decided the town would require extra policemen during the upcoming cattle season. With Meagher absent the 1874 summer had been very troublesome for Wichita, with drunken cowboys having their own way along the streets and alleys of the town. Petty crime and mischief had also greatly increased with few miscreants detained. Marshal Smith had proven himself and his too few police officers incapable of keeping order. The council realized the lawmen they required were hardened men who could handle the tough Texas cowpokes. They agreed several rugged men, possessed of courage, pistol prowess and the ability to subdue fighting-mad drunks, must be employed. A hiring committee was appointed.

Wyatt's previous application was retrieved from the rejected file and given a second look. Following an interview he was offered an appointment as a constable with the regular police force.[6] His contract was for one year but included an option clause that on expiration the city could offer a long-term contract. He accepted and was sworn in, duties to commence April 21 at a salary of $60 per month.

The offer made to Wyatt was a departure from normal procedure because Wichita generally followed the custom prevalent in other Kansas cowtowns of hiring extra deputies only for the months of the cattle drives. Appointments ranged from three to five months and all contracts ended on September 30. These short-term deputies were paid the same monthly wage as regular force constables. Wyatt was pleased to have been hired to the permanent force rather than the special unit as it would mean a steady, full-time salary during the winter months when gambling slackened. It was also good news for Mattie who was once again finding a certain appeal in the prospect of permanent residency.

To further Wyatt's satisfaction, the council had no objection to police officers working at other lawful occupations during their off-time hours. Thus, Wyatt was enabled to continue operating his faro games. When not patrolling he could usually be found in the Keno Hall or other saloons.[7] With steady money now rolling in, Mattie and Wyatt grew accustomed to a higher standard of living, a standard easily maintained through profits from the Douglas Avenue house plus Wyatt's police salary and faro.

Overall, Wyatt proved himself very capable at keeping the peace and in the process earned several accolades.[8] He became popular and respected with Wichita's citizens from all walks of life and might have stayed on the force for years, perhaps even making it his life's career, had his proclivity for getting into trouble not intervened, and his service as a city police officer not ended abruptly with a less-than-honorable release.[9]

Wyatt was approaching his twelfth successful month as one of Wichita's finest, his contract seemingly destined for renewal when he punched his way into trouble. In April 1876 Earp slugged Bill Smith, knocking him down. Charged with assault, Earp appeared in court. Mike Meagher, who was about to win the election to marshal, was called as a prosecution witness. He took the stand and detailed the assault. That Meagher was the prosecution's chief witness against Wyatt was irony indeed because the two men were very good friends. In fact, Wyatt's reason for assaulting Smith was that he felt Smith was publicly slandering Meagher.[10] The court declared Wyatt guilty and fined him $30 plus $2 court costs.[11]

The city council understandably took a very dim view of a police officer causing assault on anyone even if it was a matter of honor. The council met to consider what action should be taken. The two choices under consideration caused a split in the council. Meagher, despite testifying for the prosecution, spoke in his favor. Several councilmen argued that Earp should be reprimanded but that his contract, which still had a few days remaining, should be honored. Others agreed, providing the contract was not renewed. Others wanted immediate firing, contract notwithstanding. In a very close vote (the margin was one) it was decided to void the contract immediately. Wyatt was fired the next morning.

Although finished as a lawman, Wyatt had no intention of leaving Wichita and Mattie certainly wanted to stay. Wyatt's faro game was doing well and 12 Douglas Avenue was busy so Wyatt continued gambling. Then, two weeks later the tiger began to buck the wrong way[12] and Wyatt's luck hit the wall. With the cards suddenly turned against him he was soon as broke as he had ever been.

That Wyatt was playing a losing hand became quickly known, as observation that did not escape the attention of his enemies, including those on the council. They wanted rid of him, not only as a disgraced police officer, but also as a citizen. Seeing him without visible means of support, they discussed ways of getting him out of town. In this they found allies among several Wichita citizens who also wanted the Earps out of town.

Wyatt was in an indefensible position. He was aware not only of the unfriendly eyes watching his every move, but he also knew Bill Smith still rankled over the humiliation of being knocked down in public. Smith was awaiting an opportunity to gain some vengeance. All that was needed was an opportunity and that came a few days later.

A letter written on Police Court stationary, in handwriting suspiciously similar to that of Bill Smith, was forwarded to City Hall. Dated May 10 it contained two recommendations. The first suggested "that the Marshal enforce the Vagrancy Act in the case of the Earps"[13] ; the second urged "That the scrip [salary owing] of W. Earp...be withheld from payment until all moneys collected [by him] for the city be turned over to the City treasurer."[14] [sic]

The letter's second recommendation was a reference to allegations that Wyatt (and another police officer) had pocketed fines. The city treasurer was instructed to make a quick audit of the books. His audit discovered Wyatt had indeed collected fines from madams and prostitutes but had not turned in the fines from the madams. Wyatt, it appeared, had kept the funds to bankroll his gambling. The city fathers, with the treasurer's report as proof of wrongdoing, took immediate steps to reclaim the money from their former policeman.

Details, while sketchy, indicate enough evidence existed to fully support the charges. Wyatt — caught and knowing it — agreed to pay the amount in full providing no charges were laid. The council, who wanted the money and not a court case, agreed, with a proviso. Wyatt, the council ordered, must leave town without undue delay. It would be appreciated also, they suggested, if his entire household went with him. With the game over Wyatt agreed to all conditions. He went home to tell Mattie the bad news. Although disappointed, she immediately began to pack, a task that was becoming familiar.

So it was that all the Earps, including those women who

were using the name as an alias, left Wichita. As usual the departure was carried out without fanfare in an exodus completed almost overnight. Wyatt and Mattie headed for Dodge City while James and Bessie departed in the direction of New Mexico. The house on Douglas Avenue, once Wichita's most popular center for socializing, gaiety and ribald entertainment, reverted to George Wood and his three women, but they could not match the talents of Bessie and Mattie and they also moved on within a few months.[15] The house at 12 Douglas Avenue would never be the same without Mattie or Bessie greeting patrons at the front door.[16]

CHAPTER 18

Ɗodge City and the Gambling Circuit 1876–1879

Upon being declared *persona non grata* in Wichita, Wyatt and Mattie decided to go to Dodge City, a decision reached because a few weeks earlier Morgan had sent word of excellent opportunities there. Neither had been considering a move from Wichita, but under the circumstances, and with no other plan to fall back on, it seemed prudent to at least take a look at Dodge City which, they had heard, seemed destined to become an important cowtown. What they found upon arrival was to their liking, but both agreed it was a place suited strictly for summer consideration. Unlike Wichita, whose economy had solid year-round incentives, Dodge City was still too dependent on cattle drives. To spend winters there held little attraction for Wyatt, and none at all for Mattie. They decided to spend their winters on the gambling circuit operating in Texas and New Mexico.

When Mattie got her first view of Dodge City it was already well established as a cattle center. Four years previously the Atchison, Topeka and Santa Fe Railroad laid in tracks, and by 1874 up to 250,000 steers each year were being moved through the corral runs into cattle cars for shipment east. Mattie was pleased for she would not have wanted to go to a town not already near full peak of success or showing little guarantee of early flourish. She was no different from the Earps in that regard.

Dodge City, despite its array of formidable lawmen, was a boisterous cowtown and remained so for several years. Its summer population teemed with drovers, trail bosses, and ancillary employees driving great herds bound for the eastern market. Often two, three, and sometimes four herds arrived within a single week. Money flowed in a seemingly endless stream. The end of the trail meant payday so the town was engulfed with wranglers flush with money, raging thirsts, and an eye for obliging women. The gambling fraternity exploited to the limit those who thought they had a talent for poker and faro. Many lost within a few hours the wages earned during long weeks of hard riding.

Not everyone liked the cattle drives. Resident detractors railed against them and the red light district they had spawned. Theirs were cries in the wilderness and went unheeded because gamblers, saloon owners, madams and soiled doves were not the only recipients of the wealth. City merchants had no wish to displease the cattlemen for they were, after all, the buoyant force of the town's mercantile commerce. Banks, hotels, cafes, bakeries, farriers and dry goods stores were all profiting. Doctors, lawyers, public stenographers, photographers, gunsmiths, newsmen, wheelwrights and carpenters were enjoying the rewards as well. Even undertakers profited, though never to the grand scale the pulp writers, Hollywood and TV would later portray.

Dodge City's reputation as the most important of the cowtowns and the capital of cowboy mayhem was never claimed during its hey-day. Nor was random violence its reality. The infamy came later through folklore, dime novels, movies and television, plus a series of energetic tourist boards. Abilene had been a much bigger terminus for the biggest drives. Newton was the west's wildest cowtown, with Ellsworth a close second and Caldwell third. Delano was arguably the most lawless. Dodge City, compared with any of those towns, was fairly tame. There were very few deaths from gunfights and even fewer outright murders. Most citizens were destined to die peacefully in their beds wearing their flannel nightgowns, their clothes hanging in neat array in a closet, their boots placed neatly under the bed.[1]

Unlike many other western settlements, Dodge City could boast some semblance of planning. Important streets were wide and straight. Side streets with wooden buildings and houses in neat rows extended for several blocks. There were wooden sidewalks, some with railings. For all that, however, it was not a pleasant town. It smelled of horse, cow and oxen manure that steamed malodorously in the summer heat[2] and intermingled with a fetid aroma emanating from great piles of buffalo hides. Stacked high near the railroad tracks, the hides roasted under the relentless prairie sun as they awaited shipment to distant tanneries. Shards of rotting flesh clinging to the hides attracted black clouds of flies that swarmed the piles in tens of thousands. Approaching travelers could smell Dodge City long before the town came into view.

Front Street, the hub of the red zone, may have been a stretch of rutted dirt but Mattie and Wyatt both saw immediately that it was a goldmine. Of course, the gold would have to be extracted from the pockets of trail riders. Mattie knew that Wyatt would easily exploit those who fancied themselves card players. She also saw the street as the road to her own opportunities, viewing it as the path to personal riches.

By the time Mattie and Wyatt arrived the population was increasing daily as more and more of the sporting fraternity arrived for the summer. Wyatt, and to a lesser extent Mattie, already knew some of them. Among Wyatt's newer friends was Luke Short (1854–93),[3] a dapper gambler who would add to his fame when he shot and killed Charlie Storms and James "Longhair Jim" Courtwright in that order.[4] They also made friends with Bat Masterson. The friendship between Masterson and Wyatt seems somewhat *outre* in retrospect as in later years Masterson showed a reluctance to speak of Wyatt. Perhaps this was because, busy as he was by then creating his own legend, he considered Wyatt a rival.[5]

On the day Mattie and Wyatt first approached the town's outskirts they were both entertaining their personal dreams.

Mattie's was of financial security and a home in some exciting city she had only read about, maybe St. Louis or — dare she dream? — New York. She did not want to delay much longer for she was already beginning to show signs of the price the sporting life exacts. No longer did she exude the attractiveness inherent in the full bloom of youth. She had gained some weight and her face and eyes were already showing lines and puffiness that attested to hard living. The past five years had taken their toll to the point where she now looked careworn, older than her twenty-six years. Worse, she was beginning to develop symptoms of the serious dental disease that would plague her final years. Perhaps she worried how she would look at thirty. Mattie was well aware she was not getting any younger.

For his part Wyatt was entertaining no thoughts of settlement. His were dreams of wealth and fame, grandiose ambitions he would chase for the remainder of his life. Neither Mattie nor Wyatt realized that dreams are but reflections of the dreamer, and neither possessed the ability to direct their dreams into reality. While neither would live to see their dreams come to fruition, Wyatt came within two years of what would have exceeded his aspiration of fame and financial success.

Mattie knew that Wyatt, just as he had in Wichita, would again seek the life he craved. She knew he saw in Dodge City the two goals he desired of life: the aura of the professional gambler and the advantages that came with wearing a lawman's badge. She also knew, with a woman's unerring intuition, that once they were again embraced by Lady Luck, the setbacks endured in Peoria and the final weeks in Wichita would pass into memory. She felt certain that gambling would bring them financial success and Wyatt would again be appointed to a position as a lawman.

Mattie may not have been a profound thinker but she knew they must sort their priorities and deal with them. First, they must find a place to live. Hotels were fine for the short term but they were usually expensive, often noisy and always lacking in privacy. Besides, she did not like the confinement of a single room. Mattie wanted a house. She would leave it to Wyatt to find one, but it would be she who would decide whether it would become a house or a home. Having enjoyed the heady experience of playing the function of madam, she was tempted to reprise the role. That decision had no need to be immediate. She must first determine the likelihood of success.

Within a few days their immediate future was settled. Wyatt had easily found a saloon in which to establish his faro game. He applied for, and was granted, a position on the police force thereby gaining a place on the illustrious list of Dodge City lawmen.[6] If Dodge City's authorities were aware that Wyatt had been driven from Wichita under a cloud, the knowledge mattered not a whit. They were well aware of what lay ahead in the hot summer months and were eager to hire his gun.

Thus, with one exception, the pair was to share their next four years with Dodge City, Texas and New Mexico. Until 1879 they resided in Dodge City from April to October where Wyatt combined gambling with work as a lawman[7]; and from November until late March they dwelt in various southwestern towns, alternating mainly between Fort Worth and Fort Griffin, Texas and Las Vegas, New Mexico.

The exception was the winter of 1876, which was spent in Deadwood, Dakota Territory.[8] Wyatt and Morgan went there and started a business cutting and selling wood.[9] The venture proved less successful than the brothers had hoped, or as Lake later claimed. Wyatt, years later, told a San Francisco reporter, without elaborating on anything, that he and his brother had been in Deadwood.[10] There is no evidence to suggest the Earps went to the Black Hills town to gamble, and Wyatt himself admitted his gambling had been extremely limited. In fact, very little is known of the Earps' adventures during that winter. Several short stories written for pulp magazines from the 1930s to the late 1940s claimed the brothers did much to tame the town but all those stories were fiction.[11] Neither man was foolish enough to even consider an attempt to tame Deadwood, and in any event, they were not asked.[12] Indeed, very little reference was made of them at all. Mattie, likewise, was never in any way mentioned, but unless she stayed south with Bessie and James it is almost certain she was there. It seems likely she would have accompanied Wyatt to Deadwood for one very sound reason: after his affair with "Big Nose Kate" in Wichita during October–December of 1873 she would be unwilling to let him wander off on his own again.

Texas had special appeal for Mattie and Wyatt. James was managing a saloon in one town or another so Wyatt had a ready-made spot for his faro games and Bessie was reportedly again operating popular houses of ill repute. Though unproven, there is great probability that Mattie worked again with Bessie in Fort Worth during the winter of 1878 although not as a business partner.

Wyatt had hoped to find employment as a lawman in either Fort Worth or Las Vegas and had applied to both police departments in 1877. His applications were rejected in both cases and Wyatt, having decided to concentrate strictly on gambling, did not reapply the following years.

While in Fort Griffin, Texas in either 1877 or 1878, their old Wichita associate, Kate Elder,[13] introduced Mattie and Wyatt to John Henry "Doc" Holliday[14] (b. Georgia 1851; d. Colorado 1887). Holliday, the west's most dangerous dentist, was a fearless, deadly young man. Afflicted with tuberculosis, from which he knew he could not recover, he may have developed a death wish, which could explain his swift, often irrational, responses to deadly situations and perilous challenges.[15]

Although the popular Holliday legend depicts him as a gambler/gunfighter, he in fact spent more time practicing dentistry than gambling (and his gunfights, aside from the OK Corral affair, were limited to perhaps three, if that). He operated dental clinics, with varying degrees of success, in several western towns during his travels. During his lifetime he earned a well-deserved reputation as an excellent dentist and during his first years was honored with an award for excellence.[16] His superior skill with a drill was such that he was able to save teeth rather than pull them. He originated a filling material that could last for decades and also introduced to the profession the guarantee of "satisfactory work or money refunded."

As the years passed Holliday developed a posthumous but undeserved reputation as a sharp-eyed gunfighter. His pistol artistry is mainly legend with very little legitimacy. He actually possessed limited skill with pistols, which may explain his dislike for them and his preference for shotguns.[17]

It is also part of his legend that he was a raging drunk, but if Kate, who knew him better than anyone, is to be believed, he was not. Her statements of later years directly oppose the popular notion that the man was a hopeless, violent alcoholic. In March 1940, in one of several letters Kate wrote to a niece[18] she stated that although Doc always kept a bottle of whiskey with him, he drank only when incessant coughing caused him great discomfort.[19] She also insisted his hard-as-nails deportment was a cover for a gentle disposition.

Bat Masterson seemingly shared Kate's depiction of Doc's demeanor. Writing in *Human Life*, Masterson acknowledged that Holliday was a dangerous man but noted that most of his bravado was bluff, that he lacked physical strength and was in fact "a weakling that any healthy sixteen-year-old boy would have been able to whip." Masterson also knew Holliday very well.

Just how stonyhearted Holliday really was is very much open to question. Kate described his reaction following the Tombstone gunfight when she wrote of his return to his room in Fly's boarding house where she was waiting for him. She asserts he was visibly shaken and buried his face in his hands as he sat, sobbing, on the bed. Kate wrote, "[Doc] came in, sat on the side of the bed, cried, and said 'Oh, this is just awful — awful.' He was all broken up."[20] That is hardly the reaction expected from an unfeeling killer.

Wyatt deliberately misled Lake about his first meeting with Holliday when he stated that a saloon owner, John Shanssey,[21] introduced him when he, Wyatt, was passing through town while on the trail of the notorious Dave Rudabaugh of William "Billy the Kid" Bonney's gang. Although he did admit knowing Kate, he also lied about their first meeting. He quickly glossed over Kate by simply identifying her as Holliday's wife, omitting to mention that Kate was in the employ (as a bar girl) of Shanssey at the time. Many years later Kate set the record straight by confirming it was she who had introduced Doc Holliday to Wyatt *"and his wife*[22] who were in Fort Griffin at that time." The "wife" was, of course, Mattie. Kate referred to Mattie in other letters she wrote over the years, but never once mentioned her by name.[23] These omissions were neither through inadvertence nor a failing memory as Kate had no trouble remembering the names of the other Earp women.

Kate confirmed the Fort Griffin introduction was Doc's first meeting with Mattie and Wyatt, but said nothing about it being her first meeting with them. That it was she who made the introductions clearly indicates she already knew them. Had Wyatt and Mattie not known Kate beforehand the meeting would likely not have taken place. While it is possible that Holliday and Earp would have eventually met across a card table, they would not likely have found any reason to become friends. Such casual contact would have presented no reason to draw them together. The leathered, weathered, rough-hewn Republican boomer and the well-educated, soft-spoken southern Democrat gentleman simply had nothing in common apart from their respective prowess in card sharping. That a friendship between the two ever blossomed at all is a mystery. No two men were ever so dissimilar.

While Wyatt's lie to Lake about having met Kate for the first time in Fort Griffin was just another of his many prevarications, his reason for its telling is understandable. Had he admitted to Lake of having known Kate prior to Fort Griffin he would certainly have been pressed for more details. Further questioning could easily have opened the possibility of stumbling over details of Wichita including his history with, and his termination from, that city's police force. He greatly feared such questions for he knew well that one might have resulted in a slipped mention of Peoria, which would have exposed his taradiddle of being a buffalo hunter during 1872–3. Any such slip would certainly have risked revealing Mattie, and Wyatt (with Josephine's full-fledged connivance) was not about to admit her existence under any circumstance.

As she did in Dodge City, Mattie remained well in the shadows during her Texas/New Mexico days. Statements by Kate, postmarks on Mattie's letters to Sarah, and enigmatic references to Wyatt in local newspapers prove their winters were spent in both states. While there is reason to believe Mattie continued in the trade along the gambling circuit, proof from police reports and court records does not exist. Her activity would have depended upon the financial success Wyatt was enjoying and he was not yet so flush that his woman could be assured the role of full-time housewife. At the time their life was so transient they were living in inexpensive hotels and boarding houses.

Furthermore, real doubt exists that Mattie was even interested in a completely domestic life for she had grown used to the glitter and auditory vibrancy of nightlife. She knew her way around the sporting areas of the towns they lived in and had passed through, and she felt very much at ease among her peers. She could always make a few dollars hustling drinks in whatever saloon Wyatt was operating his faro game; and if a newfound friend expressed interest in her she could always spare some of her time for him. There was also the little matter of her increasing taste for whiskey, the occasional cigarillo and her use of opium that had progressed from occasional to habitual. Because Wyatt disapproved of such vices he would never have underwritten even a portion of the expense. Mattie would have had to spend her own coin on her favored frailties, and there was only one way she could earn that coin. Moreover, because she had chosen her lifestyle of her own volition, there is little reason to consider she would not continue in it. Furthermore, there is nothing in her known history that projects the image of a happy, apron-clad homemaker, arms covered in flour to her elbows kneading bread on the kitchen table or stirring an iron kettle filled with homemade soup.

❖ ❖ ❖

Throughout the summer of 1876, with a credible police force patrolling the streets and special deputies ready to assemble at a moment's notice, Dodge City managed to keep a semblance of peaceful exuberance. As a result, the summer passed without much serious incident. Wyatt did his share of peace-keeping, made a number of routine arrests, which added to his paycheck, quelled some minor disturbances and garnered mention in the paper on occasion. His off-duty time was spent at the gaming table. Mattie also spent the summer quietly, making no public fuss but remaining busy just being Mattie.

In mid-October she and Wyatt departed, not for Texas but for Deadwood, where they found it not to their liking. They returned to Dodge City the following April determined to avoid making that mistake again. Next winter they would go to Texas, or maybe New Mexico. The Dakotas had shown them nothing of what they sought. Meanwhile there would be a change in their Dodge City routine as well.

In 1877 town records indicate Wyatt did not resume his place amongst the town's lawmen. It appears he chose instead to devote his entire summer to faro and poker. His name does not appear on the city's salary records nor is he listed as the arresting officer in any of that year's court records. Whether his hiatus came about of his own volition or because his application was not accepted is unknown. Whatever the reason, the following year his name again appears as a member of the law enforcement team.[24]

Mattie's activities in Dodge City during 1877 are not fully known, either. She kept her usual low profile and left no record in the courts. She was never mentioned by anyone who had known her while she and Wyatt lived in Dodge City. Her present-day relatives are convinced she was playing her usual games, and considering her track record it is difficult to picture her treading any other path. It becomes even more difficult to envision her otherwise during 1878 and 1879 when Kate, her erstwhile co-worker and rival for Wyatt's affections, was actively carousing along the breadth and length of Front

125

Street for fun and profit. It seems out of character for Mattie to see Kate having a good time and making a few dollars without joining in. She would naturally consider domesticity a waste of the house Wyatt had provided for her. Still, whatever she was doing, she was being very quiet about it.

If she left no traces of her activities on Front Street,[25] neither did she leave any evidence that her house was anything but a home. Although it is known to have been conveniently located two short blocks north of Front Street[26] there is no city directory in existence to pinpoint its exact location. It is known to have been on either First Avenue or Spruce Street very close to the Union Church that fronted on First Avenue at the northeast corner where Spruce Street intersects with First Avenue. Thus, Mattie's house was either on First Avenue, a few lots to the right of the church, or a lot or two behind it on Spruce Street. In either case, because the church has been mentioned as a reference marker, her house was within a few yards of that intersection.[27]

Mattie's house was about a three-minute walk from the Front Street saloons, thus conveniently located for the operation of a brothel. If she was operating such a house she was doing so with full immunity from the law, compliments of Wyatt's influence within the town's hierarchy. He would certainly have financed the endeavor for it would not only have been a sound business investment, it would have kept Mattie busy in Wyatt's absences.

In the [Rice County] *Gazette*,[28] in its regular section on Dodge City affairs, an intriguing article appears concerning what appears to be a house of ill fame. The reporter, a Dodge City resident, refers cautiously to an incident involving "one of Dodge City's angels, in the person of — no, we will not give the name," leaving one to ponder if perhaps the reporter felt the "angel" was being protected by someone who could cause him more trouble than he could handle. Could Mattie have been the "angel" and Wyatt the protector? Perhaps. It worked in Wichita.

So anonymous did Mattie remain that for some time Wyatt's apologists (some still do) claimed she had never been in

Dodge City. The cries echo the same (equally discredited) denials about Wichita and, more recently, Peoria. Again, their arguments are based on her name being absent from court records and newspapers. Their arguments are decanted from an empty jug. Her name does not appear in the Dodge City court records because she was never arrested; and she does not appear in the newspapers because she did nothing newsworthy. Denials notwithstanding, Mattie Blaylock Earp was indeed with Wyatt Earp in Dodge City. Ed Bartholomew, in *Wyatt Earp: The Untold Story*, mentions her in nine words in one to-the-point sentence. He mentions how Wyatt arrived in Dodge City in 1876. He was driving a buggy, Bartholomew wrote, and almost as an afterthought added, "Seated beside him was a young woman named Mattie." Beyond that he makes no further mention of her, not even to puzzle over her full identity or why she was with Wyatt.[29]

Mattie never had trouble steering clear of the courts with Wyatt as her protector.[30] As for news reports, Mattie, unlike Kate who cared little one way or another what anyone thought of her, never behaved badly in public. Mattie never generated a single report anywhere she went of her being drunk in the street or that she engaged in catfights with her peers. No equivalent of Front Street's infamous tabby tussle between Alice Chambers and Kate Howe ever appeared on her resume.[31]

During her time in Dodge City Mattie saw little of Wyatt. Busy with his numerous endeavors he had no time for the mediocrity of domestication; and Mattie was likewise too busy with her own concerns to care what he was doing. Besides, in 1878 he had once again become involved with another woman, reportedly one Lily Beck, also known as "Dutch Lil."[32]

During each of the four summers Mattie lived in Dodge City court records reveal no less than forty-eight known bawds in various establishments. These women operated mainly on or near Front Street and worked without police protection. There exist newspaper estimates that at least sixty others remained unidentified to official sources. Mattie would have been among that number. One fact that should not be overlooked is that

Kate Elder arrived in town in 1878, and despite the animosity that existed between them it is unlikely they would not have resumed dealings to some degree.

Kate was very definitely an active member of the Dodge City demimonde, becoming so well known her antics along Front Street became the stuff of legend. Some stories are doubtless true, but none can be proven through court records or newspaper accounts. Kate was also protected by Wyatt as part of his friendship with Doc Holliday, so she gained none of her fame through citations in newspapers or appearances in court.[33]

One other point of significance stands out. One of Mattie's present relatives made an interesting observation to this writer during a phone conversation. When asked if she knew much about Mattie's life in Dodge City she took a deep breath, paused, then replied, "Oh, the trouble that woman could get herself into." She chose not to elaborate because, she said, her great-aunt Mattie had suffered enough through what is already known. She did, however, indicate by inference that the truth of the matter was that Mattie was very much a part of Dodge City's sporting scene but simply stayed out of the spotlight.

The winter of 1877–8, spent in Fort Griffin, was financially reasonable for Mattie and Wyatt. In the spring they returned to Kansas. Wyatt suggested to Holliday that he and Kate return with them. Doc demurred, but within a few weeks they showed up in Dodge City. What had changed their minds? Departure from Fort Griffin had been made necessary through a misadventure involving Holliday and a sore poker loser. In order to avoid a confrontation with an irate group of the loser's friends, he and Kate left hurriedly. Dodge City seemed a good destination.[34]

Contrary to legend, Holliday went to Dodge City not to gamble but to resume his dentistry practice. He opened a surgery in the Dodge Hotel and placed an advertisement in the newspaper.[35] Because he always presented an image in keeping with the profession, he convinced Kate to forego carousing. She tried hard and kept a low profile for several weeks.

Celia Ann Blaylock (aka Mattie Earp; aka Celie Earp; aka Sallie Earp). Taken in either 1870 or 1871 at Fort Scott, Kansas. *Courtesy of Arizona Historical Society.*

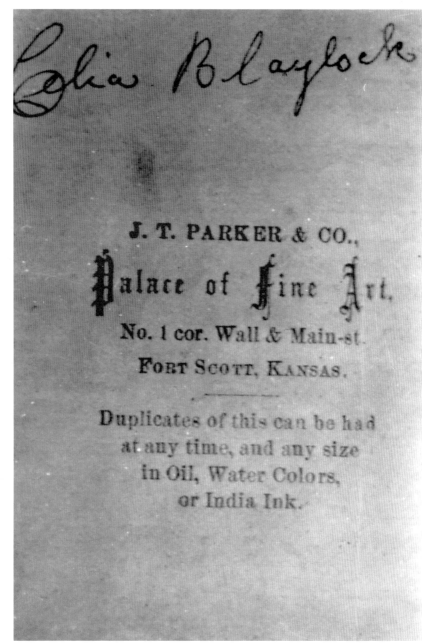

J. T. PARKER & CO.,
Palace of Fine Art,
No. 1 cor. Wall & Main-st.
FORT SCOTT, KANSAS.

Duplicates of this can be had
at any time, and any size
in Oil, Water Colors,
or India Ink.

Printing on back of the original photo of Mattie on file at the Arizona Historical Society. The signature is probably Mattie's.

Mattie's parents, Henry and Betsy. Their stern countenances indicate parental discipline may have been a deciding factor in Mattie and Sarah's decision to run away from home in 1868. *Courtesy G. Boyer collection.*

Tony Mae Blaylock, Mattie's baby sister, at about eighteen months of age. Chances are that Mattie looked something like her at that age.

Courtesy Karma Heim Lanning collection.

Above: Tony Mae Blaylock as an adult. Note the resemblance to Mattie's Fort Scott photo.
Courtesy G. Boyer collection.

Right: Sarah Blaylock married Hiram Marquis several years after her return home. Hiram was about twenty years her senior. The photo (c. 1877) was probably taken shortly after their marriage. *Courtesy G. Boyer collection.*

Wyatt Earp, c. 1871. *Courtesy G. Boyer collection.*

Wyatt Earp, c. 1883. *Courtesy G. Boyer collection.*

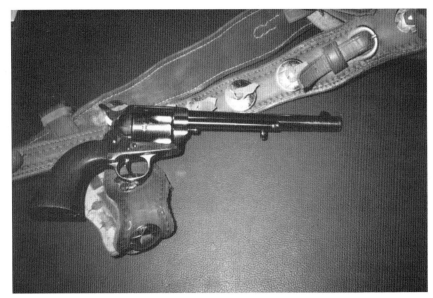

This Colt Peacemaker was owned by Wyatt Earp and might be the weapon he used in the gunfight near the OK Corral in Tombstone in October 1881. Forensic tests are being carried out at the moment in an effort to make a final determination. The pistol is part of the G. Boyer collection. *Author photo.*

This pistol was once owned by Nicholas Earp, Wyatt's father. The pistol is part of the G. Boyer collection. *Author photo.*

Douglas Avenue in Wichita, Kansas in 1865 before the railway
came in. The entire town is little more than a collection of huts.
Courtesy Kansas State Historical Society.

Wichita's Douglas Avenue, c. 1873, shortly before Wyatt and Mattie arrived.
Courtesy Kansas State Historical Society.

Modern day Washington Avenue at Hamilton Street in Peoria. The city razed the old red light district, widened the streets, and built modern buildings of legitimate commerce. In 1872, Haspel House was located on the left side of this parking lot between the gnarled tree and a large building called the Cooper Institute. The street at that time was occupied entirely by saloons, dance halls, card houses, and brothels. In the square behind Haspel House were several small shacks, each one a brothel. The old tree is the only thing remaining from those old days. *Author photo.*

The Cooper Institute has long since been replaced by the Kelly Feed Store. Jane Haspel thought the massive building would shield her bagnio from the prying eyes of Captain Gill's vice squad. She was wrong. The front door of Haspel House was approximately where the lamp standard now stands and the house extended to the far edge of the driveway. *Author photo.*

On this lot on Hamilton Street stood the McClelland Institute, home to Jennie Green, her girls, and also to Mattie, Wyatt and Morgan Earp, who had joined Jennie upon leaving Haspel House. In March 1872, Mattie's friend, Minnie Randall (aka Abbie Soder) died of an opium overdose here. This location is now home to a city civic complex. Many of those who work within are unaware of the ghosts that may yet haunt the area. *Author photo.*

Now a café and a photography studio, when Mattie moved to Globe, Arizona in 1882 to be with Kate Elder, this building was the St. Elmo Hotel. There are many indications that this was the brothel managed by Kate. Years later, Kate referred to her work in Globe as "managing a hotel." The St. Elmo, however, had become a brothel in 1882 (the year Kate leased the hotel) and remained in that capacity until 1973 when state authorities shut it down. *Author photo.*

Pinal, c. 1883. One of those small shacks housed Mattie during her final months. Its exact location is unknown. Leudke Brothers General Store is the large white building seen directly behind the tall smokestack. *Courtesy Arizona Historical Society.*

Pinal as seen from the Crushing Mill, c. 1885.
Courtesy Arizona Historical Society.

A section that remains of the old railway tracks that ran between Pinal and the Silver King Mine. *Courtesy Scott Dyke collection.*

With the butte in the background, the town of Superior can be seen to the right. Pinal's site is about two miles from Superior. *Author photo.*

The old Pinal cemetery lies some 800 yards from the old town site in the shadow of the butte in the background. This view is from Mattie's gravesite.
Author photo.

This grave is often mistaken for Mattie's; however, it is several yards away. Someone placed a plastic rose on it.
Author photo.

Mattie's memorial is not at all close to her grave. Either the person who erected this had no idea of where her grave was, or he was deliberately protecting it. *Author photo.*

Mattie's grave in Pinal's abandoned graveyard. Its marker was stolen about 1953 and has not been replaced.
Author photo.

Note: The author agreed to withhold the exact location of the grave at the request of Mattie's family members. Anyone wishing to visit it must first ask permission from the Superior Town Hall, and those approved are directed to its location.

Mattie Earp, 1885. Taken at Globe, Arizona.
Courtesy G. Boyer, Tucson, Arizona.

Inscription on back of
the photo of Mattie.

27 317

J. C. BURGE,

ARTIST,

GLOBE CITY,

ARIZONA.

First-class work a specialty.

144

Perhaps she spent quiet days with Mattie in her home near the church, while Doc tended to teeth and gums. But fate, as it is wont to do, intervened.

Dentistry soon proved too boring for Doc[36] and the stress of shunning the saloon scene did little for Kate's morale. Finally, by mutual agreement, the pact was nullified. Holliday closed his surgery, retrieved his playing cards and other paraphernalia and resumed life as a professional gambler. Kate, barely concealing her excitement, happily headed back to the sporting life.

In 1878 talk of imminent changes in Dodge City once again approached a high point. Predictions that the massive cattle drives would soon end became daily rumors. Many within the sporting fraternity started to look for greener pastures. Wyatt was one of those thinking along those lines[37] but finally dismissed the rumors for what they were and decided to stay one more summer at least.

Dodge City had been good to Wyatt and had treated Mattie well also. During their summers Wyatt had come into his own as a professional gambler and Mattie had brought no disgrace to herself, had not caused rumors and had raised few eyebrows. As the summer rolled on it produced no final omens that changes were imminent. The drovers still spent their money, the saloon girls continued to sing, dance and kick their heels high, and the merchants reaped above-average profits.

Nonetheless, Dodge City was changing and both Mattie and Wyatt were among those who sensed it. Reliance on cattle was slowly declining[38] as local corn and wheat farmers gained influence and forced change. Permanent residents began to talk again for the need of change and applied pressure where it counted, in Topeka, the state capitol.

Change, however, was being driven as much by the town's psyche than anything else. By 1878 Dodge City's artistic front had already seen an upsurge in theater agenda. There were more visits from professional theatrical and musical troupes.

Stage productions, including Shakespearean drama, were becoming more in vogue. Dodge City residents were reaching for refinement. Saloon and brothel pianists still played the usual selections of frontier favorites, but that summer the hit of the day was as unlikely a choice as could be imagined in such a rugged cowtown. Housewives, children, merchants, cowboys, gamblers, whores, parsons, lawyers, lawmen and bankers were humming and whistling the notes of a classic musical piece. Chopin's *Polonaise* in A-flat major had inexplicably swept the entire west to become the number one hit of the year.[39]

Change had also occurred amongst the town's rough-and-tumble. Serious crime was down and Wyatt's services as a police officer in Dodge City had diminished accordingly. Earp had made a number of arrests in 1876 and had been busy in 1878 with thirty-five, but in 1879 his arrests dwindled to only twelve, all minor, mainly drinking, infractions.[40] The town was definitely changing. It was time to leave.

All in all, Earp had served Dodge City quite well. While some of his activities drew notice, none were as important as he and others would later claim on his behalf. It is doubtful his service to Dodge City produced even a fifth of the heroic deeds that have been attributed to him. Despite his later claim of being the city marshal, he was never more than a deputy. The promotion to marshal was posthumous, bestowed by Stuart Lake and perpetuated by adoring fans. The claim of his shooting Bill Hoyt out of the saddle is especially suspect, as is his version of facing down the ever-dangerous Clay Allison.[41] Only fools ever faced Allison alone, so the day Wyatt met with the sanguinary gunman he was very well backed by shotguns. (Bat Masterson, shotgun cocked, stood in a doorway just across the street). Allison was no fool. Recognizing the odds against him he wished Wyatt well and left town.

On October 5, 1879 Wyatt played out his final scene as a Dodge City lawman, a minor role in the arrest of George Kennedy.[42] The popular saloon singer, Dora Hand, had been shot and killed the previous evening and Kennedy was considered the culprit.[43] Wyatt was listed in the newspaper account as being a member of the posse that brought Kennedy in, but he drew no further comment.

Nonetheless, he accomplished enough to be considered a creditable part of the city's law enforcement structure. Because he was extremely adept at buffaloing, he never had to shoot an obnoxious or belligerent cowboy. Buffaloing, it should be noted, took skill, success being dependent on surprise. In one swift non-stop motion the lawman drew his pistol from its holster and laid the barrel across the side of the suspect's head with sufficient force to render the recipient unconscious.[44] None ever knew what had hit him until he awakened and was told about it. Earp was a master of the tactic and considered it the best method to subdue hard to manage rowdies.

Mattie, during her four summers in Dodge City, had no idea she was witnessing the beginning of a legend. Did she ever feel pride in Wyatt's exploits? Did she avidly read the newspaper for mention of his name? Did she see him as a great man of action? Did she care? Whatever her thoughts, she kept them to herself.

During 1879 Wyatt, and to a lesser degree Mattie, was beginning to show signs of restlessness. Dodge City seemed to have lost some of its glitter and Wyatt had obviously lost much of his interest in his role as a lawman. As September waned, Mattie, knowing she and Wyatt would soon be leaving, dusted off the well-traveled trunks and began selecting items they would take with them. On October 9 Wyatt turned in his badge and the next night closed his faro game for the final time. A few days later he and Mattie headed west once again, but not to Texas. This time the road would lead to Arizona Territory, to a town called Tombstone. Wyatt had heard of great opportunities in the area, which, he told Mattie, was unbelievably rich in silver ore. Great wealth awaited anyone willing to look hard enough for it. The territory was opening up and other opportunities were sure to become available. They would journey to Prescott and stay with Virgil and Allie to await James and

Bessie who were coming from Texas. Then all would embark to Tombstone. Wyatt expected that Morgan would eventually show up in Tombstone as well, which would put the brothers Earp into a position to make their marks as influential personages. Mattie shrugged. By now, as far as she was concerned, one town was as good as any other. Whether in Kansas, Texas or Arizona it made little difference to her.

While news of wealth emanating from Tombstone was music to any boomer's ears, the Earp brothers considered it a clarion call, a proclamation demanding immediate action. Mattie did not know it, of course, but Tombstone was for her, and all the Earps, the crossroads in their lives. It was at Tombstone that Wyatt, his brothers and Doc Holliday would gain lasting fame (or infamy depending on one's point of view). Tombstone would also shatter the tightly knit complexity of that unusual family. Morgan would die at the hands of cowardly back-shooters. Virgil would be fortunate to survive a late night ambush. Wyatt would exact a terrible revenge against Morgan's killers, and then would flee Arizona a wanted man. Bessie Earp, who had but nine years more to live, would abandon her life as a madam forever. A sloe-eyed beauty of questionable morals would rise to a certain fame. Mattie's days with Wyatt would end permanently and she would begin her fateful journey on the final trail that would lead her to a miserable hell on earth and a tragic death.

CHAPTER 19

ℭombstone 1879–1880

Wyatt and Mattie were boomers, he by natural intuition, she by a desire to stay with her man, and astute boomers knew the signs that foretold the beginnings of the last days of easy profit. Both Mattie and Wyatt knew it was time to leave Kansas when Virgil informed them of a dusty cluster of adobe huts in the southeast corner of Arizona Territory, which was fast becoming the center for silver lodes that defied description. Wyatt and Mattie needed no further urging and hastened to Prescott where Virgil was working as a deputy marshal. They stayed with Virgil and Allie while awaiting James, Bessie and the two children, Hattie and Thomas, who were coming from Fort Worth. Mattie had never met Virgil or Allie and Allie had yet to meet Wyatt and James, so the waiting period allowed everyone to become acquainted. Mattie and Allie hit it off well, possibly because they had some common ground. Allie, orphaned at a young age, had survived a difficult childhood and Mattie was of the opinion that she also had been hard done by in her teens.

In December, in a small convoy of wagons, the group departed Prescott. The journey was uneventful, if dusty. Mattie's first thoughts upon arrival in Tombstone are not known, but she may have been dismayed, perhaps mightily. The town was much bigger than she had envisioned. She estimated the population as being close to ten thousand people, not including a large number of Chinese (whom the newspapers referred to as Celestials). She saw sprawled across the desert an array of buildings and houses, some adobe and some wooden. There were several buildings of brick in varying stages of completion, and dozens and dozens of tents. Three principal streets, Allen, Toughnut and Fremont, all wide and straight, were already crowded on either side with saloons, dance houses, hotels and card rooms. Some cafés, stores and places of recreation lined the lesser side streets. Many dozens of canvas tents, some quite large, were set up along unnamed roads that meandered, seemingly with no particular destination, among sagebrush and cacti until they narrowed to trails and dissipated into the desert. From her perch on the wagon's front seat Mattie saw hundreds of men and many women, all coming and going on their various missions, scurrying like ants at a picnic. She spotted many whom she instinctively knew to be sporting women. She may even have concluded the entire town was one big sporting district. Horses and mules, loose or attached to wagons of varying sizes, crowded the roads. In reality it was not much different than the approach to Dodge City except there was no dreadful smell and it was very noticeably bigger.

Mattie decided there was too much to do without wasting her time dwelling upon what the town might or might not be. She did notice, though, that as the Earps' wagons rumbled into town, many men appeared to take notice. Both Bessie and Mattie, from force of habit, feigning shyness, smiled as they passed. Mattie wondered if maybe Bessie was contemplating the feasibility of planning a future establishment. It was worth a thought, she decided.

The next few weeks were too busy for thoughts of business, with the men finding work and the women settling to make homes out of whatever dwellings they had been able to rent. Mattie (and Bessie, too) had already decided domesticity was the route to go, at least for a while. During the next weeks the Earps began carving their individual niches in Tombstone society. James quickly settled into his usual role when he was hired as bartender-manager of Vogan's Bowling Alley and Saloon on Allen Street. A few months later he opened his own place, The Sampling Room.[1] Virgil was quickly hired (probably on the recommendation of Territory Marshal Crawley Dake) as chief deputy to City Marshal Fred White.[2] The Earp vanguard was well established when Morgan arrived in June 1880.[3] With him was a very attractive blonde he had met in Montana, Louisa Houston, (pronounced Lou-i-za and some-times called "Lou") whom he introduced as his wife. The last of the brothers, 16-year-old Baxter Warren, arrived from Cali-fornia in 1881. Warren, during his time in Tombstone, worked at odd jobs arranged through his older brothers. One of the jobs was as security guard in the marshal's office, which gave him the opportunity to also occasionally ride on posses with Virgil.

Wyatt, despite what some believe, did not immediately be-gin to gamble. Tombstone was not an easy place to break into because gambling was tied up between two rival factions, one of easterners the other of Californians. The two factions were engaged in a serious turf war that the Earps wanted no part of, so Wyatt hired on with Wells Fargo.[4] He also served, as re-quired, as a deputy for Virgil. Most of his time he spent pros-pecting and pursuing interests with some partners. In June he was hired as a faro dealer by Lou Rickabaugh (not to be confused with the outlaw, Dave Rudabaugh) of the California group. It was through Rickabaugh that he acquired his gam-ing space in the Oriental Saloon.[5] To his dismay he was soon embroiled in the disputes between the factions.[6]

It was probably through Wyatt's influence that Luke Short and Bat Masterson came to Tombstone, arrivals considered more purposeful than coincidental. Both men bolstered the ranks of Earp's affiliates, one of whom was "Buckskin Frank" Leslie.[7] The unease between the factions settled quickly after Luke Short killed Charley Storms on Allen Street, just out-side the Oriental Saloon. An aging but still deadly gunfighter, Storms may have been brought to Tombstone for the express purpose of killing Dave Rudabaugh, but Storms got drunk one evening and challenged Short who was sober. The diminutive gambler shrugged, rose from his chair at the gambling table, told the players that he would be only a few minutes, nod-ded to Storms that he accepted the challenge. Storm left the saloon to stand on the street. Short appeared a moment later and the two stood facing each other for a few seconds. Suddenly Storms pulled his gun but Short's draw was quicker and he also had the better aim. As Storms lay dying in the street Short looked quietly down at him for a fleeting moment then, satisfied he would not get up, returned to the saloon and rejoined his interrupted poker game. Witnesses later said Short had reacted as if nothing had happened.

If Storms' death hastened the truce that followed, an equally possible cause was the formation of a vigilance committee by some concerned citizens. While the committee was never particularly active, its members did hold some well-publicized meetings and nailed impressive warning notices to poles. Often words speak louder than actions and those of the committee obviously gave pause for thought. Of the California faction the majority were from the San Francisco area and certainly aware of how deadly a determined vigilance committee could be. As well, many in the Eastern faction could recall the lethal efficiency of Indiana vigilantes when they terminated the Reno gang in 1868.[8] Neither faction wanted dealings with nightriders. The two camps agreed discretion overrode boldness and called a truce.

While their men had been looking the town over for prospects, Mattie and her sisters-in-law had also looked over their new town. As if by common resolve they all settled into domesticity. Their lives were spent strictly as homemakers during those days. Mattie was happy and resumed writing to Sarah. As usual her return address was Mrs. Wyatt Earp and she may have thought the security that had eluded her for the past years was at hand. Louisa, on the other hand, seemed not so sure of her status. To this day she remains an enigma. Letters to her family in Wisconsin indicate ambiguity regarding her marital status. Whether this was intentional or not is unsolvable. In some letters she refers to Morgan as "my husband" while in others she refers to him formally as "Mr. Earp." In none does she refer to him as "Morgan" or with his sometimes-used middle name, Seth.[9] As well, some of the letters are signed Louisa Houston, others Louisa Earp.

Bessie was apparently happy to be settled and seemed content to be referred to as housekeeper instead of "keeper of a house." She tended her home, looked after her children and, like her sisters-in-law, remained well within the shadows.

None of the Earp women drew comments in either of the two papers until the week they departed for good. Nonetheless, they were all well known to merchants and shopkeepers. During the 1930s a few pulp magazines printed articles about the Earp brothers in which their women were given occasional mention, but none ever included Mattie or Bessie. Aside from a mention in the *Epitaph* upon her departure from Tombstone in 1882 and her obituary in 1888, Mattie received no press until Frank Waters mentioned her in his book, *The Coloradans*.

Waters also wrote what was purportedly Allie's authorized biography, but the manuscript contained so much fiction and so many errors that when Allie proofread it she found it too critical of her beloved Virgil, and she never forgave him for it. She refused to sanction it and the prospective publisher backed off and it sat unpublished until 1963, some twenty years after Allie's death. When Waters did get a second chance for publication, with Allie long dead and no one else to interfere, he added to it, including quite a great deal about Mattie. The revised book, *The Earp Brothers of Tombstone*, was a hatchet job on all the Earps, including Mattie. Waters in this instance did not allow facts to get in the way of a good story.

He made his revised "biography" sound plausible by writing it in a manner similar to the first manuscript in which Allie had a hand; but there was very little of Allie's input in the second. He portrayed Allie as a naive innocent caught up in a family of no-goods. The book itself was a vehicle of mostly glaring fabrication designed to depict the four Earp brothers as power-hungry outlaws hiding behind their badges. No one, including Mattie, escaped his obvious dislike of the Earps. In fact, Waters committed quite some space to Mattie, little of it good and none sympathetic.

It was, however, the men he most fictionalized. They were lazy, unproductive and continuously looking for easy money — not excluding stage robbery — that forced the women to become the principal wage earners. He has Allie tell him of a partnership she formed with Bessie, Louisa, Big Nosed Kate and Mattie within a couple of weeks of arriving in town. Their men were having no success gaining employment so the women, in an effort to raise some household money, started a small, but soon thriving, business sewing together canvas siding and roof panels for the numerous tents being raised. Mattie had no choice but to join in because Wyatt was not working and making no effort to find work. (Waters had decided Wyatt and Doc Holliday were too busy holding up stagecoaches to worry about employment.) Before long the ladies' business proved so successful it became the family's major means of support. Within this particular fiction was Water's inclusion in the business of Louisa and Kate.

Fact: The women never formed a business of any kind.

Fact: All the Earp men were employed.

Fact: Wyatt held several jobs.

Fact: Wyatt could not have been robbing stages with Holliday because Doc and Kate had not yet arrived. Waters wrote that all the Earps, accompanied by Holliday and Kate, arrived in Tombstone en masse in 1879.

Fact: Morgan and Louisa did not arrive until Spring of 1880.

Fact: Holliday and Kate did not arrive until late in 1880.

Fact: Following a short visit of perhaps three days, Kate went to Phoenix after flatly refusing to reside in Tombstone.[10]

Within a few weeks Mattie considered herself settled, content to lead a quiet life, and she remained so throughout her entire stay. Yet it is this period in which the mass of malicious fiction regarding her is mostly centered. A myriad of novels, short stories, and a few movies depict her stumbling about in an alcohol or opium induced haze. She is portrayed as an alcoholic, cigarillo-puffing strumpet playing the saloon scene or inviting into her little house any man with spare change in his pocket. She makes a fool of herself on the streets and causes fights. She is portrayed as prowling around Chinatown,[11] her scarlet dress in disarray, in her unending quest for opium. In truth, there would be no reason for Mattie to venture into Chinatown for opium because it was equally available in the local pharmacies and general stores.

In these stories a long suffering Wyatt, driven to aggravation, first tries to salvage Mattie and then, at wit's end, searches for ways to end his unhallowed marriage. He regrets having met this immoral jade who seems determined to destroy his unsullied reputation as a fearless lawman. Finally he turns to Josephine Marcus who, in her pristine purity and piety, rescues him from his ensnaring web of despair.

If even one of the stories is true the proof is very well hidden. Not a stain of trouble marred Mattie's public image in Tombstone. Although she was admittedly drinking (she and Allie are known to have shared many an afternoon nip) she kept it private. As in Dodge City, her stay in Tombstone is notable mainly for its almost total anonymity. She was no recluse, though, for she was well known to merchants and others she had dealings with and who all knew her as Mrs. Earp. All in all she was fitting into a persona of respectability. The 1880 census simply lists her as "keeping house," confirmation that she had settled into the lifestyle of a housewife. If she was guilty of anything it was a touch of chicanery in fudging her age. The census lists her as twenty-one. She was, of course, nine years beyond that.

Mattie had no reason to behave badly or indulge in harlotry while in Tombstone. Wyatt, his brothers and his other partners were all making money through investments in promising claims. James was planning the opening of his saloon, Morgan had steady employment with Wells Fargo and Virgil was drawing a good salary as a lawman. Wyatt, having profited from endeavors in Texas and Dodge City, parleyed much of it into profitable ventures in Tombstone. By late 1880 Wyatt and partners had laid claims on several mine sites, some of which yielded moderate to high profits. There was income enough to allow Mattie and Wyatt to live reasonably well, and she seems to have been pleased with her life. Mattie was particularly thrilled when Wyatt registered one claim as The Mattie Blaylock Mine. If it turned a profit, or was ever fully developed, is unknown, but it is listed in the records archived at the Tombstone Land Office. Mattie was excited at having a mine named after her, but may have wondered why he had not called it The Celia Earp Mine.

The mine was a highlight, but her happiest day came when she and Wyatt purchased a little adobe house.[12] They had gone together to the office of James Howard, Wyatt's lawyer, business partner and good friend to sign the papers registering them as co-owners.

Had Mattie been misbehaving Wyatt would have put a quick stop to it, and she would have as quickly complied. Madams and saloons could not re-enter her life for a very good reason. Wyatt, with Mattie's encouragement, was ambitiously pursuing appointment to the newly proposed Cochise County Sheriff's office. His only opponent was John Behan, but Wyatt, who considered himself superior to Behan, was convinced he could win.

Nonetheless, neither Earp nor Behan could be sure who the governor, the mercurial and generally incompetent John C. Fremont, would favor; and there was always the chance he would select a hitherto unknown third party. To consolidate their positions they entered into an unlikely pact. They agreed the winner would appoint the other as under-sheriff at a good salary. Wyatt thought the pact was made in good faith. He knew less about John Behan than he had thought.

Wyatt had not considered Tombstone for permanent settlement until the possibility of being named county sheriff led him to realize there was big money in politics. Suddenly he changed his mind about settling down. The office of Cochise County Sheriff would be the perfect outlet for his talents. When Wyatt told Mattie of his plans she encouraged him, not because she was much enamored of Tombstone, but because she was tiring of the constant moves. She was also bitterly cognizant of the relentless approach of her next birthday. Though not yet old in years, the pace of the past ten years had aged her and subverted her spirit. She welcomed an opportunity for permanent settlement.

From her first day in Tombstone Mattie devoted her time to Wyatt. She kept their home clean and tidy and prepared his meals on the days he was not in the hills or on posse duty. The new life suited her. What was most important was his coming home at night. Even after he began gambling in the Oriental, with sessions lasting well into the night, he was coming home.

Her new life seemingly revitalized her. During the morning she did her housework while Wyatt slept. Later, she and Allie would venture downtown to buy vegetables and other commodities. Occasionally they enjoyed lunch at a little café owned by an energetic Irish lady named Nellie Cashman.[13] Sometimes they lunched in the dining room of one of the town's hotels. Evenings, when Wyatt had gone to work, became her lonely times. For someone long familiar with a night routine, adapting to daylight is never easy, and Mattie had long been a night person. As the lonely evenings wore on she became to feel more and more alone. She tried but before long her old friend, "John Barleycorn," began to call. As more time passed he called more often. Very soon the two were spending all their evenings reminiscing of times from the not-so-distant past.

Memories and loneliness, however, were not her only reasons for drinking. Neither was her acquired taste for whiskey. Recent revelations indicate she was already afflicted with a severe medical condition[14] and whiskey held the pain in check; but it was not until she moved to Globe in 1885 that the pain progressed to the point where only laudanum had effect.

Laudanum, the Old West's painkiller of choice, was so easily obtained that availability became its real tragedy. Doctors, often recklessly, recommended it for a wide variety of complaints ranging from cancer to headaches. A combination of opium and alcohol, it was assuredly efficacious as a painkiller but it was also of such potency an overdose invariably proved fatal. Mattie knew the dangers of laudanum and would not have used it needlessly, and certainly not recklessly. No proof exists that she used it in Tombstone. In fact, stories of her using it to excess are fiction and speculation from those who have shown her in a demeaning light.

Mattie while in Tombstone drank whiskey, no doubt too much, and used opium also, perhaps too often. Well aware of the danger they presented in combination, she would not have used them together. Mattie may not have been the brightest spark among the embers but neither was she a muggins. How much opium Mattie was using in Tombstone is open to debate but probably no more than was considered socially accepted. The drug at the time was popular in all levels of nineteenth century society[15] including Mattie's. Legal to manufacture and sell, it was inexpensive and never in short supply. The debate is not about Mattie's use of the dream dust but rather the degree of usage. Claims that she lived in a perpetual opium-induced haze are nothing more than efforts to increase her value as a fictional anti-hero. There is absolutely nothing to indicate her use of opium was above the norm for the era. She would not have used it to alleviate pain, as whiskey was much cheaper and would more easily dull whatever pain her medical condition was causing at that stage in her life.

CHAPTER 20

When Dreams Fade and Die 1881–1882

Until spring of 1881 Mattie saw a great deal of Wyatt and they spent time together. After that she rarely saw him as he was gone for long periods in varied pursuits.[1] He and his partners were spending increasing days in the hills staking claims on everything from potential mines to water rights. He was able to keep his faro games going when he was out of town by placing them with dealers[2] whom he hired from among trusted friends. Wyatt, as one of Virgil's deputies, also regularly rode as a posse member, mostly in pursuit of members of the Clanton gang.[3] Investigating the Clantons' activities, particularly in cattle rustling, had become almost a full-time job for Virgil and Wyatt in their capacity as lawmen.

Mattie was certainly aware her husband and his brothers were being paid handsomely by a cartel of businessmen and politicians to provide protection against the Clantons. If she worried about his safety, she also knew he was capable of looking after himself. Meanwhile, knowing the future held promise, she was content to live her lonely existence making the best of the situation. The situation, however, was about to change.

Mattie's loneliness soon escalated with the arrival in Tombstone of a vivacious man-eater named Josephine Sarah Marcus (1861–1944). Her arrival heralded the beginning of the end of Mattie's relationship with Wyatt. Josephine, known variously as Josie or Sadie,[4] the new live-in mistress of Sheriff John Behan arrived during the spring of 1881 to take up residence in a house she had bought but had foolishly registered the deed incorrectly.[5] They lived together only a few weeks until Behan alienated Josephine and the liaison quickly become stormy. As her ardor towards Behan cooled, she turned her limpid eyes in Wyatt's direction.

When Josephine flashed her sparkling dark eyes towards Wyatt he was smitten at first glance, seeing her as a welcome oasis and respite from Mattie, of whom he was tiring. From the moment Josephine decided Wyatt was the man most likely to rescue her from Behan the sparks of passion flew, but it was Mattie who was burned. Wyatt took up with the sagebrush seductress, secretly at first, but later quite openly. Mattie pretended not to notice.

When Governor Fremont announced his choice for county sheriff it was Behan he named. Wyatt, though disappointed, did not lament. A deal, after all, was a deal and under-sheriff was a high rung up the ladder. He was also aware John Behan was an undirected man who would not likely remain sheriff for long. Wyatt was willing to accept a secondary role for a time. Also on his side was that the next sheriff had to be elected. He felt confidant he could defeat Behan at the polls. Meanwhile, Wyatt would simply await the call from County Sheriff Behan.

Behan, now safely ensconced in office, pulled one of his trademark double-crosses. He named as the county's under-sheriff Harry M. Woods, a crony who was also editor of the anti-Earp newspaper, *The Daily Nugget*. When Behan reneged on his deal with Wyatt he antagonized all the Earps and they turned against him, not only because he had gone back on his word but in appointing Woods he had rubbed salt into the wound. From that point the Earps regarded John Behan as several degrees lower than a desert viper.

Meanwhile, Mattie had become aware that the affair Wyatt and Josephine were conducting was no longer a discreet liaison. Her suspicions increased when Wyatt began coming home later and later. By this time she fully expected he would move out but, for his own reasons, he did not leave. He remained with Mattie while Josephine continued to live alone in her house, remaining there until Behan forced a foreclosure. She then moved into residence at Mrs. Young's boarding house, which was well ordered, sedate and, above all, strictly respectable.[6]

Mattie maintained her outward *sang-froid* by continuing to seek solace with Allie and Bessie, both of whom tried to help but without success. Mattie may have mishandled the situation but she was not without support. Allie counseled Mattie to hang onto Wyatt as best she could and Mattie tried, but as the strain increased so did her drinking.[7] She relied more and more on Allie and it was during this period that Virgil began to lose patience with her. He felt she was taking up too much of Allie's time, and perhaps he was right.

Although Allie and Bessie rallied to her side there was little they could do; and it would have been folly to approach Wyatt on Mattie's behalf, and both knew it. Because none of the Earp women had an ironclad guarantee of domestic permanence, they understood the reality of Mattie's situation. To the Earp boys, never paragons of fidelity, only family blood was the tie that ultimately counted. Their women were considered only as additions, expendable, easily replaced.

As the weeks wore on Mattie withdrew deeper into the bottle, but she never created a public scene.[8] She never confronted Josephine, and if she did discomfit Wyatt in any way it was in the privacy of their home. Her restraint may seem surprising, considering her quicksilver temper and splenetic nature, but she knew the futility of fighting over it. She was fully aware of his weakness for women, especially pretty ones, and that his philandering nature was nothing new and would not change anytime soon. Mattie had survived his affair with "Big Nose Kate" in Wichita and had not been permanently cast aside for "Dutch Lil" in Dodge City so, having emerged the victor in both events, she was certain she would survive and again prevail. The fact that Wyatt was still coming home at night convinced her he would eventually tire of Josephine.

Confident that time was on her side, Mattie watched and waited. She, it seems, had forgotten the marriage that had begun as a business arrangement had never been a true love match.

While Mattie struggled with her personal demons Virgil and Wyatt were struggling with a dilemma of a different nature. As lawmen they were expected to maintain order, no small feat considering the extent and influence of the lawless element and hostile factions in a town where shootings were above the average of the wildest towns of the Old West.[9] The Earps' major concern was with the Clantons and their associates, but they also had troubles stemming from an uncertainty, and overstepping, of jurisdictional limits. Virgil, although city marshal, was constantly in conflict with County Sheriff Behan whose invariant attempts to override him were, at the very least, vexatious.

The Clanton gang, headed by Newman "Old Man" Clanton (b. c1830; d. Aug. 1881), included legendary outlaws John Ringo,[10] Pete Spence,[11] and "Curly Bill" Brocius. Another gang member, albeit of lesser note, was William "Billy the Kid" Claiborne (d.1882).[12] Clanton's three sons, Phineas, called Phin,[13] William, called Billy and Isaac, called Ike, were also part of the gang.[14] Ike, the gang's weakest link, was an abject coward, acknowledged by all as a "mouth fighter," a man who talks up a fight then runs from it.

The Earps also had to contend with a group of politicians and businessmen (remembered as The Ten-Percent County Ring) who, with the backing of Behan and Woods of the *Daily Nugget*, sanctioned Clanton. Among the Earps' backers was John Clum, owner/editor of the *Tombstone Epitaph* and the powerful Wells Fargo. During 1880 and 1881 verbal battles raged unabated between the two newspapers.

The first sentence in the final chapter of the Clanton–Earp saga was written in August 1881 when Newman Clanton and several gang members were driving a herd of rustled cattle northward from Mexico. They were cornered in Skeleton Canyon and in the gunfight that ensued Clanton and several of his riders were killed. Ike, Phin and Billy Clanton, none of whom had been present, immediately accused the Earps of having ambushed the group. The Earps had been present but denied arranging an ambush, claiming regular troopers of the Mexican Army trailing the rustlers started the shooting.[15] From August until October small skirmishes, mostly verbal, were fought between the two factions.

The final violent scene was played out during the early afternoon of October 26, a chilly Sunday.[16] Shortly after 1:00 p.m., Virgil, Wyatt and Morgan Earp, accompanied by Doc Holliday, faced down five members of the gang on Fremont Street near a vacant lot between the residence of W.A. Harwood and Fly's boarding house where Holliday lived.

Because countless volumes have been written about the shootout there is no need to recount more than basic details here. The shootout, inaccurately called The Gunfight at the OK Corral, lasted about thirty seconds. Ike Clanton, true to form, took to his heels at the first shots and was quickly followed by Billy Claiborne leaving Billy Clanton, Frank and Tom McLaury alone. All three were killed and Morgan and Virgil were wounded. Virgil was hit in the leg while Morgan suffered two wounds. One was minor, but the other — a bullet had nicked a vertebra — was serious. A deviation of even a fraction of an inch could have either killed him or left him paralyzed. Holliday came close to injury when a bullet struck his leather holster. The bullet deflected but its impact left a large, sore bruise on his thigh. Only Wyatt, at all times an open target, emerged unscathed.[17]

There are those who suspect the gunfight had been preplanned by the Earps,[18] but if that was true no one informed Wyatt or Virgil because both were caught totally unprepared. When Wyatt returned home from his Saturday night poker session in the Oriental it was well after midnight. He told Mattie he intended to sleep into the afternoon. Thus, he was sound asleep even as the first phase of the ensuing fight was developing during the morning. He was still sound asleep when an excited messenger, Ned Boyle, appeared at the door shouting Wyatt's name.

Mattie was in the kitchen preparing lunch when Boyle called to Wyatt that Ike Clanton, armed, was searching for the

Earps. Mattie, a little bewildered and worried by the urgency in Boyle's voice, knew something was afoot. Wyatt, displeased by the sudden awakening, made no immediate effort to get up. Some time elapsed before he rose and dressed. Not until after 12:30 p.m. did he strap on his guns and leave the house. Mattie had looked on in nervous silence as Wyatt dressed and kept her eyes on his back as he walked through the yard to turn down Fremont Street toward the town's center.

Mattie's first notification of the gunfight is not known and there is nothing on record indicating she had accompanied Allie and Louisa when those two hurried to the scene. It is likely she was there and no one had thought to mention her presence. It would not have been the first time she had been overlooked, nor would it be the last.[19] Had she been at the scene of the gunfight, she would have observed the aftermath of a disaster. The acrid smell of black powder still hung heavy in the becalmed air. Dozens of onlookers who had gathered milled about, discussing and speculating on what had happened. In the alleyway lay the McLaury brothers, motionless in death. Dr. Goodfellow was tending to Billy Clanton who still lived but, though mortally wounded, remained unwilling to go gently into that long goodnight. He made several futile attempts to regain his feet while continually demanding his gun and cartridge belt. Finally, exhausted, he fell back and remained still. Although unable to move he continued an ongoing but weakening harangue against the Earps and Holliday.

Holliday had already vacated the scene to return to his room in Fly's boarding house where he found uneasy comfort with Kate who had come to Tombstone for the weekend.[20] The Earp brothers, two of them bloodied but alive, had regained their composure and were preparing to leave. Morgan, under doctor's orders to remain prone and not to move, was lifted onto a dray wagon that had been brought up to transport him to Virgil's house for further treatment. Virgil, nursing his leg wound, rode with Morgan. Wyatt and James walked with the women.

Once the Earps had left, the bodies of Frank and Tom McLaury were removed to the undertaker's parlor. They were soon joined by that of Billy Clanton who had spent an extra final hour of his life raining curses on the Earps in general and Doc Holliday in particular.

Somewhere in the crowd Josephine Marcus had also watched, having rushed to the scene upon hearing of the gunfight. Years later she described the scene and her actions to her biographer, saying she had arrived after the shooting had stopped, but remained discreetly in the crowd instead of rushing to Wyatt's side although she could see he was unharmed. It is this unusual action that suggests Mattie had indeed arrived and was at Wyatt's side. (Josephine had not up to that point admitted Mattie's existence to her biographer, and had no intention of ever doing so.)[21] Josephine's description of Wyatt's and Doc's actions in the shooting's aftermath is more than somewhat suspect.[22] It seems very clear it was Mattie who was escorting Wyatt to Virgil's house while reassuring him that Morgan and Virgil were going to be all right.

At the mandatory inquest, presided over by Justice Wells Spicer, Sheriff Behan, as expected, sided with the Clantons and *The Daily Nugget* recorded the proceedings with the Clantons in mind while the Earp viewpoint was reported by *The Epitaph*. Ike Clanton pushed for indictments of murder against the Earps and Holliday. The evidence they presented was confused, convoluted and contradictory. Ike Clanton testified the McLaury brothers and his brother had all been unarmed. Upon hearing this Wyatt remarked wryly that obviously Morgan, Virgil and Holliday had shot each other.

Morgan, recovering from his wounds, did not attend the hearing. Holliday attended but was never called upon to testify. In another perplexing twist, Wyatt was permitted to read his testimony from a prepared statement, thereby exempting him from cross-examination.

In his final verdict Spicer exonerated Virgil, Wyatt, Morgan and Holliday on the grounds that Virgil, as city marshal, had been attempting to uphold the law with assistance from lawfully appointed deputies. He found the cowboys had been in clear violation of city ordinances. Though it was not wholly accepted (Judge Spicer later received threats against his life) majority opinion agreed in retrospect it was the only decision possible under the circumstances.[23] Nonetheless, the Earps were a spent force within Tombstone's political framework.

The gunfight had barely ended when the town council suspended Virgil as city marshal. Wyatt, Morgan and Doc Holliday were also ordered to relinquish their badges. Suspensions, normal procedure in any mandatory enquiry's outcome, were usually temporary but this time, despite the exonerations, there were no reinstatements.

However, the turn of events did not deter the Earps. They would stay in Tombstone, they decided, as Virgil was determined to regain his appointment as city marshal and Wyatt remained convinced he could win the next election for county sheriff. Neither man seemed to realize the chances of accomplishing either goal lay solidly between zero and nil. Whatever prospects the Earps might have had in Tombstone, they all had been shot down in the thirty-second gunfight.

Mattie, as did Allie and Louisa, feared the Clantons would retaliate. They worried not for themselves but for their husbands. In the Old West not even the most hardened criminals would deliberately harm women or children. Thus, they had little reason for personal fear and indeed none of the women were ever harassed, insulted or in any way provoked. Wyatt, Morgan, Virgil and Holliday, on the other hand, were fair game and knew the Clantons would attempt some form of retaliation. They remained alert and vigilant. Slowly, things returned to normal — or appeared to.

Morgan recovered from his injuries and returned to his work with Wells Fargo. Holliday, never varying his routine, played poker each night as if unconcerned about what the Clantons might do.[24] Virgil also recovered from his injury but, with his badge gone, was at loose ends. He gambled at times in the Oriental Saloon and engaged in business with mining partners. Wyatt seemed disinterested enough to continue with his faro games and tending to his mining claims.

At home, though, he was so distracted and moody the distance between himself and Mattie increased. He was even less attentive to her than usual, though he was certainly aware she was heavyhearted with the turn of events. To Mattie it was clear his thoughts were with Josephine. Still, because he continued to come home each night, he obviously had no intention of moving out.

It was late on December 28 when the Clantons struck. Virgil, having just left the Oriental to return home after an evening of cards, stepped onto Allan Street a second before the roar of shotguns shattered the night's silence. He staggered a step or two, turned and collapsed slowly to the ground. Though severely wounded, Virgil had not been killed. Regaining his feet he staggered back to the saloon where quick medical attention by Dr. Goodfellow, who arrived within minutes of being summoned, saved his life. Virgil, drifting into and out of consciousness, was carried to his home.

Witnesses reported seeing three men in a nearby alley just before the shots were fired. From the descriptions given, Wyatt and Morgan determined the four had been Pete Spence, Johnny Ringo, Frank Stilwell[25] and Ike Clanton. They were further convinced that Will McLaury,[26] brother of Frank and Tom, had paid them to kill Virgil. Wyatt produced Ike's hat, which he claimed to have found in the alley. Ike countered by insisting Earp had planted it there to cast suspicion his way, but offered no explanation how his hat had come into Wyatt's possession. Interestingly, none of the other three suspects ever endorsed his claim.

Now certain of further retaliation, Wyatt rented rooms for everyone in the Cosmopolitan Hotel. Virgil was carried to the hotel where Allie had prepared a sick room. Though he had not been killed in the ambush, his wounds were so severe he hovered on the verge of death for several weeks and remained bedridden for several more. Wyatt, Mattie, Morgan and Louisa prepared for an indeterminate stay.[27] James and Bessie, feeling they had nothing to fear, remained with the children at home and Holliday could see no reason to leave Fly's boarding house.

Virgil's confinement proved very difficult for Mattie because Allie remained constantly at his bedside, refusing to leave for more than a few minutes. As a result she was deprived of company in the very time of her greatest need. She would gladly have spent time with Bessie, but Wyatt forbade her to leave the hotel.[28] By the time he eased his strict edict Mattie's small room had became a prison.

Mattie's hopes took a happy upward turn on February 13, 1882, when Wyatt hustled her to the office of B.L. Peel, a Justice of the Peace. He explained to her he had arranged a loan on their house and her signature was required. James Howard, Wyatt's attorney and business partner, had agreed to loan Wyatt $365 for ninety days at 2 percent per month interest. Wyatt had tendered the house as collateral. Her first thought was that they would be leaving Tombstone, something she wanted. When she had time to give it further thought she decided ninety days seemed too short a duration to indicate a possible departure was being contemplated. In fact, Wyatt (and Virgil as well) had no intention of leaving.

Dismayed or not, Mattie signed the document. Had she looked at the paper carefully she would have noticed several changes had been made to the original document. Some lines had been added and several words had belatedly been pluralized but because her business acumen was so limited she probably did not notice the changes. Had she noticed she might have realized the alterations to the document indicated Wyatt had offered the house without her consent.[29]

If Mattie did notice the changes Wyatt obviously explained them to her satisfaction because she signed the paper. Whether she knew how Wyatt intended to use the money remains unknown, but in the long term she did not figure into the equation anyway. Regardless of her degree of willingness, she had signed away her house.

The loan fell due on May 14. When no payment was forthcoming Howard made application to foreclose and took possession of Mattie's little adobe house. Of course, she was not there to see the transfer of ownership.

CHAPTER 21

Farewell to Tombstone March 1882

Mattie had hoped her dreams would come true in Tombstone, but instead they ended in anguish during late evening of March 17. Morgan, Wyatt and some friends were playing pool in Bob Hatch's Saloon and Pool Hall when suddenly the quiet was shattered by a gunshot and the sound of breaking glass. A bullet, fired through the back door window, smashed into Morgan's back ripping into vital organs as it passed through his body.[1] Wyatt rushed to help his stricken brother. Others hastened to seek a doctor.[2] Another ran to the hotel to find Louisa who hurried to his side. Morgan held her hand until, thirty minutes later, he gasped one last, short breath and died. His life ended thirty-nine days short of his thirty-second birthday.

The *Epitaph* account of the shooting made note of the presence of Virgil[3] and Allie and of James and Bessie,[4] but neglected to mention Louisa[5] and Mattie. No reasons are known why Mattie would not have been there, but several have been offered over the years. The most persistent suggestion, which is difficult to dispute, implies she was in her hotel room in an opium-induced sleep.

If Mattie missed Morgan's final minutes she would have felt even greater sorrow, as she had very much liked Morgan. She had laughed at his jokes, enjoyed his sense of humor and thought him less inhibited than his brothers. She also worried his impetuous spirit would lead him to grief. She, Wyatt and Morgan had shared adventures over the years. Some had been fun, but others — the experiences in Peoria for instance — had not been at all enjoyable.

Wyatt hovered near his dying brother, paying no attention to anyone. Morgan had always been his favorite. When Morgan breathed his last Wyatt stood up, stared a long moment at the shattered body, then turned and in the company of others departed into the night.

Virgil, accompanied by Allie, James, Bessie and Louisa, returned to the hotel. They all knew from the manner in which Wyatt had brushed by everyone on his way out of Hatch's that the Clanton gang was going to pay dearly. Indeed, soon all Tombstone would know.

Mattie wondered if they would now leave Tombstone. While she, Allie and Bessie had discussed the possibility at various times, all three knew their husbands had no interest in their views. All were adamant in their refusal to leave. Virgil, besides fighting for reinstatement as city marshal, intended to run to ground the men who had ambushed him. Wyatt was equally firm in his reasons to stay. James could see no advantage in leaving as his saloon was doing very well and he was not being bothered by the Clantons. How this latest turn of events would affect the brothers' thinking was a question that Mattie, without doubt, asked herself.

However, the situation did indeed change their thinking. James was first to come to grips with reality. He knew it was once again time to move on, that the Earps no longer had a future in Tombstone. James knew it. The women knew it. It would fall to James to convince Virgil and Wyatt.

Reason eventually prevailed after some hours of discussion, and once agreement was reached plans were quickly formulated. Virgil, Allie and Louisa would accompany Morgan's body to Colton, California for burial. James, when he sold his saloon, would follow with Bessie and Mattie. Wyatt would remain in the area to settle scores. Warren, already on his way from Colton, would ride with Wyatt, Doc Holliday, and several others who wished to assist Wyatt in his quest.

On March 19 the majority of Earps departed Tombstone for Tucson. In one of the wagons holding their possessions was a pine box containing Morgan's body. Wyatt, Doc Holliday, "Texas Jack" Vermillion, Sherman "Mysterious" McMaster and Jack "Turkey Creek" Johnson rode along for their protection. From Tucson, Virgil, Allie and Louisa[6] would board the westbound train.[7]

At the Tucson depot Virgil, McMaster, Vermillion and Johnson guarded the women while Wyatt and Doc oversaw consignment of Morgan's coffin to the baggage car. Then Wyatt assisted Virgil up the steps to a passenger coach and made certain he was comfortable. Once Allie and Louisa had settled beside his brother, Wyatt departed without another word. He did not want to upset anyone by warning them that Ike Clanton and Frank Stilwell had been spotted lurking in the shadows at the far end of the depot. As the train eased away from the platform Wyatt and friends, guns already drawn, watched the train until it was engulfed by the darkness. Then they turned to the business at hand.

Ike Clanton and Stilwell had journeyed to Tucson intent on ambushing the Earps as they boarded the train but, as they hid in the darkness, they realized they were too outnumbered to carry out their plan. Then they realized they had been seen. Ike, true to his fashion, wasted no time in running away. Stilwell, left alone to fend for himself, also tried to run but the five men were already upon him. Unable to find a hiding place he was doomed. Pistol shots rang out followed by the roar of a shotgun. Then silence reclaimed the evening.

The following morning a railroad employee on a routine checking of the tracks found Stilwell's bullet-riddled body not far from the depot. Wyatt and friends had delayed their departure only long enough to kill Frank Stilwell. His was the first name on the list to be crossed off.

Having determined Stilwell was dead, the men boarded a train to Contention, a mining town not far from Tombstone, where Warren was waiting with horses. They saddled the waiting horses and without further delay rode out to pick up the trail of the men they were certain had ambushed Virgil and killed Morgan. They rode into the hills, made camp and awaited daybreak. The following morning they began the quest for vengeance.[8]

CHAPTER 22

The Road to Pinal 1882–1887

O n March 24, 1882, James, Bessie and Hattie, accompanied
   by Mattie, departed Tombstone[1] for California.[2] Stories
that emerged some years ago of Mattie staying in Tombstone
are totally untrue. Her departure was considered newsworthy
enough that it was reported in the *Epitaph*. There is no mention
in later editions of her having returned, an event which would
have been considered equally worthy of mention.

Despite leaving under unhappy circumstances, Mattie obviously thought she was about to renew life with Wyatt. She
had never been so wrong at any time in all her thirty-two years.
Mattie arrived at Colton on March 27 for temporary residence
on Nicholas and Virginia Earp's farm. By August she realized
her husband was not going to return to her. Following his
manhunt of the Clanton gang in the Arizona hills and a short
sojourn in Colorado, Wyatt had gone directly to San Francisco
to be with Josephine. Either directly or through a third party
he informed Mattie she was on her own. When she learned
her future would not include Wyatt Earp she was heartbroken,
her spirit shattered. She could not understand why and did
not believe she had done anything to deserve such treatment.
She steadfastly refused to accept the facts, admitting them not
even to herself, for quite some time. Eventually, however, she
let her thoughts be known to anyone who would listen.

The facts were no secret to Allie and Bessie who had long
known that Mattie's addiction to opium and alcohol and her
shrewish[3] manner had driven too many wedges between the

172

two. Wyatt, feeling she would never change, saw the opportunity to leave and seized it. Whether it was sans regret is very much open to question because, had Josephine Marcus not come into his life, he likely would have stayed with Mattie, perhaps even succeeding in straightening her ways. No doubt he would have taken an occasional mistress as he had before but Mattie, as in the past, would have accepted the situation rather than lose him altogether.

Wyatt's affair with Josephine began as had his other trysts. It never progressed to cohabitation in Tombstone even though Josephine, at least for a while, had her own house. There are lingering questions of how seriously Wyatt took the affair, at least in the beginning, for it appears his initial interest in Josephine was basically lukewarm. Throughout their entire time in Tombstone Wyatt and Mattie stayed together. They shared their house and their bed, she attended to his laundry and cooked his meals; but the most significant aspect to the situation was that Wyatt came home at night however late the hour. In fact, Mattie and Wyatt were together the morning of the infamous gunfight. He had been roused from Mattie's bed, not Josephine's. It was Mattie, not Josephine, who had watched with an indiscernible concern when Wyatt rushed from the house that fateful Sunday morning. It was she, not Josephine, who offered comfort to Wyatt after the shooting ceased. After moving to the Cosmopolitan Hotel they stayed together and never for one instant did he consider leaving her alone in harm's way. Wyatt also insisted that Mattie go to Colton when the time came to leave Tombstone, when he could just as easily have left her to fend for herself.

So, why did he not do that? Again, the answer will never be known. Perhaps he was trying to find the answer himself when, a few days before he drew his final breath, Josephine recalled he suddenly awoke, looked thoughtful for a moment, and said, "Supposing...supposing." She thought he might have been thinking of events in Tombstone. Was he thinking of Morgan? Of the gunfight? Of Mattie? Or all that had happened? He ended his thought by saying, "Oh, well!" and fell asleep again.[4] He obviously had not been able to find the answer, either. Regardless, not until he realized that Tombstone was a dead issue for the Earps did he decide that life with Josephine was preferable to life with Mattie.

Sometime during the waning days of August, Mattie packed her well-traveled trunks and said her tearful goodbyes. Allie and Bessie promised to keep in touch. One of the men, probably James, drove her to the railway depot where she bought a one-way ticket to Phoenix. Seeing her trunks placed safely aboard he helped her find a seat in a quiet parlor car. Perhaps he gave her a quick kiss on the cheek and wished her luck.

Mattie's decision to return to Arizona[5] had not been lightly made. She had contacted Kate whom she knew was managing a brothel in Globe,[6] and Kate sent word the welcome mat was out. Kate may not have liked Mattie all that much, but she knew and understood her torment. Hers was the empathy one rejected woman has for another. Kate had felt the same anguish for weeks after saying farewell to Doc Holliday a year before. She had also suffered heartache when cast aside by Wyatt Earp in Wichita. She had simply resolved their bygones should indeed be put behind them.

So the die was cast, but why did Mattie choose as she did? Deserted wives were no rarity in the Old West, but very few turned to brothels or saloons. The vast majority found other means of support. In 1882, not yet thirty-three years of age, she was not too old to find employment, if only as a domestic. Had Mattie returned to Iowa her sisters — Sarah certainly — would have helped her during that trying time in her life. She might eventually have met an older man who would have been happy to call her his wife. Why, then, did she return to her old ways? The answer can never be fully answered, but known facts that point to it contain little of an attractive nature.

Mattie was well aware she could not return to Iowa. She was addicted to opium, her drinking was out of hand and she could at times be an unreasonable termagant. She had already entered the penultimate phase of her life. With Wyatt no longer part of her existence her world had become a void. Just as her demeanor had driven Wyatt to his final decision, so also did it prohibit her return to Iowa. Mattie considered herself incapable of holding a job even if she could find one. Holding that to be true, she decided to go to Globe, join Kate, and begin again what she felt was her only station in life.

The journey from Phoenix to Globe was by stagecoach and was not pleasant. The road, sixty rough, dusty miles, was flat until the Pinal Mountains were reached. Then began a series of dodgy ascents and steep descents along a twisting, narrow trail.[7] On the route were small towns and settlements where brief stops were made. One such stop was a little mining center named Pinal. One wonders if Mattie took any notice of the town at the time.

Once in Globe, Mattie settled in, easily adjusting to her new surroundings. She and Kate slowly pushed aside the coolness between them and Mattie soon decided she liked Globe. She pined for Wyatt and what she believed she had lost, but did not let it weigh so heavily on her mind that she lost her sense of reality. Globe's sporting district was lively and relatively lucrative. More importantly it was safe. The police force ensured the town's soiled doves remained unharmed, secure, and protected. A payment was levied monthly for the service with rates that met with general approval. It was part of the cost of doing business but safety, after all, has its price. This protection, incidentally, continued until the mid-1970s when Globe's last brothel closed its doors permanently.

A photograph Mattie posed for in 1885 at The Photograph Gallery (the studios of J.C. Burge, artist), suggests that Globe treated her reasonably well. Burge's motto — "First Class Work a Specialty" — was stamped on the back of each photo and served as the banner for his weekly newspaper ad. The ad invited one and all to his studio, but for reasons unknown he never included the address. Sole reference to his studio's location was an oblique statement: "Opposite Somerville's Bakery." Apparently the bakery's location was no secret because The Photograph Gallery prospered for many years.

Mattie was evidently satisfied with the photo because she kept it. Her dress is stylishly formal, evidence that her love of finery and flair for style had not diminished. Her neatly groomed hair indicates that Globe had at least one good

175

hairdressing salon. Mattie, however, is a vivid contrast to the happy young lady of the photo taken fourteen years earlier. In 1885 her mouth is firmly set, the wistful smile gone. No coy glance hints at the presence of an unseen admirer. She appears heavier than in her Fort Scott photo and much older than her thirty-five years. Hers is the stern look of an unhappy, care-worn, bitter woman. In her eyes is the look of heartache. While there are no outward signs of illness, her dental health, it is now known, was already at a critical stage. Her teeth were badly decayed, her gums susceptible to painful abscesses that inflicted intense pain that would plague her throughout her final months of life. The cavities and abscesses had not yet reached the level where only laudanum could bring relief so, for the moment, folk remedies and whiskey sufficed.

The first three of Mattie's four years in Globe were reason-ably happy. During this period she added to her silver brace-lets that had became a sort of trademark. She and Kate may even have been having some fun along the way. Globe, with a well-attended music hall and other venues of entertainment, was a regular stop for road show companies. Troupes of tran-sient actors regularly performed dramas and operettas. Gilbert and Sullivan (HMS *Pinafore* may have brought bad memories to Mattie) were still popular with road companies. Mattie may not have had much interest in fine arts, but it seems likely that Kate, who did, would have taken her for an occasional eve-ning out. Mattie may have begun to enjoy that part of life she had never before taken seriously.

According to the late John D. Gilchriese, Mattie's life be-gan to unravel the afternoon she sighted Wyatt and Josephine walking together along Broad Street[8] when Wyatt was in town checking some gambling interests. They did not see her, or if they did no sign of recognition was given.[9]

According to Gilchriese[10] Mattie was extremely upset to see the prosperity Wyatt had bestowed on Josephine.[11] She complained to Kate it was she, Mattie, who should be on Wyatt's arm, wearing the fine clothes and sporting the brace-lets and jewels. Kate, though sympathetic, could do nothing to console the distraught Mattie. Shortly after, Mattie began drinking heavily again and may also have increased her opium habit, which in all likelihood she had never ceased. The Broad Street incident, if true, would certainly have begun her ultimate decline and, perhaps, trigger an early stage of mental breakdown. Nonetheless, it was about this time she began telling anyone who would listen that her husband, Wyatt Earp, after having ruined her life had deserted her.

Most who were subjected to her lamentations must have wondered whom she was talking about, as at that point few had heard of Wyatt Earp. There would have been some who recalled hearing of a man of that name who had been involved in a gunfight in Tombstone, but very few would have had first-hand knowledge. There might have been one or two who recalled Wyatt Earp from Dodge City or Wichita, and their recollections would unlikely give them reason to discount her claim.

Then, Mattie suffered a further tragedy in a life that had been a series of disappointments. The final setback came one spring morning in 1887 when Kate told her she was leaving Globe. Doc Holliday had written to her asking if she would come to Colorado to be with him in his final days. Knowing death was not far off he wanted nothing more than to spend those days with Kate.

Even had she wanted to, Kate could not refuse his final request. During the almost eleven years of their tumultuous love–hate relationship, an attachment had been forged that could not be broken. The bond was too strong, too infrangible, their lives too intertwined to allow one to end life any other way but in the company of the other. Kate had no choice. She would have to go to Colorado to be with Doc in his final weeks.[12] Kate set about finding a buyer for her share of the business, a task that posed no problem. She had no trouble finding a buyer and likely made a tidy profit.[13] She left for Colorado during May.

Kate's announcement was a terrible blow to Mattie's soul. In her fragile state of mind she felt she was being deserted once again. Receding deeper into the shadows of dismay and discontent she increasingly found solace in her only remaining friend, John Barleycorn, who, ever faithful, stayed with her even into her final hour.

However, the fact Mattie remained in Globe until October clearly indicates she had not intended to leave. Her departure seems to have been a sudden decision suggesting rather clearly that the new owner had told her to leave. There was no room for a soiled dove, drunk, disheveled and aged beyond her years. Such was the grim reality of the trade. Mattie, once again finding herself alone, out of aces and unable to remain in Globe, decided to move to Pinal. Why Pinal? It is a question asked many times by many researchers. The logical answer is that without Kate she no longer had a friend and confidant. Worse, she no longer had a guiding hand. Mattie had always needed friendship, support and direction. She got it first from Wyatt, then from Bessie, then from Allie and finally from Kate. On her own, Mattie had always tended to stray aimlessly. Now she was again adrift on a sea of indecision. Perhaps she saw Pinal as being as good as any other town for a woman in her straits; but the decision was more likely dictated by limited funds. Pinal was a very short distance from Globe, so she bought a one-way ticket and boarded the stage. One can only imagine her thoughts as the coach rumbled along Broad Street towards the trail leading west. Mattie had begun her venture down the final miles of the trail she had followed for twenty years of her tormented life.

CHAPTER 23

The End of the Road October 1887– July 1888

P inal. One can also only imagine Mattie's thoughts when she saw her new town. She could have felt nothing short of dismay when she peered through the coach's grimy window to glimpse the town about which she knew so little. As the coach moved slowly along the rutted main street, the town may have seemed even more forlorn than she could have believed. The horses gingerly stepped between the ruts as the stage, proceeding slowly, rocked sharply, first left then alarmingly right. On both sides of the street were weather-beaten, ramshackle buildings that appeared to grow directly from the dirt piled high along the roadside. Most were closed, windows boarded, owners long departed. There were no sidewalks. Mattie, who had known bustling towns and exciting cities, would have been truly dismayed.

Pinal was small but had a certain sprawl. It had one main street, quite long. It sloped slightly, perhaps five degrees, higher on the northwest side. Leading from both sides of the main street were several short side roads. Along both sides of those roads stood rows of small wooden shacks, few of which had more than two rooms. All stood neglected and many were vacant, their previous owners having already left for greener fields. At the far southwest end of town stood a two-story building of brick and wood, its appearance suggesting the builder, having not brought quite enough bricks, had finished it with wood. A sign of peeling black and white paint identified it as the Pinal Hotel. Mattie would stay there a week or two, perhaps a month. She had no choice as it was the only hotel in town and it would take her awhile to find a cabin she could inhabit.

Main Street's other prominent building also boasted two stories. It too was weathered for the years of blistering sun had faded the white paint to gray. Wind-blown abrasive sand had peeled much of the paint from its boards. A land shift, likely the same one that had given the entire street its noticeable slant, had left the stately pillared veranda with a noticeable tilt. A large sign read simply Leudke Bros. A clutter of barrels, mining implements and other hardware strewn across the veranda told passers-by that this was a general merchandise store.

To its right were two small buildings, one vacant. It was constructed of indeterminate material encrusted with dirt. The other, of fieldstone construction, was the town's primary saloon. A hand-painted sign announced it was The Bank Exchange Restaurant & Ale House. Below those words was painted a boast of being "Open Day & Night" while smaller letters informed everyone the new owner was one Joe Mc-Court. He had simply painted his name above that of the previous owner, Charles F. Murray, then painted a thin line through Murray's name and let it go at that. Obviously, with times tough and about to get tougher, spending money on a new sign was pointless.

Just beyond the saloon were another three even more nondescript buildings, two wooden, one brick. All were anonymous and empty. At the far edge of the town, east of the hotel, stood the St. Louis Brewery, owned by August Werner who also owned the town's remaining retail liquor store and its adjoining beer garden.

A sign above the door of an empty building averred that Pinal had once had a newspaper. In fact at one time two had enjoyed good circulation. *The Drill* ceased publication in 1884 leaving the field to the *Pinal County Record,* and its final edition had gone to press in 1886. Since then the only newspapers available to Pinal residents were those brought in by stage at irregular intervals from Phoenix, Globe or Florence; but rumors the stage would soon by-pass the town meant an end to printed news. One wonders if Mattie was aware at the time that she had opted for a dying town. She was certainly seeing nothing indicative of prosperity or even an illusion of permanency. Both had long since disappeared.

Even during its boom days Pinal had never suggested permanency; towns like Pinal were never founded with that in mind. Boomers and miners were well aware mining towns rarely lasted longer than ten years. Pinal was not considered an exception. Any continuity Pinal was likely to offer would be to those consigned by death to the little cemetery located 800 yards west from the main street. Everyone was aware that only in dying would there be found constancy in Pinal.

During the town's first weeks, hundreds of men had arrived in search of silver. Some had tents, but many more made homes in caves in the cliffs abundant in the area. Some built shacks, makeshift and flimsy, but these were few because no one intended to stay longer than necessary. The miners were there for quick wealth and quick departure. Many left almost as quickly as they had arrived.

Many claims were staked, worked, sold or abandoned but only one mine, Silver King, produced ore rich and abundant and prospered for many years.[1] An abandoned army outpost called Picket Post became the site of the Silver King's ore-crushing mill. Day after day, year after year, huge ore wagons rumbled the two miles from mine to mill, and to this day ruts marking the route remain visible.

Between the two sites some 2,000 men gained steady employment. It had been they who had built small houses and sturdy shacks along Pinal's side streets. With the Silver King as its base, Pinal's economy boomed and soon merchants and entrepreneurs arrived to set up the usual array of businesses[2] such towns attracted. Pinal's economy remained viable until 1884 at which point a downturn began. This was not because the lode was expended, but because America's abandonment of the silver standard caused the market to soften profoundly. The mine's management cut back production, and laid-off miners began to move away in search of work elsewhere.

By 1885 the mine's production had been so drastically curtailed, Pinal's population had dwindled to about four hundred. In 1886, the Silver King's owners gave notice the final month of operation would be October 1888.[3] Without the Silver King, Pinal was doomed. As more of the population departed, several businesses, including most of the remaining saloons and gaming houses, closed.

By spring of 1887 Pinal was no longer wealthy. The Silver King,[4] the richest silver mine in Arizona's history, had removed hundreds of millions of dollars in silver ore from its ever deepening shafts but now there was only enough output to sustain work, often part-time, for the three hundred who remained. They had not stayed in optimism for the town's future, for they knew it had none. They stayed in the hopes of having one final year of more or less steady work. Pinal was dying and everyone knew it. By October 1887 only two hundred workers remained on the payroll, and only half would see out the final year.

Closing the mine meant nothing would remain. It was Pinal's destiny to become a ghost town, and even that status was soon lost forever.[5] Within fifteen years the entire area the town had occupied would be fully reclaimed by the restless desert sands, the ubiquitous cacti, omnipresent sagebrush, coyotes, and small desert rodents.

Pinal's importance to Mattie, indeed her only reason for staying, was her knowledge that some of the few remaining miners would spend money for female companionship. In her room in the hotel, and later a little shack she occupied, she was able to entertain sufficient clients to bring in enough money to pay her rent and keep her in food, whiskey and occasional grains of opium.

When Mattie arrived the county sheriff was William Mc-
Gee but he, not intending to seek re-election in March, rarely
ventured outside of Florence, the county seat, and he never
went to Pinal. It was not until March 1888, after Mattie had
been there almost five months, did the new sheriff, John Peter
Gabriel,[6] pay a visit to the town to reacquaint himself with the
population and to reopen a small building he had kept during
his earlier terms in office.

Pete Gabriel was an old style lawman who made a point
of knowing everyone and meeting newcomers to his county.
He showed interest in the nature of newcomers' business
and, when necessary, enquired about their intended length of
stay. When he made his post-election visit, he met Mattie, but
whether he met her in the Bank Exchange Saloon or in her
rooms is unknown. What is known is that she, who knew well
the ways of lawmen, and Sheriff Pete Gabriel, who fully understood bawds, got along genially.

Gabriel found nothing objectionable about Mattie. He
asked his usual questions, wished her well and took his leave.
As did most lawmen of the era, he had a quite liberal point of
view. Never unduly concerned with moral issues, he insisted
only that Pinal County's sporting women give him no trouble.
Gabriel learned a great deal about Mattie and became well
aware of her relationship with Wyatt Earp.

Mattie also became a patient of the town's only remaining
doctor, Thomas H. Kinnaird, MD. How often she saw him and
for what treatments is not known. If any records he kept still
exist, they have not been found in existing archives. Dr. Kinnaird tended to Mattie as best he could. It is his signature that
authenticated her death certificate.

Mattie became known in Pinal to others besides her clients. She acquired several casual friends,[7] enough for respectable social contact. It was through these friends that Mattie's
story became entrenched in the lore of the Superior area. She
told those friends, as she told everyone, that she did not understand why Wyatt had deserted her. She had been known as
Mrs. Wyatt Earp in Wichita, Dodge City and Tombstone and
many places between. She told some of her friends about her

days in Peoria. She told others that Wyatt had named a silver mine for her. She told those friends that Wyatt Earp, her husband, had ruined her life. How much detail she divulged is not known, but she told them enough to gain sympathy.

Among her good friends were a Mexican man and his wife. They were very likely close neighbors as it was they who helped her as best they could. For many years after her death they faithfully tended her grave. There was also a sixty-five-year-old laborer, an enigmatic man from the east named Frank Beeler, who listened to her tirades against Earp, offered encouragement and hoped she might find a better life. All would figure into her final days.

Whatever questions her friends may have asked of her, the one they do not appear to have asked was the most important: Why, when she left Colton, did she return to the profession she had put behind her? She knew the answer but shared it with no one, including her sister. Sarah had long known Mattie's situation and probably tried to influence her to give it up. She would have wanted her sister to make a new, better life for herself, if not in California, then back home in Iowa.

Adding to the mystery of why Mattie chose the path she did, Josephine Marcus told Mabel Earp Cason[8] many years later that Wyatt had sent money to Mattie on a fairly regular basis. She insisted the amounts were sufficient to assure Mattie the necessities of life and that Wyatt continued sending money until he was notified of her death.[9] If that was indeed the case, Mattie had little reason to choose as she did. Even a small annual allowance would have afforded her reasonable comfort. It was an era when a loaf of bread cost three cents, beef three cents a pound, poultry twenty cents for an entire chicken and eggs were one cent each, less if purchased in lots of two dozen or more. A full-skirted gingham dress could be bought for $2 and a fashionable taffeta dress for $5.[10]

That Wyatt Earp deserted Mattie is a fact, but it also appears he harbored serious reservations about it. Had he truly intended all along to forsake Mattie? If Josephine's statement to Mabel Cason is to be believed, he obviously felt enough responsibility towards Mattie that he sent her money.

Mattie of course realized the finality of her circumstances before she went to Globe, but while there her suffering had increased dramatically. Finally, truly alone in her torment, she saw only bleakness in her future. Those were the reasons that she, a dying woman, chose Pinal, a dying town, for her final refuge. In all likelihood she knew full well the day she departed Globe that the stagecoach to Pinal would convey her along the final miles of her personal road.

inal Curtain

When Mattie arrived in Pinal she spent her first weeks in the Pinal Hotel and had not taken long in getting established. The saloon and Werner's Beer Garden, both a short walk from the hotel, became her contact points for the first few weeks, so she spent evenings between the two places. Shortly thereafter Mattie moved to a sparsely furnished shack just off the main street that would become her final home. Werner closed the beer garden in December leaving only the saloon for socializing, but by then her clients knew where she lived so she had no need to go out often. Nearly every evening, especially when her health began to so noticeably fail, Mattie would sit outside her door watching the skies change from daylight's cerulean blue to sunset's variable tones of red, purple and yellow. The evening reverie became her only joy in life. Unless a client or a friend dropped by to keep her company, she would sit alone as the day's heat gave way to cool evening breezes. It is during this period of the day when desert blossoms release fragrances that mingle each with the others. To Mattie the desert flowers were indeed lovely. She was able to lose herself in her thoughts and for a couple of hours push aside Pinal's dreariness and that of her own frail existence.

From her vantage point Mattie could hear the sounds of the main street's activity. She could watch people walk along the wheel-rutted, dirt corridor that separated the fading buildings that represented the dissolution of Pinal's yesteryears. Staring into the umbra of contrast within the darkling shades she perhaps sensed the twilight of her own tragic life. Mattie's eyes, dimmed by whiskey and opium, scanned the buildings that, like fatigued sentinels of a vanquished army, stood slouched in defeat, the peeling, faded paint their battle-stained uniforms.

Of the few businesses still operating the day Mattie arrived, at least half had closed during the winter. McCourt and Werner still monopolized the town's liquor trade but Werner, having closed his beer garden for the winter, had not bothered to reopen it. A clothing store, preparing to close forever, was offering huge discounts on the remaining stock of denim work shirts and pants. Leudke's General Store now handled the bulk of Pinal's diminishing mercantile business. The hotel now catered to so few visitors nearly all its rooms were closed, their furniture sold. Mattie had bought the furniture in her room when she moved to her two-room shack. Friends had helped her move.

The shack had two rooms but only one was fully furnished. The main room held a bed, bureau and a wooden table with two chairs. On the table sat a kerosene lamp to provide light at night. Near the only window stood a small wood-burning stove. Beside the bed on a stand was an earthenware washbowl and pitcher. To the left of the bed was a door that opened to the second room. It was empty save for a wooden bedstead and a straw mattress the former inhabitant had left behind along with the stove. A few yards behind the shack stood a privy, called locally an earth-closet.

Mattie had spent the winter watching the town slowly disappear around her. By mid-April the small remaining population was housed in a few tiny houses and shacks standing lonely among the dozens of others, all empty. The mine had been reduced to one shift comprised mostly of casual laborers who had stayed to work until October on an on-call basis. Now they, too, were preparing to depart. Pinal, in a scene typical of so many once thriving mining towns, was undergoing its death throes.

If Mattie, on this her final evening, had entertained any thoughts of walking down to the saloon she decided against it. The saloon no longer held interest for her. Merrymakers' laughter she had once so enjoyed had long since been muted. Laughter now was seldom heard in the saloon, or anywhere in Pinal for that matter. Her own interest in life had declined to such a degree that even personal hygiene had come to mean little. Upon rising in the morning a splash of water, an occasional lather of soap and liberal applications of attar of roses sufficed. Her once fashionable clothing was no longer kept neat and clean. Her disinterest had begun at least three months before and had spiraled swiftly downward during the last five weeks. Her concerns this night were centered on her aching teeth, her whiskey supply and the temperament of men who might call.

Mattie wondered if Frank Beeler might drop by. She wanted someone to talk to and her bottle held enough for two. Frank and Mattie got along well.

"We are birds of a feather," Mattie once told him and Frank agreed that indeed they were.

Frank was Mattie's best friend. He was from some eastern state (some think Pennsylvania, but no one knows for sure) but there had been a great many years between his departure from his eastern home and his arrival in Pinal.[1] Some twelve years before he had staked a claim a few miles from town along Queen's Creek. The ore samples failed to assay enough to make further exploration viable so, as did most men with failed claims, he tried to sell it to newcomers. When none took the bait Frank hired on as a laborer at the Silver King. He earned good money for a few years until whiskey eventually took him in its grip. His work suffered and by 1886 Frank Beeler was no longer considered reliable for steady employment. His hours were eventually cut until he was called for work only occasionally.

Beeler knew Mattie better than did anyone in Pinal. She may have looked upon him as a father figure or, perhaps, an older brother. Perhaps he looked upon her as he might have regarded a wayward daughter. She told him her troubles and he listened patiently as he drank her whiskey. He knew the pain she suffered was both physical and from a broken heart, but was not sure which was worse. He knew she was sick and he knew its cause, but he also knew he could do nothing to help. He wanted to help her but was unable to translate concern into advice, either medical or friendly. So he did the next best thing. Because he was rarely busy, every day he called to check on her, adapting his daily routine so he could call every morning. He would also drop by during the evenings, if she was not busy, of course.

Frank was also aware how pointless it was to suggest she quit drinking. He, and others, had tried, and she had laughed, so he never mentioned it again. Her laughter hurt, but he understood. Such advice, coming from Frank Beeler, must have seemed to Mattie as akin to a fox telling a ferret to stop raiding the hen house. Frank did his best, but however good his intentions, the aspiration was illusion; his helplessness was reality.

As Mattie sat outside her little house alone in the gathering gloom of her final night an impish breeze brushed her bare arm. She shivered, pulled her mantilla tighter and shivered again. In the zephyr's chill she may have felt the passing of her final days.

Her reverie was interrupted by a stranger calling her name. She looked, waved and beckoned to him. She would not spend the night alone after all.

It was morning when Frank Beeler looked in on Mattie.[2] He had peered through her window the previous evening, saw she had company and had quietly left. He had not called again, but this morning she was alone so he went inside. Because she was sleeping he sat quietly at the table. Mattie turned slightly and the blanket slipped away from her arm. Frank noticed the silver bracelets she always wore were missing. He wondered where they might be. He knew they were the only items of value she had left.

Frank had not been there long before she awoke.

"Oh!" she remarked, startled. "Frank! Hello. I didn't hear you come in."

"You were sleeping," Frank replied, "so I stayed quiet. Didn't want to wake you up."

Mattie rubbed her eyes, smiled weakly and relaxed against her pillow.

"Do you want anything?" he asked.

"I don't feel at all good. Pour me some of that," she replied, pointing to a beer bottle on the table.

Frank lifted the bottle, removed the cap, sniffed it cautiously, decided the liquid within was whiskey, poured a splash into a cup and handed it to her. She took a couple of swallows then returned the cup to Frank and he poured her another shot. Locating a second cup he poured himself some of the liquid. Between them they emptied the bottle.

"Frank," Mattie asked, "can you get me some opium?"

Frank shook his head. He told her she needed sleep, not opium. He tried to take her mind from the subject by asking about her bracelets. She looked down at her arms then glanced towards the table. With a shrug she vaguely replied they were lying around somewhere. Suspecting that perhaps her visitor of the previous evening had stolen them, Frank looked here and there but found only the brooch she always pinned on her bodice. He placed it beside the little tin cash box on the shelf above the bed. He hoped the bracelets were under her blanket.

Mattie, realizing Frank would not get her opium, asked if he would go to Werner's for whiskey. Bowing to the futility of argument, he took some coins from the tin box and departed. Before he closed the door he looked back. Mattie had closed her eyes.

Upon his return Mattie awakened. She apologized for being such trouble to him but she needed another favor.

"Frank, will you go to Luedkes' and get me some laudanum?"

Frank took more coins from the box and retraced his steps along the dusty street.

Beeler had no idea of how much laudanum he should

buy but the storekeeper knew the amount Mattie usually purchased. He gave Beeler a green bottle filled with liquid. Frank asked how much was in a dose.

"Varies," came the reply. "Usually between ten to twenty drops. Mrs. Earp will know. She has bought quite a lot over the last few months. Her teeth are giving her hell."

"Actually," he added, "she's been using more than usual lately. I reckon she is in a lot of pain."

"Yes," Frank replied, sadly. " Yes, she is."

Frank was correct. Mattie's decaying teeth were worsening. If she had seen a dentist in Globe,[3] for whatever reasons the work was never completed. When her teeth ached she could treat them with popular nostrums,[4] but they were no longer effective by the time she arrived in Pinal and there was no dentist there to turn to. When the roots began to abscess, the pain became so intense she began using the fast-acting laudanum. Still, ever mindful of the fatal danger of tincture of opium, she used it only when whiskey did not alleviate the pain. Thus, throughout winter and spring, she managed to keep the pain within bearable limits.[5]

By February 1888, however, increased doses of laudanum had become necessary. Mattie, no longer able eat solid food without great difficulty, finally stopped in favor of broths and whatever could be mashed. The resultant weight loss further weakened her. Her face became more lined; her skin grew sallow.

Her dental problem was only part of her pain. Her broken heart, beyond mending, became too intense for her to endure. Her physical pain combined with her mental state to eventually bring her to the decision she felt was no longer avoidable. She saw no way out. She began to talk of suicide. At least twice, friends restrained her.

Frank Beeler knew what was ailing her. Mattie's dental suffering was common knowledge, but Beeler's statement at the inquiry indicates another ailment, perhaps cancer in its final stage. One of Mattie's present-day relatives suspects cervical cancer. A case can also be made for a venereal disease, syphilis and gonorrhea being rampant amongst those in Mattie's profession. Either, as they progress to a final stage, very often brings intense pain.

Frank hastened back to Mattie. He had been promised a couple of hours of much needed work if he would report at one o'clock. Now, though, feeling the effects of the early morning whiskey, he had lost track of the time,[6] but knew it was not much past nine o'clock.

"Can you sit with me awhile?" Mattie asked.

Beeler, pulling up a chair, nodded as he removed the cap from the laudanum bottle.

"How much of this do you want?" he asked as he took a cup from the bedside table.

"Twenty drops," she replied.

"That seems like a lot," he remarked.

"No," Mattie replied. "It's the right amount."

Beeler, still thinking the amount excessive, counted fifteen drops into her cup.

"Do you take it straight?" he asked.

"No," Mattie replied. "Pour in just a little whisky. I will tell you how much."

Beeler dribbled in a small amount of the liquor, stopped when Mattie instructed, and handed her the cup. She downed it in one swallow and within minutes was sound asleep. Beeler, reluctant to leave her alone, stayed at her bedside. The whiskey bottle drew his attention and unable to resist temptation took a swallow from the bottle. Then he went to the next room, lay on the mattress and dozed off.

Beeler awoke with a start, alarmed that he might be late for work. Rising quickly he went to the other room, glanced outside at the sun and was relieved to know he still had time to get to the mill. He checked on Mattie and was pleased she was still sleeping. She seemed fine, so he left.

Beeler, having worked his promised few hours and with new money in his pocket, decided to stop at the saloon before looking in on Mattie. He stayed a little longer than he had intended, so when he arrived at Mattie's he was a little unsteady. He managed to open the door quietly and peered inside. Mattie was still sleeping. He saw the whiskey bottle on the side table, lifted it and shook it. It was empty. He returned it to the table. He also noticed the laudanum bottle was empty as well but the significance failed to register on his whiskey clouded mind. He was relieved to find she was breathing quietly, yet even through his haze, he sensed something was not right. Taking Mattie's wrist he felt for a pulse. The pulse had a regular beat. He latched the door, went to the other room, lay on the mattress and fell asleep.

Tom Flannery, a thirty-year-old laborer, was also concerned about Mattie and often dropped in on her during the evenings. On July 3 he had worked late, but after work came by to check on her. He was surprised to find the door locked. She always left it open. He knocked. Receiving no answer he peered in the window. He could see Mattie in the bed. She was alone so he knocked again, harder. His persistent knocking awakened Beeler who stumbled groggily to the door and unbolted it.

"Is Mattie alright?" asked Flannery, entering the room.

Beeler nodded, pointing to the bed.

"Sound asleep," he whispered. "And no wonder. She drank a bottle of whiskey while I was away."

"She doesn't look at all comfortable," he observed. "I will see if I can move her a bit."

Flannery lit the lantern, approached the bed.

"Did you say she drank the whole bottle?"

"It was near to full when I left," Beeler said, "but it was empty when I came back." Then he added, "She took some laudanum, too."

"Laudanum?" Flannery asked. "How much?"

"She wanted twenty drops," Frank replied, "but I only gave her fifteen. Twenty seemed like a lot."

"Was she drinking whiskey *with* the laudanum?" he asked Beeler.

The younger man picked up the bottle. "This is empty," he remarked.

"When I was here she had it with just a sip of whiskey," came the reply. "She must have finished them both while I was gone."

Peering at the motionless figure, Flannery could see black spots on Mattie's arms and face. He knew what they signified. Feeling for a pulse and finding no trace he ran to the street to find Dr. Kinneard. Beeler, confused by the younger man's quick departure, also left. In his befuddled mind he thought he was supposed to report for work.

It was 8:15 p.m. when Flannery located Doctor Kinnaird, who was on his way home. As the two hurried to Mattie's place, Flannery explained the situation. Seeing the two men in such a hurry caused others, curious, to follow. Kinneard went directly to Mattie while Flannery lit the kerosene lamp from the table. He held it as the doctor made a quick check on the inert figure.

Beeler, meanwhile, had gone some distance before he realized he had already been at work. Retracing his steps he was surprised to find a group of men standing inside Mattie's room watching the doctor work to revive the inert woman. After a few minutes the doctor stood up and drew the blanket upwards to cover her. The black spots contrasted with the paleness of death. There was no need for him to speak. The group understood. The woman they had known as Mattie Earp had passed beyond. Sadly, slowly, mostly silent, they filed out into the gathering dusk.

The doctor turned to Frank. "Is there any whiskey here?" he asked.

"No," Frank replied. "She drank it all when I was gone to work."

"I see," said the doctor as he turned to leave. He did not explain to Frank what it was he saw, nor did he elaborate upon the unusual question.

Kinneard and Flannery left together, but Beeler remained. Almost shuffling he moved to the table, sank slowly to a chair, his face masked in sorrow. Folding his arms atop the table he cradled his head upon them. Frank Beeler wept, his heaving shoulders attesting to his anguish. An intense sadness gripped him. He had failed his friend when she needed him most.

Frank sat alone in the darkening room. The lamp went out but he did not relight it. He would stay with Mattie until morning when the undertaker would come to take her away. He sat quietly, thoughts running through his mind. He had failed his friend and he could not shake the thought. Through the open door he heard a soft, melodic *chideary-chideary-chideary*, the trill of a nearby Crissal Thrasher calling to its mate. Frank had heard the call often but had never before paid much attention. He listened for a reply. None came.

CHAPTER 25

We, the Jury, find...

In the early morning hours two Mexican women arrived at Mattie's house, gently ushered Beeler from the room then set about preparing Mattie's body for burial. The women, wives of mine laborers, lived nearby and had befriended her. According to a Superior resident, a descendent of one of the women, the two had helped Mattie, especially during the last three months when her pain had been so intense. Without regard for Mattie's lowly social status, they had given aid and comfort to her during her final weeks. Now, for a final time, they went together to prepare her for her final place of rest. After washing Mattie's wasted body and carefully brushing her hair they wrapped her in a clean white sheet. Then they said a prayer. When the undertaker arrived these kind, thoughtful women gave her over to him and his assistant. The two men, perhaps touched by the commiserations of the women, took extra care in the transfer of the frail body to the pine box that would be her final bed.

At 11:00 a.m. the mandatory inquest, convened by County Coroner Benson, was called to order. With the coroner was a jury of six men chosen at random, Sheriff Gabriel, Doctor Kinnaird, three witnesses and Wood Porter, the recording clerk. There may have been some spectators. The coroner explained the procedure for the enquiry and instructed the jurymen to listen well to the evidence given and statements from the witnesses for it would be they who must determine the probable cause of death. They would also attempt to resolve if Mattie Earp had met her death by suicide, accident, or at the hands of a person or persons unknown.[1]

Frank Beeler was called as the first witness. He related the events of July 3 but his memory, muddled by whiskey, dimmed at times. He confused several of the day's sequences and certain time periods in the order of events. The second witness, T.J. Flannery set the times of the evening events straight and his times were verified by the third witness, S.E. Damon, who basically knew very little of what had occurred, but was able to confirm the time of the doctor's arrival.

With the testimony ended, the jury retired to consider the case. Out only a short time, it returned a unanimous verdict that death was caused by opium poisoning. The jury had also decided Mattie had committed suicide by intentionally drinking a nearly full bottle of whiskey in conjunction with a full bottle of laudanum. Coroner Benson agreed with the jury's verdict and dismissed them. Those who had befriended Mattie also agreed with the verdict.

The jury, there can be no doubt, had delivered a correct finding. Despite some recent theories suggesting Mattie was murdered, she did not meet her death through foul play or under circumstances even vaguely suspicious. That she had gotten up from her bed to retrieve the laudanum from the shelf, leaves no doubt she had acted deliberately. Mattie knew exactly what she was doing.

With the inquest ended, Celia Ann "Mattie" Blaylock Earp, prostitute, alcoholic, opium addict and secret second wife of Wyatt Barry Stapp Earp, sometimes farmer, horse thief, pimp, brothel keeper, occasional lawman and professional gambler, was conveyed the remaining 800 yards of her life's tormented trail. She had found the permanence she had sought with final rest in the Pinal graveyard.

Pinal County did not allocate public funds for funeral services, nor was it excessively charitable for burials of indigents, transients or suicides. Thus, Mattie was assigned a pauper's grave. The county disbursed $5 for the cost of the pine box, plus $2 to the anonymous man who had dug the grave. Shortly after the noon hour of July 4, 1888 Mattie Earp was lowered into the cold and final darkness of her assigned space.

Frank Beeler, the loyal friend who might have saved her had he remained sober enough to see the immediate problem, attended the burial. So did Flannery and some others. It is not known if the sheriff attended, but it seems likely he would have as he had also befriended Mattie. Perhaps one or two of the merchants whose stores she had patronized were there as well. Maybe someone recited a short prayer on her behalf. It would be nice to think it was Frank Beeler who later set up the simple wooden board that identified her grave for almost sixty-three years. To their lasting credit, the family of one of the Mexican women[2] who had befriended Mattie adopted the gravesite. The family still tends it.

So far as is known there was no eulogy. What could anyone have said of Mattie Blaylock Earp? No one really knew her and those in Pinal who did were well aware of her addiction to opium, her dependence upon whiskey and laudanum, her animosity towards her husband, and her intense hatred of the woman who had replaced her. A eulogist would have been hard pressed for words.

Mattie's life had not been a success. She brought forth no children to mourn her passing. She amassed no estate of great worth nor did she leave a legacy, not even a minor legend to expand upon. Her single claim to fame is having married a man who would years later become a fabricated legend. In the places where she plied her trade she remained virtually unknown. She had spent her life in pragmatic anonymity, appearing in only one census after 1866. She left indelible marks only in Peoria and Wichita, all in police records under assumed names. Elsewhere, because Wyatt Earp protected her in his capacity as law officer, she made no court appearances, had no arrests and, except for one mention in Tombstone, remained unnoticed by newspaper reporters. All in all, everything said and done, Celia Ann "Mattie" Blaylock Earp did not distinguish her thirty-eight years. Her death and burial attracted no more attention than six short lines in the Globe newspaper.

On July 5, the day following Mattie's interment, Sheriff

Gabriel packed her belongings into the two trunks that had accompanied her to Pinal from Fort Scott, Peoria, Rice County, Wichita, Dodge City, Tombstone and a dozen stops between. Her entire estate consisted of a few items of clothing (some very fashionable and obviously expensive), a collection of letters, several photos, some jewelry and the incidental items a woman collects during a lifetime. It is not known if her silver bracelets were among them. The county claimed the few coins in the tin box on the shelf above her bed as partial defrayal of the $7 her burial had cost.

The trunks were tagged and transferred to a storage space in the sheriff's office in Florence, the county seat. A letter was written by Coroner Benson to Mattie's sister, Sarah Marquis. Tersely, in the manner of such letters, Sarah was given the particulars of Mattie's death, the findings of the inquest and the subsequent verdict. It ended by informing Sarah her sister's trunks would be sent to her upon receipt of $23, the cost of stage and rail shipment to Iowa. The county would await her reply.

Sarah sent the required amount whereupon the trunks were forwarded. Sarah and her husband placed them in the attic where they remained, more or less forgotten, for many years.

On July 7 Mattie's death was reported in Globe's newspaper, *Arizona Enterprise*, as an item in a column covering county events. It is short, only 28 words in six lines. It reflects a flippant attempt at humor by an unknown, disinterested reporter.

Mattie Earp, a frail denizen
of Pinal, culminated a big
spree by taking a dose of
laudanum on Tuesday and died
from its effects.
She was buried on the 4th.[3]

The reference to "a big spree" flies in the face of reality. Mattie was certainly not in the midst of a wild party on Tuesday, July 3, 1888. On that hot July day, her pain, both physical and from her broken heart, was at last brought to a merciful end by Pale Death, the grand physician who cures all pain.

Epilogue

For seventy years Mattie Earp remained as forgotten as the trunks in Sarah Marquis's attic, eluding all the researchers and historians engaged in the recovery of Old West lore. Those who had known her kept silent, perhaps themselves wondering what had happened to her. Two who knew were Wyatt Earp and Josephine Marcus, and they weren't talking.

During the six years Mattie resided in Colton, Globe and Pinal, Wyatt and Josephine traveled from place to place attempting to cash in, sometimes successfully sometimes not, on various schemes and interests. During that time they lived together but never claimed to be married, an indication that Wyatt was honoring his marriage status if not his marriage vows. Certainly something was restraining Wyatt and Josephine from proclaiming their arrangement as a marriage.

The "something" was Mattie. Mindful that she was Wyatt's wife, and very much alive, both continued in their efforts to erase her memory and name from the slate. Neither mentioned her to their personally selected biographers until Josephine did, many years later and then only because she was left with no choice.[1]

Josephine began calling herself Mrs. Wyatt Earp during 1889, informing all and sundry that she and Wyatt were indeed married. Josephine's sudden change in status suggests two letters had been mailed from Pinal County that day in July of the previous year. Her emphasis that she was Wyatt's second wife was so successful writers and historians thereafter always referred to her as such. Josephine claimed she and Wyatt had exchanged vows before the captain of a yacht while at sea beyond the three mile limit.[2] Josie was seemingly unaware that captains of yachts were not authorized to perform marriages. As had Wyatt's marriage to Mattie, this one also failed to produce a confirming certificate, and none has as yet surfaced.

Alvira "Allie" Earp, Mattie's good friend, never went so far as denying her existence, but she never mentioned her either.[3] In fact, all the Earps maintained resolute silence. All were aware of Mattie's return to Arizona although they may not have known she had left Globe. While Mattie was in Globe, someone, either Wyatt's sister, Adelia Earp Edwards, or Allie, mailed her a small photo of a cute little girl named Virginia Edwards, known as "Ginnie." She was Adelia's daughter and Wyatt's niece and, therefore, Mattie's niece as well.

Why the amnesia? No surprises there. Wyatt's branch of the family tree was very secretive. The brothers had always banded together in defensive mode whenever they felt endangered; and it mattered not whether the danger was real or merely perceived. The trait was no less ingrained in their women, so they also instinctively reacted in like manner when the perceived danger indicated Wyatt would be acutely embarrassed if his treatment of Mattie became known. They coalesced to the point of shielding the generally disliked Josephine, not for her sake but to protect Wyatt. Profound silence, the Earp version of circling the wagons, worked well for nearly seventy years until one day when Mattie's ghost decided to work some rascality. By that time only nieces and nephews remained and, unable to deny her existence, they simply claimed to be unaware of a woman named Mattie and hoped the issue would go away. It didn't.

When Sarah Blaylock Marquis died in 1906, at age fifty-four, her son, Osmond Hiram Marquis, inherited her estate. Among the goods and chattels were two trunks that, Marquis knew, had belonged to his Aunt Celia. He left the trunks in the attic and forgot about them. He also knew she had been married to a man named Wyatt Earp who had abandoned her. He was also aware his aunt had died under tragic circumstances in Arizona, but was unaware of the details. He recalled discussing his aunt with his mother when he was a small boy. She had shown him some pictures and had read to him snippets of letters she had received from her sister. He remembered asking why the letters had so suddenly stopped. Sarah told him only that his aunt had died of a broken heart. He was too young to understand.

In 1932 Marquis heard of a man named Wyatt Earp who was emerging as a legendary hero and wondered if he had been his Aunt Celia's husband. However, he did not pursue the matter until another twenty years had passed, by which time Wyatt Earp had become famous in film and legend. Marquis decided he should learn whether his Aunt Celia and been married to this particular Wyatt Earp. One quiet day in 1952, Marquis decided the trunk's contents might be a good starting point for some answers. Going to his attic he wrestled the remaining trunk (one had been given away several years previously) downstairs and opened it in the light of his living room. He scanned items both familiar and not familiar. He carefully examined a package of letters of which the most interesting was the coroner's letter from Pinal County which explained the details of Mattie's demise. There were two photos of Mattie, an obviously expensive dress and some lesser articles of everyday clothing. The picture of Virginia Edwards caught his attention, as did a tiny bible. On the bible's flyleaf was an inscribed dedication[4] to Wyatt Earp. Hiram had no inkling what this meant but felt it was important.

Uncertain of how his finds might impact on the Earp myth but determined to find out, Marquis mailed an itemized list to the Beeson Museum in Dodge City. He was aware the museum had artifacts concerning Earp's days in that city, but he was not aware that its curator, Merritt Beeson,[5] was avidly pro-Earp in every regard. Had he known he would probably have chosen a different tack.

In his letter Marquis described the mementos, the bible and the photos. He also mentioned his aunt, Celia Ann Blaylock, had been married to Wyatt Earp, that he had deserted her and that she had committed suicide. Marquis' letter had an impact on Beeson — all negative. Shocked and alarmed, he hid the letter in an unused filing cabinet but, fortunately, did not destroy it. He never replied to Marquis who, unfortunately, neither followed up on the letter nor tried another avenue.

Marquis's letter remained in the cabinet for about three years, well hidden, until the day Mrs. Beeson decided to sort the files. She found the letter and read it in fascination. Mrs. Beeson did not necessarily share her husband's desire to shield Earp at any cost and set about authenticating the details.[6] She contacted Marquis who sent her copies of what he had. Shortly thereafter Mattie's two photos were established as genuine, the little girl's photo was verified as being that of Ginnie Edwards[7] and the tiny bible, it was determined, had been presented to Earp by two Dodge City lawyers, Sutton and Colburn, both of whom had been Wyatt's colleagues. (Some think this verifies a story that Earp had been a deacon in the Unity Church. Others are equally convinced it had been presented to him as a tongue-in-cheek joke.)

The revelations caused a storm in Dodge City where Earp was (and still is) considered an authentic hero and a major tourist industry. The news caused equal amounts of concern and dismay within the ranks of Earp disciples who had eagerly espoused Lake's interpretation of the man. There was a great outcry, but the truth was too revealing to be denied.

Further investigation followed in which it was proven a marriage, with or without ecclesiastic blessing, had existed between Mattie Blaylock and Wyatt Earp and that he, following his shameful desertion, attempted to keep her a secret. The superlative marshal's boots had obviously encased feet of clay. Alas! Wyatt Earp, whom Stuart Lake had aggrandized a knight in shining armor and a paragon of virtue, had been neither. Earp stood exposed as a mere mortal subject to worldly temptations in his eager pursuit of fame and fortune. Earp adherents, gasping and sputtering in dismay, rallied to discredit Mattie.

Rushing headlong into the ever-widening breach, they insisted Mattie's connection with Earp had been nothing more than the righteous lawman's determination to rehabilitate a saloon whore. Mattie, they insisted, spurned Wyatt's efforts to help her return to the narrow path of social nicety. Worse, not only had she betrayed his trust, she had also stolen his trunk which held his prized possessions, the little bible and niece Ginnie's photo.[8]

Disregarding mounting evidence, they even refused to accept Tombstone's 1880 census in which Mattie is detailed as Mrs. Wyatt Earp, housewife, age 21, residing with Wyatt Earp in their co-owned house. If Mattie was guilty of anything at the time, aside from her opium habit, it was for shaving nine years from her age.

Her detractors declined to submit any evidence to support their claims because, in fact, they had none to offer. A particular case in point is Virginia's photo. It not only repudiates the possibility of theft, but also conclusively proves Mattie had remained in touch with Wyatt's family,[9] perhaps as late as 1885. When Mattie was deserted Virginia was barely two years old. At its earliest the picture was taken after Mattie had left Colton.

In the face of all evidence available there was no doubt that Celia Ann Blaylock, who first became Mattie Blaylock and then Mattie Earp, was indeed Wyatt Earp's second wife and that he had deserted her in March 1882. It was she whom he and Josephine undertook to suppress, and almost succeeded, because seventy years passed before an aged man became curious about a dusty trunk in his attic.

Following Marquis's death his widow donated the items to institutions, museums and individuals seriously researching the Earp saga. Mattie's photos and the Dodge City bible went to the Arizona Historical Society. Her letters to Sarah went to relatives while other artifacts and mementos were given to friends. Hopefully the letters will be produced someday to throw more light across the mystery of the woman who was Mattie Earp, Wyatt's secret second wife.

Postscript

Over the years, just as it had totally repossessed Pinal, the desert reclaimed the town's graveyard. Although nearing the point of obliteration today it is not difficult to find, but getting to it can be a minor adventure. The rutted trail that must be taken is fully capable of destroying the suspension of any vehicle with less stamina than a four-wheel-drive SUV. Large rocks, precariously placed by nature, protrude from the ground menacing the oil pan of any vehicle with low clearance. For years the area surrounding the graveyard was used as a dumping ground. Mounds of broken glass lurk in wait threatening to shred tires.

One can walk of course, but different hazards abound. From the main road the south route is a steep, rutted grade and from the north turn-off at the old Silver King Mine the road is a mile of rough, deep ruts. Snakes, scorpions and black widow spiders must be kept in mind. Cacti and thorny bushes brush against legs and arms, so a sturdy long-sleeved shirt and denim pants are recommended. Occasionally a lone coyote will watch from a safe distance.[1] Walking is not for the faint of heart or the short of breath.

Eventually however, all hazards bypassed, the trail ends at what was once an orderly cemetery. Most graves now remain only as mounds of earth while others are fully overgrown with prickly pear cacti, thorny brush, sagebrush or desert grass. None of the original wooden markers remain, so unless one knows who lies in a given place, identification is impossible.

There are a few stone markers but the names and dates are eroded, most almost totally beyond readability.

When the startling news emerged that the Mattie Earp who had died in Pinal had been married to Wyatt Earp, someone made his way to the old cemetery. He crept through the overgrowth, found Mattie's grave, and stole her wooden marker. The family tending the site made a replacement. When it was also stolen the decision was made to leave the grave unmarked.[2] Her "family" continued to tend it and, aided and abetted by residents of Superior, kept the exact location secret for several more years.

Eventually, one of Mattie's three great-nieces contacted Superior authorities regarding the grave. The site location was revealed to them when one of the nieces visited Superior and was introduced to the matriarch of the family who tends the grave. Together they visited the site. Since then others, this writer included, have been privileged to look upon the exact site of Mattie's grave. The residents of Superior guard Mattie's privacy, so others who just drop by see only a memorial that is some distance from the grave.

Happily, Superior is expanding its historical society. On the agenda is the restoration of the graveyard. This is an ambitious and formidable task but already volunteer hands have cleared several long-neglected graves. The area has been recently declared a historical site and placed under protection of the federal parks department. This assures that anyone caught damaging or interfering with graves or stealing markers or other artifacts will face prosecution under federal statutes. Penalties can be very severe.

APPENDIX 1
Coroner's Inquest Report

Certified Copy of Original Inquiry Into the Death of
Mattie Earp In Pinal Arizona Territory. July 3, 1888.[1]

Inquisition on
The Body of Mattie Earp,
Deceased

Filed July 21, 1888
W. Wood Porter,
Clerk

In the matter of the inquisition held upon the body of Mattie
Earp, deceased, the following named witnesses were sworn
and testified as follows:[2]

Frank Beeler being duly sworn on his oath says:

Q. What is your name, age, occupation and residence?
A. My name is Frank Beeler. I am 65 years of age. I am a laborer and live in Pinal, Ariz.

Q. State to the jury all that you know about the cause of the
death of the deceased.
A. The woman felt sick and I knew pretty well what the sick-
ness was as I had waited on her once before when she was this
same way. I went to her room here in Pinal day before yesterday and looked in the door. I asked her if she wanted anything

as I was in the habit of doing some chores for her. She said no she didn't want anything. She was lying on the bed and a man was lying there in the bed beside of her. During that day I didn't go there again but yesterday I went there about 8 or 9 in the morning and I asked her if she wanted anything and she said come in here and sit down I want to talk to you.

I went in and sat down and she said she did not feel well and pointed around beside the stand to a beer bottle that stood there. I took the bottle out. It contained whiskey about one fourth full. And she and I drank it up. She said then that she wanted to get more whiskey and some opium or Laudanum as she wanted to try and get some sleep. While she was lying there I said where are your bracelets and she said I guess they are around here somewhere. I could not find them but I found her breastpin. I put it up on the wall.

She then said I would like to have you go to Leudke's and get me some Laudanum as I cannot sleep. She then said go to Werners and get some whiskey. I went there and got fifty cents worth of whiskey and took it to her. Then she wanted me to go and get the Laudanum. I went to Leudke and he gave me a small bottle of Laudanum and I took it to her. I asked Leudke how much one ought to take of that to make them sleep and he said he didn't know but that she had been taking it for a long time. When I went back with the Laudanum I said I don't know how much a dose is and she said pour me about twenty drops. I counted out about fifteen drops and said how much whiskey do you want in it and held the glass up and poured it out until she said when I had enough. She then took it and drank it.

She then said come and sit down and talk and I said how do you feel and she said better and that she thought she could sleep. I sat there about an hour and then went in the other room as I was feeling the liquor. I laid down and about that time Flannery came to the door and I then went out and I was gone for about two hours when I went back to her house and as I wanted a drink I looked around for the whiskey but couldn't find any and the whole bottle of Laudanum was gone.

I felt for her pulse and her heart and they seemed to be beating allright and she seemed to be asleep. I sat down there for an hour or two and then went out as I thought she was asleep. I was away about two hours and then went back and saw a number of persons in the house. The Dr. was one of them and seemed to be trying to restore her. The Dr. asked me if there was any whiskey there.

Q. What time of day did you get the Laudanum from Leudke?
A. I cannot tell but it was in the forenoon and I gave it to her right away.

Q. What time was it when you went back there last and found the Dr. there?
A. It must have been four or five o'clock.

Q. Were you sober during the day, yesterday?
A. I cannot say that I was though I was able to attend to business.

Q. Wasn't you pretty drunk in the afternoon?
A. I was. But I didn't give to her any Laudanum when I was drunk.

Q. What did you do with the bottle after pouring her the Laudanum?
A. I sat it up on the shelf.

Q. Was she up during the day?
A. Yes.

Q. Why did you feel her pulse when you went in?
A. Because I saw the Laudanum was gone.

Q. Was there Laudanum enough in that bottle to have killed any person if they had taken it all in your opinion?
A. I don't know how much it takes. I do not think I gave her an eighth of what was in the bottle.

(Signed) F. Beeler

Submitted & Sworn to
before me this 4th day
of July, AD 1888

W.N. Benson,
Acting Coroner, Pinal
County, Arizona (sic)

T.J. Flannery being duly sworn on his oath says.

Q. What is your name, age, occupation and residence?
A. My name is T.J. Flannery. I am 31 years of age. I reside in
Pinal, Ariz. Occupation laborer.

Q. State to the jury all that you know about the cause of the
death of the deceased?
A. I went to her room here in Pinal last night about eight
o'clock or a little after and knocked on the door but no one
answered. I had not seen her since Sunday or Monday. The
door was opened very soon by Beeler who said that deceased
was lying on the bed asleep. I went in and saw by the position
that she was lying in that something was wrong as she would
not be that way unless something was wrong. I lit a light and
went up to the bed and looked at her and her arms and face
were covered with black spots. I supposed she had been taking more Laudanum and had taken too much and was dead
or dying.
    I felt her pulse and found they were not beating. I asked
Beeler what she had been taking and he said he gave her some
Laudanum and that she had taken the whole bottle. I then
started out for the Dr. and met him as he was going home. He
went in and tried to restore the deceased but could not do so.
It was about half past eight when the Dr. got there.

Q. What condition was Beeler in when he came to the door to let you in?
A. I did not pay much attention to him. I do not think he was drunk.

Q. What is the name of the deceased if you know?
A. Mattie Earp.

(Signed T.J. Flannery)

Flannery is then recalled:

Q. Did you ever hear the deceased threaten her own life?
A. I have. Earp, she said, had wrecked her life by deserting her and she didn't want to live.

(Signed: T.J. Flannery)

Submitted & Sworn to me
& before me this 4th day
of July AD 1888.

W.N. Benson,
Acting coroner.

S.E. Damon being duly sworn on his oath says:

Q. What is your name, age, occupation and residence?
A. My name is S.E. Damon. I am 31 years of age, occupation laborer and I reside in Pinal, Ariz.

Q. State to the jury all that you know about the cause of the death of the deceased.
A. I do not know anything about the cause of the death. I know she had been drinking heavily for about three months and I have severally [sic] times taken whiskey away from her. About three days ago she said she was going to make away with herself as she said she was tired of life.

(Signed: S.E. Damon)

Subscribed and sworn to
before me this 4th day
of July AD 1888.

(Signed) W.N. Benson,
Acting Coroner, Pinal
County, Ariz.

I hereby certify that the above and
foregoing are true and correct depositions
and were taken by me in the Inquisition upon the body of Mattie Earp, deceased, held July 4th, 1888.

(Signed) W.N. Benson,
Acting Coroner, Pinal
Pinal County, Arizona.
July 12, 1888.

APPENDIX 2
The St. Elmo Connection

In early 1940 the woman known as "Big Nose Kate" Elder was rediscovered by a Dr. A.W. Bork who was doing research on elderly Arizona citizens. He was interviewing a Mrs. Mary Cummings,[1] a resident of Pioneer's Home in Prescott when his subject, perhaps inadvertently, informed him she had once been known as Kate Elder. Bork, who instantly recognized the name, was both surprised and pleased at his discovery and was elated when Kate granted him a more in-depth interview. From her, Bork learned that after Doc Holliday died she had remained in Colorado. In March 1890 she left the sporting life forever when she met and married a man named George M. Cummings.

They were married in Aspen and from that point onward she worked hard at becoming a respectable lady. She reverted to her given names, Mary Catherine, and she and Cummings found work at a mining camp, he as a blacksmith, she as a cook. Cummings, unfortunately, was an alcoholic and Kate left him in 1899 but did not sue for divorce.[2] As Mary Cummings she had continued for many years working successfully towards respectability, and in 1930 was granted admittance to Pioneers' Home.

Kate told Bork she had lived from 1880 to 1887 in Globe, but gave vague answers to questions about her activities there. She said that in 1882 she had "purchased" a lease on a hotel[3] for $500 and managed it until 1887. She did not name the hotel and Bork, either because he was in awe of this amazing old lady or thinking she had forgotten in old age, did not pursue the question. Dr. Bork may not have been aware that in the

Old West the word hotel often had two definitions.[4] Had he known, he might have been more inclined to press the issue. He would have found that Kate's "hotel" was located on Broad Street.

Broad Street, Globe's main thoroughfare during the period in question, was divided into two sections. The north section was the sporting area while the south was the respectable part of town. Today, North Broad Street remains a link to the Old West. The division line, in effect the town's deadline, was Mesquite Street. Respectable women in 1882 did not venture alone north of Mesquite, for the area was a strand of saloons and other sinful places. A saloon of the 1880s era still operates but now caters to respectable townsfolk and tourists. It is not far from where Kate's "hotel" was located.

Globe's extant records contain nothing indicating the town ever issued a hotel license to a Kate Elder, Haroney, Holliday or Fisher. Nor is there a record of her having been employed as the manager of a hotel. The logical explanation, considering Kate's profession at the time and that she referred to the place as a hotel, is that she had purchased a share in a brothel. It is on this point that the case becomes interesting.

At 474 N. Broad Street there stands an old, wide, two-story, wood and brick building. Several years ago the ground floor was divided into two sections and remodeled into two separate businesses. The upper story of the structure however was not altered. A restaurateur and a photographer eventually bought the building.

One half of the ground floor is a fashionable restaurant, La Cassita. The other half is home to Michael Collett & Co., a photography studio. The morning I visited Globe I met the owner of the photography studio. He is a member of a local historical group [not affiliated with the Globe Historical Society] hoping to restore the area to symbolize its checkered past. We discussed Big Nose Kate, her presence in Globe and her claim of once managing a hotel. We discussed the building's history, at least as much of it as is known. Mr. Collett told me he and his group are convinced this was the "hotel" Kate operated during her seven years in Globe.

He invited me to look at his half of the top floor. Entry to the upper floor is gained from sidewalk level through a recessed door, a locked steel grill preventing casual entry. The door opens to a well-worn staircase leading to the second floor. It is also fairly steep but we arrived safely at the top onto a small landing (too small to be called a foyer). An electric doorbell (circa 1920) above a sign with faded lettering informs the visitor: "Ring for Service." The bell no longer works, but in the 1880s service was likely gained by sounding the clapper of a small brass bell.

On each side of the landing is a door. The one to the left was locked and the owner was not available. I was told behind that door is what was once a fine parlor. The door to the right allows entry into the business side of the place. It opens to a narrow hallway on each side of which are several small rooms. Today all are in various states of disrepair but are undergoing slow restoration.

It was an interesting tour. Each room betrayed the occupation for which the hotel was famed (or ill famed, if you prefer). In each room, always in a corner, can be seen a section of floorboard showing two sawn lines about ten inches apart. At one end of each section a drilled hole, the circumference of an adult's thumb, allows the cover to be lifted. Below is space for safe storage of money and other valuables. In these recesses (they were called "hidey holes") the soiled doves hid their valuables from clients who were not always trustworthy. A trunk, a rug or a washstand always covered the boards. Their presence alone betrays the building as having been a brothel.

During its long and interesting history The St. Elmo Hotel served as a bona fide hotel for only six or seven years.[5] Built about 1874 as a one-story hotel it retained its legitimacy until 1882. In 1878 local Freemasons convinced the owner to build a second story for their use as a temple until they could build a permanent temple. The Masons departed in 1881 whereupon the owner converted the second floor into rooms, changed its line of endeavor but kept the name.

When Kate invested her $500[6] it was Globe's premier brothel, and remained so until 1975. During its ten decades of operation it suffered two major fires, each of which caused damage to the interior but none to the structural integrity. Following each fire, repaired and refurbished, it resumed operation as a thriving bordello, sometimes under new owners.

Was The St. Elmo the place Kate told Dr. Bork she had managed? It seems so. The present owners and others involved in researching Globe's history are quite convinced it was. Although no fingerprints, so to speak, exist as proof, the supposition seems valid for several reasons.

From its inception Globe was a rough, tough, wide-open mining town with several houses of ill fame. None however was big enough to be called a hotel. After 1882, when The St. Elmo joined the "society of soiled doves, it was commonly referred to simply as "the hotel." Kate, by referring to her occupation in Globe as managing a hotel, undoubtedly meant she had been the madam of "the hotel" and the $500 "lease" was actually a "share."

While it is very probable that in the not-too-distant future the answers will be forthcoming, they will not be easily found. The history of Globe's red light district is difficult to unearth for two reasons. The first is that no brothel was allowed to operate unless madams or keepers paid the police force for protection. This assured there was never any trouble in the houses because the police responded very quickly upon being summoned. Disorderly clients were arrested and always charged with "being drunk in public," a generic term covering a multitude of situations. The troublemaker knew it was unwise to upset the police by explaining to a judge why, and where, he had been misbehaving, so he merely pleaded guilty, paid a small fine (usually $2) and quietly left town. Because no newspaper items can be found indicating arrests had occurred in a house of ill fame and, because no madam, keeper or bawd was ever charged, one can easily get the impression that such places did not exist.

The St. Elmo Hotel was no exception. From its first day as a house of ill repute to the summer day in 1975 when it closed forever, its various keepers and madams paid the protection premiums. As a result none was ever arrested, and neither were any of the soiled doves who graced its halls and hid their precious items in the hidey-holes under the floor boards.

The second difficulty in researching Globe's scarlet past is a reluctance to discuss the matter by those who wish the town had not been so lively. The town's official historical society, at least on the day I visited, displayed little desire to discuss 1880s activities north of Mesquite Street. Questions about Big Nose Kate drew ambiguous replies.

"What does the record say of Big Nose Kate?" asked the enquiring mind.

"Very little," was the answer. "A woman called Big Nose Kate once resided here but little is known about her."

"How much is little?" asked the enquiring mind.

"Oh, really very little. Nothing worth pursuing."

The answers gave the impression the society wants Kate forgotten. Questions concerning Mattie Blaylock Earp, drew even vaguer reactions. There were never outright denials, but there were no affirmations, either.

Silence often speaks loudly. The enquiring mind was left with the distinct impression that Kate and Mattie not only imprinted their dainty footprints in Broad Street's chalky dust, but their fingerprints were all over the rooms and hallways of The St. Elmo Hotel. Sadly, time has swept them away.

Meanwhile, the small determined group slowly works to uncover the secrets of The St. Elmo Hotel while also investigating local traditional lore that tunnels under Mesquite Street allowed surreptitious passage from the respectable side of town to the red light area. Thus Globe's respectable menfolk had easy access to favorite bordellos without fear of being seen by respectable people in general, and ministers, wives and mothers in particular. If there were in fact such tunnels, there should still be access to them to some degree. Most will have collapsed over the years, of course, but enough should remain for purposes of confirmation. Globe, it seems, harbors an interesting chapter of Old West history; and Big Nose Kate, Mattie Blaylock and The St. Elmo Hotel were all part of it.

APPENDIX 3
A Question of Identity

It was once thought that Sarah Haspel, daughter of the infamous Jane Haspel, might have been the mysterious woman from the Beardstown Gunboat who informed the court she was Sarah Earp, Wyatt Earp's wife. Sarah Haspel was not Mrs. Wyatt Earp. It was Mattie Blaylock who, on September 9 1872, identified herself as Sarah Earp and informed the Peoria court that she was Earp's wife. She had simply used her sister's name as a quick alias. The resultant mystery went unsolved for years as several theories were raised in efforts to identify Sarah Earp, wife of Wyatt.

The suggestion that she was Sarah Haspel at first glance seems possible, but the errors it contains render it unfeasible. An unusual notation in the *Daily National Democrat* for September 10, 1872 caused the confusion:

"Sarah Earp, alias Sally Heckell, calls herself the wife of Wyatt."

Alias Sally Heckell? No one knows where the reporter got that name. Heckell, or anything remotely resembling it, does not appear in any arrest records, court records or the *Daily Transcript*. The notation in the *Daily National Democrat* is purely a case of a reporter's error. His mistake led, many years later, to Sarah Haspel being identified as Mrs. Wyatt Earp.

The first error: Sarah Haspel was too well known to the Peoria police and Judge Cunningham for her ever to be booked or charged or tried under an alias. The reporters who covered the police beat all knew her and would have identified her immediately. The woman who on that morning identified herself as Sarah Earp and Mrs. Wyatt Earp was totally unknown to all concerned.

The second error: Sarah Haspel is listed as Sally only twice, the first occurring in a census entry and the second in a court appearance in October 1871. Sarah called herself Sally when she was in the employ of Thankful Sears, Peoria's alpha madam. The 1870 US Census (Peoria) appears to list her as Sally Haskell, white, prostitute, age sixteen, born Bloomington, Illinois. Close inspection of the enumerator's printing of the surname that looks like Haskell reveals only a case of poor printing. When the page is viewed under a magnifying glass the "k" in Haskell is clearly a poorly formed "p". The name given was in fact Sally Haspel. Enumerators' spelling, printing and writing often left much to be desired.

Error three: This is the most important of all. Sarah Haspel was not among the women arrested in the Beardstown Gunboat. In fact, she had no connection whatsoever with either the gunboat or with John Walton.

Error four: Had Sarah Haspel been in the courtroom calling herself Mrs. Wyatt Earp that morning, Mattie would have objected strenuously. In all probability she would have attacked poor Sarah.

A proponent of the Sarah Haspel as Sarah Earp theory has suggested that Sarah Haspel, calling herself Sally Earp, journeyed with Wyatt from Peoria to Wichita. There, he theorized, she partnered with Bessie Earp as the Sally Earp co-charged with Bessie for keeping a brothel.

The errors in this hypothesis are all counteracted by indisputable facts:

Fact one: Sarah Earp was Mattie's alias.[1]

Fact two: A farm near Peace, Kansas in 1873.

Fact three: Wyatt and Mattie were continuously together from 1871 until March 1882.

Fact four: The theorist was apparently unaware that Mattie and Wyatt had lived with Newton and his family at Fort Scott for several weeks in the autumn of 1871 before going to Peoria.

Fact five: One year later, in September of 1872, Mattie and Wyatt again appeared, bags in hand, at Newton's door at his new farm near Peace in Rice County, Kansas. Many years later one of Newton's descendants declared when Wyatt appeared at her father's farm in 1872 he was with Mattie and she was Wyatt's wife. Had Wyatt appeared with Sarah Haspel, even Newton would have displayed some curiosity, and his wife would certainly have objected.

Fact six: Shortly thereafter Wyatt rented a small farm down the road. There for most of 1873 he and Mattie lived quietly on their own acreage.

Had Wyatt taken up with Sarah Haspel in Peoria, and if she had been the Sally Earp of Wichita, what had Wyatt done with Mattie? The theorist offers no answer to this important question. In fact, Sarah Haspel does not enter into the equation in the slightest. Wyatt Earp could not have relegated Mattie into some sort of exile between Peoria and Dodge City.[2] The thought that Mattie would have quietly gone into such an exile is nonsense. It is not remotely possible that Sarah Haspel[3] was the Sally Earp of Wichita records.

Also interesting to note is that after Wyatt and Mattie departed Peoria there is no further mention of Sarah Earp or Mrs. Earp in newspapers or court records.

APPENDIX 4
Madam of Mystery

Mattie Bradford quietly emerged from the dealings at 12 Douglas Avenue on June 4, 1874, the day after Mattie and Bessie were released on bail. She disappeared just as quietly on September 16, the very day the Earp women were acquitted. Nonetheless, for three months and twelve days, she put an entirely different spin on the case. Obviously, the Earp ladies had at least one more trick up their skirts, so to speak. It seems exceedingly strange indeed how her arrival and departure coincided so precisely with Bessie and Mattie's court dates. Coincidence? Hardly!

Mattie Bradford is on record as having been the madam at Bessie's place, yet she remained completely invisible during her entire stay. Like the Cheshire Cat in *Alice in Wonderland*, who disappeared at will leaving only its smile, Mattie Bradford's name was all she left in Wichita, and it appears only in court records.

Marshal Smith was obviously charging madams even when he didn't know who, or where, they were, because on June 19 Mattie Bradford entered the records with three charges as a "keeper." Baldwin's law firm, acting on her behalf, entered guilty pleas and paid fines totaling $46. Interestingly, the first two charges brought fines of only $12 and $14 dollars. The $20 fine, the usual amount, was levied against the third charge.

Because court clerks did not record reasons for judicial decisions, it is unknown why the lesser amounts were imposed. Bradford was, however, fined the usual $20 in July, August and September, and also paid on her behalf through Baldwin's law firm. Her September fine, her last, was paid a week after she vanished.

Mattie Bradford, the Wichita madam who was never seen, never appeared in court, never talked to anyone and whom not a single old timer could recall, quietly vanished without a trace leaving only her name in the court records. She appears in no census and has yet to be found in court records or police files in any other western town or city. The madam who never was remains as unique to Wichita as Sarah Earp had been to Peoria.

What made Mattie Bradford necessary? The answer is simple. She was the solution to the gravest dilemma that could ever face Mattie and Bessie. Troubles that seemed trivial when Marshal Smith charged them with running a house of ill fame had suddenly escalated when Justice of the Peace Mitchell invoked the seldom-used judicial prerogative of refusing to accept a guilty plea. Lesser minds than Mattie and Bessie would have been able to figure out the motives behind his maneuver and both realized they had to shed the madam label. They decided to let someone else grace the court records as the madam of 12 Douglas. The "someone else" was the elusive Mattie Bradford.

Marshal Smith was not the only one confused. Mattie Bradford so obscured the overall picture that Mattie Blaylock Earp went undetected for years. Researchers, thoroughly confused, could not agree whether Mattie Blaylock had been in Wichita with Wyatt. Their confusion created two schools of thought.

One group was convinced — rightly it turned out — that Sally Earp was just another Mattie Blaylock alias. The other contended Mattie Bradford was Sally Earp. What they could never explain was why Bradford and Sally Earp, if they were the same person, appear in the records at the same time. Nor could they explain why Bradford lasted only a matter of weeks. The issue remained unanswered for years, going nowhere, while bewildered researchers tried to sort it out.

One issue that perplexed the researchers was the matter of the city's official census. The March 1875 census confirms Bessie's resident status and her occupation, which is listed as sporting, leaving no wonderment there. Mattie Bradford was long gone. There is no mention of Mattie Blaylock under Celia Blaylock, Mattie Earp or Sally Earp. Either she was not home, or, more likely, she deliberately eluded the enumerator. Wichita author Ann Wrampe eventually proved that Mattie did reside at 12 Douglas Avenue.

To Mattie Blaylock, also known as Sally Earp, the house was indeed a home. Accounts from several old-timers — recorded in Ms. Wrampe's *Wichita Township's Soiled Doves* as well as in Ed Bartholomew's book[1] — mentions Mattie Earp as being "well known" to them. Other old-timers recalled both Bessie and Sally Earp, and what is more interesting is the number who recalled that Sally had also been called Mattie. All acknowledged the two women were partners in the house and all agreed Bessie had been the principal madam.

Ed Bartholomew, a gatherer of Earp lore, was among the first to suspect Mattie Bradford[2] was fictional, and he also suspected Bessie and Sally had been partners and that Sally had also called herself Mattie Earp. For some reason he never pursued those suspicions, which were confirmed years later by Ann Wrampe in her study of Wichita's brothels and their inhabitants. Ms. Wrampe did not cite the Bartholomew book as reference, as she obtained all her information from local sources and interviews with some very elderly citizens.

One of them, a virtual eyewitness to the events at 12 Douglas Avenue, was known as "Captain Sam" Jones. Although very old when interviewed, he easily recalled Bessie's house as his grandmother had been the cook in Bessie's house from 1874 to 1876. During that time Jones was a little boy who spent much of his time helping her with kitchen chores and running errands for the girls. They tipped him twenty-five cents per errand, most of which were to the liquor store. Other errands were to local saloons when the girls would write notes to their steady clients and Jones would deliver them. He easily recalled Bessie, Sally and Kate Elder, but had no recollection whatever of seeing, or even hearing of, Mattie Bradford.[3] He also told Ms. Wrampe that Sally Earp was also known as Mattie Earp.

APPENDIX 5
The Etiquette of Ignominy

Between 1865 and 1910 thousands of teenage and adult females, footloose and vagrant, drifted nomadically to western cities, towns and mining centers. Finding no work, many entered prostitution through lack of choice or desperation. Sporting women encountered little difficulty finding work, but soon discovered the life was not what they perhaps thought. Opulent houses were the exception, not the rule. The women's lives were not a mad whirl of parties and they did not amass great sums of money; few gained even a modicum of fame or fortune. Most stayed awhile and then departed, usually without notice. A few left traces of their being, and on occasion one would meet a lonely man in search of a wife and settle down.[1]

Most, however, found only graves, often unmarked, in the boot hills of short-lived towns and mining camps that dotted the western territories. They died in their 30s or early 40s, broken in spirit, ravished by alcohol, opium, venereal disease or tuberculosis, sometimes all four. They died lonely deaths, often amidst squalor. Many perished violently of beatings, knife or gunshot wounds. Although there are no specific figures available, from the young ages and cause of death as "opium (or laudanum) poisoning" listed for so many, it appears that an inordinate number committed suicide. For many soiled doves, their retirement package was a bottle of laudanum and a quart of cheap whiskey, a lethal combination costing about seventy-five cents, but it guaranteed eternal quietus.

Madams knew the town doctors who would — and did — care for their girls, but not on retainer or on regular weekly visits; and along with the diseases and injuries that occurred in

224

the sporting life, some of those doctors would no doubt have dealt with abortions as well. Many of the girls, and certainly the madams, were also pretty adroit with the administration of slippery elm and other herbs that would deal with pregnancy situations, although during the 1800s prophylactics and birth control devices were available from pharmacies, and were likely used. Children that were born to the girls would usually be sent to an orphanage and some would be adopted privately in far-off cities; and some of the girls kept their babies. Mattie had no children, nor does anyone know if she was ever pregnant, but she was, in all likelihood, wise in the ways of prevention.

All large towns and cities had a sporting district[2] where up to several dozens of bawds plied their trade.[3] Few western settlements, even those little more than a cluster of tents perched precariously on some obscure mountain, could not boast at least one soiled dove to entertain and comfort lonely miners.[4]

Frontier brothels were an integral part of the Old West. For years historians and scholars have pondered the subject and several studies have been published. The definitive work, however, remains a future tome. Because of the vastness and complexities of the subject, several volumes would be required for proper coverage. Indeed, it may never be written.

Although those in the trade appeared to be free spirits unencumbered by precepts, there were rules of protocol and etiquette to be followed. Red light districts[5] were usually confined to one area of town. Often the railroad tracks[6] separated the sporting area from the respectable district, but sometimes a street intersecting the town's main street was designated the separation line and became known as the deadline.[7] By 1870 established boundaries distinguished which area was which. Nonetheless, a discreet madam could successfully run her house within the respectable part of town.[8]

By-laws were passed by town councils intent on keeping sporting women apart from respectable women. (There was no prohibition on respectable men visiting the sporting district, a double standard that functioned, alive and well, in every western town.) The by-laws allowed sporting women to cross the deadline during morning hours to shop, attend to banking matters, visit a salon, milliner or keep appointments with doctors or lawyers. On Sundays they could attend church services, providing the sanctimonious congregation would allow them entry.

In the main, though, by-laws were merely sugar coatings intended to appease moralists. They were rarely enforced because in fact they were not enforceable. Most sheriffs and city marshals allowed houses to operate freely providing no trouble was caused. Elected officials could ignore neither the voting power of the sporting alliance nor their financial input to civic coffers. Sheriffs, marshals and their deputies were drawn mainly from the sporting fraternity, so they had vested interests.

Brothels handled the majority of carnal commerce. Large houses operated along the lines of a social club with impressive parlors and well stocked bars. Many had a card room and entertainment. Some even offered dining facilities. Madams allowed clients plenty of time to socialize with their women over drinks. It was good business because clients paid for the time through high bar profits, in which the girls shared. At the far end of the parlor a hallway, sometimes hidden behind lavish tapestries, led to rooms along both sides. This was called the line and the women who inhabited the rooms were referred to as being "on the line." Small houses had none of these trappings. In those houses the women did not fare well as a rule.

House residents paid the keeper[9] a percentage of their earnings to cover room and board and protection. Protection came through deals with the police chief, city marshal, sheriff or town council. Sometimes, as in Wichita, protection was bought through pre-set fines paid in court. Under that system — really a form of business license — madams and residents pleaded guilty each month in court and paid a set fine. Smart madams retained lawyers to attend court, enter the guilty pleas and pay the fines. That way no one had to appear in person.

Saloon women followed a different protocol. In many jurisdictions ordinances against saloon prostitution made discretion necessary, so owners referred to their girls as hostesses or entertainers. Ostensibly they entertained patrons with song and dance routines, but the real money was made in the back rooms and in the promotion of drinking and gambling. Working on percentage, the "entertainers" patrolled the barroom exuding smiles and good will while coyly enticing lonely drovers to try their luck at the gambling tables. "We have the only honest games in town," they purred. "Our dealers are all gentlemen of culture."

While the patron awaited a place at a card table or gaming board the girls continued their sales pitch. "Try our excellent imported whiskey, honey. It is sold only to special customers like you who appreciate finer things."

Of course, the gentlemen operating the gambling tables were skilled dealers who knew where the bottom cards were. The excellent imported whiskey was cheap rye or corn liquor in an ornate bottle with a fancy label and an exorbitant price.

On the other hand, if the patron had eyes only for the "showgirl," that was also satisfactory. It was, after all, part of the etiquette.

TIME LINE

1848 Mar   Wyatt Barry Stapp Earp born in Monmouth Illinois.

1850 Jan   Celia Ann Blaylock born in Johnson County, Iowa.

1868   Celia Ann runs away from home with sister Sarah, age 15. Begins calling herself Mattie.

1869   Wyatt Earp moves to Lamar, Missouri.

1870   Sarah returns home. Mattie goes to Fort Scott, Kansas.

    May   Wyatt Earp marries Urilla Sutherland and leases a farm near Lamar.

    Nov   Earp elected Lamar's town constable.

1871 Jan   Urilla dies. Wyatt fired and departs Lamar. Goes to Pineville, Missouri to farm with his father, Nicholas.

    Mar   Wyatt arrested in Ft. Smith, Arkansas, skips bail, returns to Missouri.

    Summer   Wyatt moves to his brother Newton's farm near Fort Scott. Meets Mattie.

    Autumn   Mattie & Wyatt go to Peoria. Meet Morgan.

1872 Feb   Wyatt arrested in Peoria in February as a "keeper" of The Haspel House, a brothel.

    May   Again arrested as a "keeper" of a brothel (the McClellan Institute) and spends thirty days in jail in lieu of a fine.

	Sep	He and Mattie (alias Sarah Earp) are arrested in the Beardstown Gunboat, also a brothel. Both leave town after court appearances and paying fines.
1873		Mattie and Wyatt farming in Rice County, Kansas.
	Nov	Wyatt goes to Wichita, Kansas. Opens a faro game in a saloon.
	Dec	Mattie goes to Wichita. Meets Bessie Earp and Kate "Big Nose Kate" Elder.
1874	Jan	Mattie registers on court records. Mattie, (alias Sally Earp) joins Bessie in partnership in brothel at 12 Douglas Ave.
	Jun	Mattie and Bessie arrested. Granted bail pending trial.
	Sep	Case dismissed. Mattie and Bessie resume business.
1875	Apr	Wyatt hired by Wichita police force.
1876	May	Wyatt hauled into court for striking City Marshal Smith. Found guilty, is fined and then fired. All the Earps leave Wichita.
	Jun	Mattie and Wyatt arrive in Dodge City, Kansas where Wyatt joins police force.
1876–79		Mattie and Wyatt spend winters in Texas and/or New Mexico on the gambling circuit.
1879	Sep	Mattie and Wyatt leave Dodge City. After a stop in Prescott Arizona, they arrive in Tombstone, with James, Bessie, Virgil & Allie in December.
1880		Morgan and Lou arrive in Tombstone. Doc Holliday arrives in late autumn.
1881		Wyatt takes up with Josephine Marcus.

	Oct 26	The Earp/Clanton gunfight on Fremont St. (known as The Gunfight at the OK Corral).
	Dec 28	Virgil shot from ambush. Not killed, but seriously wounded.
1882	Mar	Morgan murdered from ambush.
		The Earps depart Tombstone. Mattie goes with James and Bessie to Nicholas Earp's home in Colton, California. Wyatt and several friends roam Pima county avenging Virgil's ambush and Morgan's murder.
1882	Aug	Mattie moves to Globe. Takes up residence with Kate Harony, also known as Kate Holliday, Kate Fisher, Kate Elder ("Big Nose Kate").
1885		Mattie has her photo taken at a Globe photo studio.
1887	May	Kate leaves Globe.
	Oct	Mattie goes to Pinal.
1888	Jul 3	Mattie takes fatal overdose of laudanum and whiskey.
	Jul 4	Coroner's jury returns verdict of death by suicide. Mattie buried in pauper's grave.
1888		Pinal County ships Mattie's trunks to Sarah Marquis' home in Iowa. Wyatt learns of her death.
1889		Josephine Marcus announces she and Wyatt have married. (No date given. No marriage certificate has yet been found).
1929	Jan 13	Wyatt Earp dies in Los Angeles. The cause of death is listed as chronic uremia.
1931		The Wyatt Earp legend begins with publication of *Frontier Marshal*.

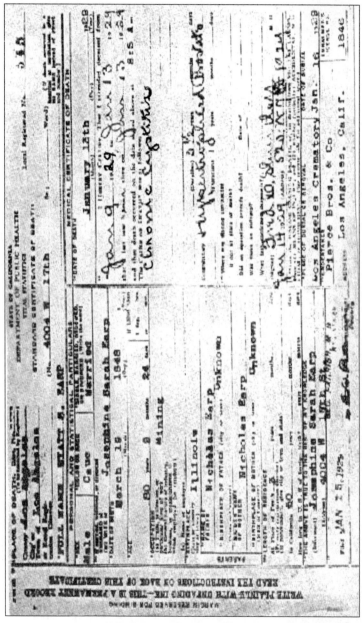

Wyatt Earp's death certificate.

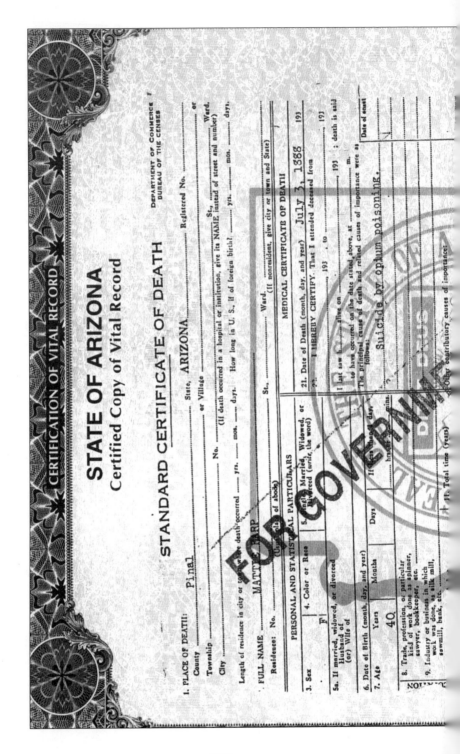

CERTIFICATION OF VITAL RECORD

STATE OF ARIZONA
Certified Copy of Vital Record

STANDARD CERTIFICATE OF DEATH

DEPARTMENT OF COMMERCE ?
BUREAU OF THE CENSUS

1. PLACE OF DEATH:

County .... Pinal ....   State, ARIZONA   Registered No. ....

Township ....   or Village .... or .... Ward.

City ....   No. ....   St., ...   Ward.

(If death occurred in a hospital or institution, give its NAME instead of street and number)

Length of residence in city or town where death occurred .... yrs. .... mos. .... days.   How long in U. S., if of foreign birth?   .... yrs. .... mos. .... days.

FULL NAME .... MATTIE EARP ....

Residence: No. ....   St., ...   Ward.   (If nonresident, give city or town and State)

(Usual place of abode)

PERSONAL AND STATISTICAL PARTICULARS

MEDICAL CERTIFICATE OF DEATH

3. Sex   F

4. Color or Race

5a. Single, Married, Widowed, or Divorced (write the word)

5a. If married, widowed, or divorced
Husband of
(or) Wife of

6. Date of Birth (month, day, and year)

7. Age   Years   40   Months ....   Days ....   If less than one day, ... hrs. .... min.

8. Trade, profession, or particular kind of work done as spinner, sawyer, bookkeeper, etc.

9. Industry or business in which work was done, as silk mill, sawmill, bank, etc.

21. Date of Death (month, day, and year)   July 3, 1388   193.........

22. I HEREBY CERTIFY. That I attended deceased from
.... 193......... to .... 193......... ; death is said
I last saw h......... alive on .... 193......... m.
to have occurred on the date stated above, at .... m.
The principal cause of death and related causes of importance were as follows:
.... Suicide by opium poisoning. ....

Other contributory causes of importance: Date of onset

18. Total time (years)

FOR GOVERNMENT USE

232

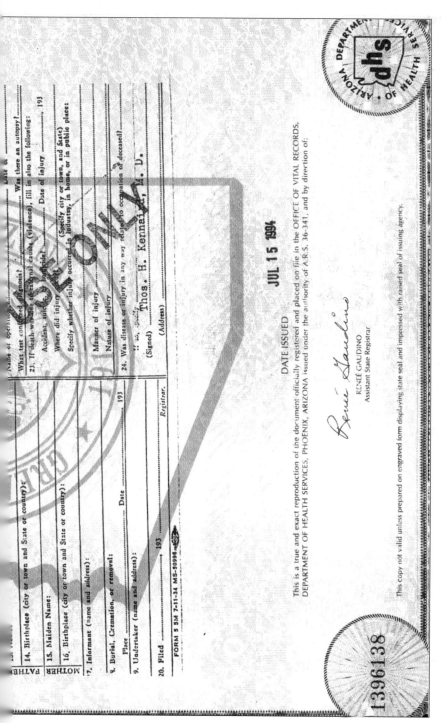

MOTHER | FATHER

14. Birthplace (city or town and State or country):

15. Maiden Name:

16. Birthplace (city or town and State or country):

17. Informant (name and address):

8. Burial, Cremation, or removal:
Place _____ Date _____ 193

9. Undertaker (name and address):

20. Filed _____ 193 _____ Registrar.

FORM 5 5M 7-11-34 MS-50998

Name or operation _____ Date of _____

What test confirmed diagnosis? _____ Was there an autopsy? _____

23. If death was due to external cause, (violence), fill in also the following:
Accident, suicide, or homicide _____ Date of injury _____ 193

Where did injury _____ (Specify city or town, and State)

Specify whether injury occurred in industry, in home, or in public place:

Manner of injury _____

Nature of injury _____

24. Was disease or injury in any way related to occupation of deceased?

If so, specify _____ Thos. H. Kennel, M. D.

(Signed) _____
(Address) _____

DATE ISSUED

JUL 15 1994

1396138

Mattie Earp's death certificate.

Doctor

James M. Cunningham

Vice Magistrate

City of Peoria

January 27th 1871. —

Book C.

last entry

March 26, 1872

234

256

Police Court.

City of Peoria } Feb. 26. 1872 complaint by Policeman
   vs   } McWhirter for locking and bringing
George Kendall } at a house of ill-fame vs. Kendall
Mag. $1.30   went to McWhirter and returned bench
Transcript 105   with the clerk in court.
   $2.35   to fees on affidavit for a charge of
Paid 10¢   Oram and the same was granted and
Bal $1.70 the papers sent to the Constable, Esq. Arte.

McWhirter D   McWhirter
  Use   D   Police Magistrate

City of Peoria }
ss. } Feb. 26, 1872. Geo. Randall by
vs. } the Marshal W. Hockley and Geo.
Wyatt Earp } Found at a house of ill-fame.
Warrant issued to Marshal to arrest in
and returned Served with the deft. in
Mag. $1.50
Marshal's Costs
    $2.35
Paid 105
Bal $1.30

Deft. files an affidavit for a change.
Notice and the same was granted
then the papers sent to Geo. Monroe
Esqr. J.P.

Westchester JP
S. Spe. JP

Arrest of George Randall and Wyatt Earp, February 26, 1872.

Police Court

City of Peoria
508 Etc

Morgan Earp

Feby 26, 1872. Complaint by Wm
McWhirter for keeping and being
found at a house of ill fame in
Warrant & Returned served with the deft

Mag $1.50
Warrant $1.05
$2.35
Paid $1.05
Due $1.30

In conv.
Deft files an affidavit for a charge of
venue and the same was granted
and the papers sent to Wm Rorennier
Esq. P.Jo.

_____

J. C. Cunningham
Police Magistrate

Jo. McWhirter SD
Ya SD

Arrest of Morgan Earp, February 26, 1872.

Police Court   Oct 11, 1871

City of Peoria }
365   vs
Sally Haspel
Ellie Crow
Jane Haspel

May # 5.85
Feb 3. 1.05

Oct. 11. 1871. Complaint by Mr. Mayes, Police
order for keeping house of ill fame
... warrant issued to Mayes and
... defend's were arrested with the defendants
... present and ready for trial.
... B. Baldwin sworn for defts. testi-
... were subpoenaed as witnesses called on leaving
it is ordered that the deft's Sally Haspel
and Ellie Crow be fined each in the

Costs $1.50   sum Ten dollars and that the deft
Spec. 1.50   Jane Haspel be fined in the sum of Ten dollars
Withd. 2.00   dollars — and that they each pay the
Lies Ex 75   Costs against respectively
Lies Ex 75
Lies Ex 75   Oct 11. 1871. Exts or all depts

Sally Haspel June 1870
                        Oct.13. 1876 Ex. ex Crow delivered   Costs 3.95
                        $11.50 Reard. paid to Magistrate, no   Ellie Crow June 10.00
                        deft property found "Eecate balance   Costs 3.95
                        Oct.16.1871. Ex. ex Sally Haspel returned   Jane Haspel June 20.00
                        no property found. Oct.16. 1871 Ex. ex   Costs 3.95
                        Jane Haspel balance $25.00 Rare
                        and paid to Magistrate
                                                                    Police Magistrate

Record of arrests following raid on Haspel House, October 1871.

Police Court.

City of Peoria } January 13, 1872. Complaint by Samuel
vs } L. Gill, Supt. of Police, for frequenting
Minnie Randall and being found at a house
Lizzie Gardner of Ill-fame. Warrant issued to
Fritz White S. L. Gill and return made with
James Dougherty the defendants in court and each
William Randall for trial.

Geo. Horschber, F. M. Wasson, Chas. Keney,
H. C. Lincoln, O. Peirce & Wm. Peirce were sworn
as witnesses and on hearing, it is ordered
that the City of Peoria have a judgment a-
gainst each of said defendants for the
sum of thirty dollars fine. And that they
each pay the costs of prosecution against
them respectively—
January 13th 1871. Exs. issued Saml. Randall Jany $30.00
                                          Costs 2.35

Witg. vs
Randall 2.35
Gardner 2.35
White 2.35
Dougherty 2.35
Randall 2.35
5 Costs 1.75
Sala. Sa. 1.75

Record of arrests following raid on Haspel House, January 1872.

Mattie White is possibly an alias for Mattie Earp as no prior or later records exist for this person, and Mattie Earp is known to have been in the Haspel House in January 1872.

NOTES

INTRODUCTION

1. The murder by vigilantes of Henry Plummer, the honest sheriff of Bannack, Montana, is an example of how legend corrupts truth.

2. The term "Wild Bill" had nothing to do with wildness. It was about long hair. Most men with long hair were called "Wild Bill." Western annals abound with "Wild Bills."

3. Masterson, born in Henryville, Quebec, Canada, was named Bartholomew. (Records of St. George Parish, Rouville, PQ) He later dropped Bartholomew for two new names, William Barclay. [*KSHS Quarterly*, Vol. XXX1, No.4 (1965) "Diary of a Buffalo Hunter 1872–73."]

4. King was actually Anthony Cook, a fugitive who had joined the army under his alias in order to escape civilian justice. [Miller & Snell. *Why the West Was Wild*, p322.]

5. The common belief that he was called "Bat" because he smacked down felons with a fancy, silver-topped cane is Hollywood hype. He handled felons, as did every other lawman, with a gun.

6. *Frontier Echo*, February 11, 1876 (Jackboro, Texas).

7. Earp's total time as lawman totals less than four years. All but one of his appointments was temporary. Most were three to six month terms. [KSHS & ASHS]

8. A euphemism much used in newspapers of the period denoting the lifestyle of a red light district resident.

9. A play on words. Preachers have long been called "men of the cloth" but in this case "green cloth" refers to the felt covers of gaming tables.

10. Soiled dove, sporting woman, cyprian, frail denizen, and fallen angel were all popular euphemisms for prostitutes. [See 1840–1910 newspapers.]

11. Bat married Emma Walters on November 21, 1891. Five days short of their 30th anniversary he died of a heart attack. [O'Connor, Richard. *Bat Masterson*, p152.]

12. Tincture of opium. Once used with little restraint for all ailments, laudanum remained popular into the mid-1940s. Codeine-based drugs, safer and controlled by law, replaced it. [*B.C. Drug Compendium*, 1998]

13. The journals of several western doctors have found their ways into various historical societies, but to date Mattie's various aliases have not shown up in their patient lists.

14. In Greek mythology Lethe was the underworld River of Forgetfulness. Its water erased unwanted memories. [*Oxford Encyclopedia*]

15. Wyatt told Lake he had returned from California in 1868 to study law under his grandfather's tutelage. Lake either never knew, or Wyatt had conveniently forgotten, that Grandfather Earp had died in 1853 when Wyatt was only five years of age. [Lake, S.N. *Frontier Marshal*.]

16. One example was Earp's feat in arresting Ben Thompson, the famed Texas gunfighter, in Ellsworth, Kansas on 18 August 1873. Earp was not in Ellsworth. He was hoeing corn on his farm near Peace, Kansas. Thompson surrendered to James Miller, the town's mayor. Myers, Roger. www. cowtownswest.com. [See also Ellsworth records at KSHS.]

17. Josephine feared Mattie far more in death than she ever had in life. This fear caused her to discourage Wyatt in his efforts to gain recognition. Earp, however, craved fame and persisted. Before he met Lake he approached writers and moviemakers, including William S. Hart, offering to relate his adventures as a lawman. None showed any interest. Hart listened but could not shake suspicions that Earp was being less than truthful. He turned him down. He remained friendly, though, and attended Earp's funeral. So did Tom Mix, the great screen cowboy, who had also declined to portray Earp in a movie.

18. Canadians do not adulate their Old West lawmen; it matters little what they accomplished. Canadian history abounds with lawmen that accomplished as much, and more, than Wyatt Earp ever did. None are famous to any great extent.

19. One exception was Galeyville resident James C. Hancock who in a letter to *The Epitaph* in 1933 wrote, "I often wonder why it is that none of his [Earp's] biographers ever mention his first wife, Mattie. The poor girl died in San Francisco many years ago. I have heard it stated that he would compel her to go into a place against her will and make money for him to gamble on." Hancock's facts were wanting, but he obviously knew of Mattie and her connection with Wyatt Earp. Hancock was also extremely critical of *Frontier Marshal* in a letter dated October 14, 1934 to one Joe Chisholm of California. [John Gilchriese collection, Tucson, Arizona]

CHAPTER 1 ❖ The Road to Fort Scott

1. Reports that Celia Ann's birthplace was Fairfax are incorrect. Fairfax (Fairfax Township, Linn County) was the nearest town so she was registered there. The registration reveals she was born at her home in Monroe Township, Johnson County. [Iowa Historical Society]

2. Mattie's other siblings were Martha Jane (1843–1872), Marion (1848–1868), William (1855–1878) and Tony May (1867–1941). Marion served in

the Union Army and was wounded, which led to his early death. With the exception of Tony May, none of the children lived long lives.

3. Some writers of western lore have stated that Mattie left home in 1866 at age sixteen. Mattie was three years older than her sister so, in 1866, Sarah was still only thirteen. 1868 is in keeping as the year of departure. [US Census, Johnson County, 1860.]

4. Information about Sarah was obtained from Tony May's granddaughter, Tony Gene Vynsand, who also gave insight into Mattie's home situation. Mrs. Vynsand was extremely helpful and very generous in her assistance. [Phone conversations with author in 2003.]

5. Nine years later, on May 14, 1878, in Linn County Iowa, Sarah married Hiram Marquis, a widowed farmer twenty-six years her senior. They were drawn to each other through circumstance and situation. In him she found a reasonable man who treated her kindly and provided a decent life. He found in her a wife who presented him with a son, Hiram Oswald (1879–1952). Marquis, like most widowers, was lonely, but his age thwarted his chances of marrying a woman of childbearing age. The family appears in the 1880 census as Sarah, age 27, Hiram, age 53 and Hiram Oswald, age 1. [US Census. Linn County, Iowa, 1880.]

6. A nineteenth century expression indicating a woman of lost virtue. [*Brewer's Dictionary of Phrase and Fable*]

7. Greeley neither originated the term, nor is it what he wrote. John Balsone Soule of Indiana, publisher of the *Terre Haute Express*, had earlier written, "Go west young man." Greeley liked the words and added, "and there build up a home and future." He put it into an editorial and, like many catchy phrases, public usage soon condensed it to its present state. Greeley tried to credit Soule, but received no response to his efforts.

8. Lamar is not likely to have been on their list as their mother had close relatives there. They would not have wanted to encounter any of them. [K. Lanning, email October 2004.]

9. Sarah reappears in the Johnson County 1870 census, but Celia Ann of course does not. That census was compiled in October. The section for Sarah's last address is blank. Sarah's age is listed as 17, a further indication she had not yet turned 16 when she left. [US Census, 1870, vol. 121, p414, line 12.]

10. A survey taken by Joe Snell of the Kansas Historical Society shows the favored aliases of Old West prostitutes. The top three were Mattie, Hattie and Fannie in that order (others were Minnie, Bessie and Flossie). [Boyer, Glenn. *Wyatt Earp: Facts* Vol.3, p21.]

CHAPTER 2 ❖ The Silence of Time

1. Alice Tubbs, also known as "Poker Alice," and Eleanor Dumont, also known as "Minnie the Gambler," were two such "ladies of the green cloth."[Author's files]

2. This eased a little in 1873. A Scottish entrepreneur, Frederick Harvey, started railroad depot restaurants. Young ladies, carefully selected, were trained as waitresses. Called "Harvey Girls," they lived and worked under strict supervision. [*True West*, December 93, p10.]

3. Appendix 5: The Etiquette of Ignominy.

4. One researcher waggishly suggested that the sisters, masquerading as men, joined a group of buffalo hunters. Another, equally facetiously, suggested Mattie met Wyatt at a buffalo camp. The first surmise is improbable, the second impossible. Wyatt Earp, despite popular myth, was <u>never</u> engaged in organized buffalo hunting.

5. Appendix 5: The Etiquette of Ignominy.

6. A January 21, 1870 census lists: Mattie Hall, age 19, female, white, courtezan [*sic*] [from] Iowa. The census was taken at Junction City, a small cattle center near Abilene, Kansas. The address was a ten-woman brothel owned by one James King. The surname differs from Mattie Blaylock's known aliases and therefore must be considered inconclusive, but there are several interesting coincidences. [R. Jay, Maryland researcher. Email to author dated July 17, 2003.]

7. Photo posing had swept the entire continent. People from all walks of life eagerly spent up to two dollars to pose for their photograph. Outlaws on the run dared hesitate long enough to have their pictures taken. (In some cases it proved their undoing as the law was then enabled to obtain copies to adorn Wanted posters.) Politicians, Indians in full regalia, farmers, businessmen, husbands and wives, entire families, parsons, gamblers, whores, judges and lawyers appeared dressed in their best clothing. Ranch hands and ridge riders posed, as neatly dressed as their worn denims would allow, usually holding their favorite rifle or pistol.

8. From 1868–71 there are many ads for Parker's grocery stores, but few for his photo studio. J.T. Parker, a man with extensive business interests, is listed in the city's 1871 Commerce Census. [Fort Scott *Weekly Monitor*]

9. Pillars and steles came in various heights to accommodate posing. The type of stele Mattie rests against was about 36" high, an indication she was about 5'3" tall. [Kodak-Eastman Ltd. Archives, Rochester, NY]

10. Monthly wages in 1871 ranged between $24 and $40, with males usually earning the higher levels. An example is that of schoolteachers. Male teachers were paid $33 and female teachers drew $27. Brothel women could net several times that amount within two weeks. [www.kancoll.org/books/cutler.html]

CHAPTER 3 ❖ Enter Wyatt Earp

1. In 1956, in his book *The Coloradans*, Frank Waters exposed Earp as having feet of clay, including his connection with Mattie. Vehemently denounced by Earp aficionados, Waters held his ground. The revelations encouraged Earp's detractors, many of whom were eager (at least figu-

ratively) to exhume and gnaw on his bones. Many of their accusations were unfounded, but others were factual.

2. While living in Lamar in 1869, Earp met and married Urilla (Rilla) Sutherland. On January 10, 1870, Nicholas P. Earp, the groom's father, solemnized the marriage in his capacity as Justice of the Peace. The new-lyweds leased a small farm close to town and there is every reason to believe that Wyatt and Rilla were happy in their new lives. The 1870 census lists Wyatt as white, twenty-two years old, a farmer. It lists Urilla as white, twenty-one years old, keeping house [Housewife]. [US Census, Barton County, Missouri, 3 Sept. 1870, p28, Farm 214]

3. The baby was either stillborn or died from the same illness that afflicted Urilla. No official records — birth, death or burial — for the baby have been found [Mrs. Mabel Cason's letter to the Monmouth, Illinois news-paper dated January 29, 1957. Boyer, G. *Suppressed Murder of Wyatt Earp*, pp 78–80.]

4. In fact, he was known to have no great love for toilsome work of any kind. In later years, when he was prospecting, he often hired down-and-out men, many of them old friends from Tombstone, to do the pick and shovel work on his claims.

5. Newton's mother was Nicholas's first wife. Nicholas wed three times. His famed sons were by his second wife. His third marriage (very late in life) produced no children. [Boyer, Glenn. "Those Marrying Earp Men," article in *True West*, March–April 1976.]

6. Some claim the Sutherlands considered Wyatt the cause of Urilla's death, citing neglect. Others claim the dispute began with the marriage, sug-gesting the Sutherlands were angered because it had been one of neces-sity. That cannot be the case as in the September census, the birth and the deaths disprove the claim. Both tales can be relegated to files of anti-Earp mythology. While Wyatt and Rilla were husband and wife there was never trouble between the Earps and the Sutherlands. The trouble occurred after Rilla died, and its cause was Lamar's illicit liquor indus-try, a business in which both families were heavily engaged. [Boyer, G. *Wyatt Earp: Facts*. Vol. V1, pp 6–10.]

7. Missouri lawmen routinely made raids on stills. Nicholas Earp's time in Kentucky's bluegrass country allowed him to master the art of keeping an illicit distillery mobile and well hidden. Because its location was all but impossible to pin down, it was never raided. The Sutherland broth-ers lacked such sophistication. They operated from one location. As a result their still was raided as often as any of the others. [Boyer, G. *Wyatt Earp: Facts*, p9.]

8. The night the five men attacked Wyatt he, accompanied by Virgil, was making his rounds. It happened that James (and perhaps Morgan) were nearby so they rushed to their brothers' assistance. Within a few minutes a general street brawl was underway. The melee, according to various

accounts, lasted anywhere from ten minutes to twenty minutes with both sides giving as good as they got. There were no decisive victors but the Sutherland and the Brummet boys joined the lengthy list of those who learned the hard way that anyone who threatened one Earp must also contend with the others. [Ibid.]

9. The loyalty the Earp brothers possessed for each other was that which many families dream of but few attain. This was never more evident than in 1882 when Wyatt and Warren, in the company of friends, hunted down and killed the men they held responsible for the ambush that had seriously wounded Virgil and those they considered as having murdered Morgan. James was no less devoted but went his own way for the most part. He had little to do with Wyatt's political schemes. On several occasions, however, he wore a deputy's badge. [Ibid.]

10. Barton County Court Records, 1871.

11. Earp *pere* was also in trouble. A couple of his financial deals had gone sour and he wouldn't pay. In classic Earp fashion he left town. His brother, Jonathon, took the heat but was acquitted. [Boyer, G. *Wyatt Earp Facts* Vol. V1, p11.]

12. A recent movie, *Wyatt Earp* (1993) stars Kevin Costner as Wyatt and Mare Winningham as Mattie. Facts are ignored and the timeline of events is generally incorrect. The film is historically flawed and the screenplay is mostly fiction. One scene has a despondent Wyatt set his house ablaze before leaving Lamar. This can be dismissed as just another slice of Earp fiction.

13. Present-day Oklahoma. Its law was administered from Arkansas.

14. An interesting side story has it that Wyatt was arrested in the company of a man and a woman in a buggy. When the sheriff, who suspected they were Wyatt's cohorts, questioned them they claimed Wyatt had ordered them to stay with him, emphasizing his point over the sights of a pistol. They told the sheriff Wyatt had threatened to kill them if they testified against him. (Coincidentally, Shown and Kennedy also claimed Wyatt threatened them in like manner.) The sheriff released the couple. Years later a story emerged speculating the two were Mattie and either James or Morgan. They had arrived to help Wyatt drive the horses north. The story still surfaces every so often despite having been exposed years ago. Wyatt had yet to meet Mattie, James was living in Aulville, and the man and woman had genuine identities. Nonetheless, the reason they gave for being with Wyatt has never been fully accepted.

15. Wyatt was also fortunate his apprehension pre-dated the 1875 appointment of Judge Isaac Parker to the Fort Smith court. Parker, although basically a man of some compassion, was not called "the hanging judge" without reason. [Tuller, Roger H. *Let No Guilty Man Escape*. University of Oklahoma Press, 2001.]

16. $8,000 by today's currency standards. [www.westegg.com]

17. Nicholas had $500 set aside to pay against the mortgage on his new farm. When Wyatt jumped bail, the money was forfeit. Nicholas was duly evicted. [Boyer, Glenn. *Wyatt Earp: Facts* Vol. 3. 1997.]

18. Some thought — and some still do — that this was the beginning of Wyatt's gambling and lawman era. It was not. In his book, *Ben Thompson: Man With a Gun* (NY 1957), Floyd B. Streeter depicts Wyatt as a gambler in Hays City, Kansas in 1871. Accused of cheating he was run out of town. The story is untrue.

In *Frontier Marshal* Lake has Wyatt, a visitor to Ellsworth, Kansas volunteer to act as a lawman. Single handedly he arrests Ben Thompson on August 15, 1873. This is one of Lake's better fantasies, but in fairness to Lake, Earp may have fed him the story by quoting details he would have known as Thompson's contemporary. No records or news accounts mention Earp being in Ellsworth at the time. Thompson made no mention of Earp in his account of the Ellsworth incident. Streeter didn't mention it. Bat Masterson, whom Lake named as one of his sources, never mentioned Earp being in Ellsworth either. It appears Earp injected himself into the situation for Lake's benefit and Lake bought it in good faith. [Myers, Roger. From a copyright article on his website, http://cowtown-swest.com, and in emails to the author in 2002.]

19. These disclosures negate the fiction that Newton held a serious grudge against Wyatt for running against him in Lamar. That Newton named his son (born August 1872) Clyde Wyatt further indicates no such feud existed. It does, however, bolster the "rigged election" theory at Lamar. [Boyer, G. *Wyatt Earp: Facts* Vol. 3, p20.]

20. Letter dated May 9, 1955 and underline is in the original letter. [Gilchriese collection.]

21. Claims of being a buffalo hunter were a popular dodge to explain long periods of absence. It was easy to lose oneself, figuratively and literally, among the vast herds of buffalo that roamed the plains. The deception was made easier by claiming constant moves from one camp to another, never staying long enough to make much impression on the memories of others. It was small wonder that Lake had such trouble accounting for Wyatt's life up to his resurfacing in Wichita. Lake was not aware that Wyatt had spent almost two years at Lamar although Wyatt, without going into details, did tell him of his marriage to Rilla.

CHAPTER 4 ❖ "I, Mattie, Take Thee, Wyatt..."

1. Josephine Marcus, the third Mrs. Earp, knew Mattie and Wyatt were married, but seemingly had no real idea how long they had been together. She told her biographer, Mabel Cason, the marriage was "already on the rocks" when she met Wyatt in 1881 and that he and Mattie had been together for "ten or twelve years." [The Cason Manuscript. Courtesy of G. Boyer, 2002.]

2. Mattie's letters were in Hiram Marquis's possession until his death in 1952. Despite a determined search they have not been found. Hopefully, one of Hiram's descendants kept them and they are not lost. They could perhaps shed more light on Mattie's fall and decline. [Author]

3. Hiram Marquis confirmed in 1952 that Mattie wrote from Dodge City (1876–79) and Tombstone (1879–82). [Boyer collection. Various correspondence to Mrs. Cason and Mrs. Ackerman regarding the Josephine Earp biography manuscript.]

4. Montana Territory (now Montana, Idaho, Oregon and Washington) and Canada's Northwest Territory (now Manitoba, Saskatchewan and Alberta) had no laws governing common-law unions. The rules for these areas changed upon the granting of statehood and province status.

5. In 1882, shortly before they left Tombstone, Wyatt and Mattie signed papers on a loan against the house they co-owned. When they bought the house in 1881 Mattie signed as Mrs. Wyatt Earp, as she did on the loan agreement. The purchase of the house indicates Wyatt considered Mattie his lawful, wedded wife and the second paper confirms it. [Papers on file at Arizona Historical Society.]

Chapter 5 ❖ Mattie Meets Her In-laws

1. Wyatt had two other sisters, Martha and Virginia. Both died at young ages.

2. The second story of The Dexter, a saloon Wyatt co-owned with Charlie Hoxey in Nome, Alaska during the 1898 gold rush, was a well-appointed brothel. It was the first two-story building in Nome. Mattie would have liked The Dexter because it had the elegance she had always wanted. Had she and Wyatt stayed together, she would have been proud to be its madam. Mattie, of course, by then was no longer in the picture. [Morgan, Lael. *Good Time Girls of the Northwest*, p169.]

3. Prescott, Arizona Territory, in 1878–9.

4. Newton's status as Garden City Town Marshal is confirmed in a letter From Alice Earp Wells to John Gilchriese, dated May 9, 1955. [Gilchriese collection]

5. No record of the marriage has yet been found in Illinois State files. [Author]

6. Earp Virgil W. Occ. Bartender. Res. Water St. Bs [bluff side] 5b Irving St. [5 doors behind Irving St.] Peoria City Directory (1870–71), section "E," p72.

7. While at Lamar, Virgil lived on his father's farm (line #212 on the census). He is listed as "Grocer." One would not have wanted to be late paying the tab at month's end. [US Census, Barton County, Missouri, September 1870, p28.]

8. Virgil and Rosilla are listed as living in Lamar. Listed as his wife is: Rose, age 17, white, born France. [Missouri Census, Barton County, September 3, 1870.]

9. Rosilla disappears from history in 1871. She may have died, run away or, quite possibly, returned to her family in France. To date no one knows.
10. Range detectives were gunmen hired by cattle owners' associations for the purpose of "apprehending and discouraging rustlers" the associations' quaint way of saying "kill them." Range detectives certainly apprehended and discouraged rustlers and none are known to have ever brought one in alive. Tom Horn was the west's most famous range detective. He was framed and hanged for a murder he undoubtedly did not commit. His real crime was in knowing too much about the darker side of The Wyoming Cattlemens' Association. [Author's files]
11. The jury's verdict was both unanimous and justified. Warren's death on the barroom floor was his 15 minutes of fame. [Author' files]

CHAPTER 6 ❖ Haspel House

1. The Peoria city directory was compiled annually. Data was collected during January to mid-February. Printed in the final week of February, its distribution began the first week of March. [Steve Gatto in email to author, February 2003.]
2. Virgil's residence on Water Street was almost the dead center of the sprawling red light district. [*Peoria City Directory* 1870]
3. In February 1872 a brothel known as The Bartlett House was operating in Peoria. James at the time was involved with Nellie Bartlett Ketchum, who later became his wife. She was a long-time madam who often called herself Nellie Bartlett, the name similar to the madam running The Bartlett House. Although circumstantial, it is possible the two were one and the same. Against the thought, however, is that Wyatt and Mattie did not stay there but instead moved into the Haspel House.
4. The telltale information lay unnoticed until 2002 and might well have remained uncovered for another 130 years except for a chance discovery by a sharp-eyed archivist at Bradley University. While searching files on this writer's behalf she came upon a Magistrate's Case Book that revealed Morgan's and Wyatt's activities in the red light district during 1872. [Bradley University, Special Collections, Earp File]
5. *Daily National Democrat.* September 10, 1872.
6. Also referred to in newspaper accounts as "Bunker Hill" because of its reputation for violent street fights.
7. Haspel House and its neighbors are gone now, leveled years ago in a massive urban development scheme. Where once stood the porch on which Mattie and Wyatt welcomed their clients only the maple tree, now old and gnarled, remains in lonely vigil. The urban transformation was intense. The entire sporting district was swept clean. The shacks all disappeared. New buildings went up. Streets were widened to accommodate boulevards and medians. Areas between the pavement and sidewalks were landscaped. The waterfront, once a clutter of railway

tracks, wharfs, and warehouses, was converted to parkland. The Cooper Institute that once cast its shadow across Haspel House is gone, replaced by a large hardware store that now dominates the corner. Rear windows of the elegant Mark Twain Hotel overlook a parking lot that was once the city's most infamous courtyard.

8. Haspel never attained her goal. She remained minor league until she remarried and, apparently, left the business. Her entry in the 1876 census is ambiguous. Her occupation appears as "housekeeper" whereas all other women on her block are listed as "keeping house." The census taker made no notation why he singled her out in this manner. Perhaps he was indicating she was a madam on a street of housewives, or vice versa. [City of Peoria Census 1876]

9. Jane's husband eventually divorced her retaining custody of the boy. About 1875 Jane remarried. She still lived near the waterfront but may have renounced her immoral ways because her son was allowed to live with her. [Peoria Census 1876]

10. The 1870 census lists Mary, then ten years old, as "a domestic." The census taker, fully aware of the infamy of Madam Sear's house, noted the little girl's tender age and wrote in the margin beside Mary's name these cryptic words: "God help you." [US Census, Peoria 1870]

11. It is unknown if Carrie Crow was an alias. She eventually disappeared from Peoria records and was heard of no more.

12. The tree, a red maple, has survived the years and is still there. Now much taller, it has added a great many rings to its trunk. [See photo, taken in 2003.]

13. The fines levied that day against Jane and each girl were, by present-day equivalents, $485.00 and $335.00 respectively. [www.westegg.com/inflation]

14. Fines for those in the sex trade were steep compared to other offences. Penalties for public drunkenness or street fighting, for example, ranged from $1.50 to $3.00. [Peoria newspapers. passim]

15. City of Peoria (1870) Census, page 999, entry 502, line 15

CHAPTER 7 ❖ Mattie's Peoria

1. Peoria has since spread far beyond her 1872 boundaries; the population has increased tenfold. Many of the old houses remain, but now asphalt roads come within a sidewalk width of the ornate doors. The hedges and expansive lawns are gone. Many of those stately houses now serve as housing for students attending Bradley University. This excellent educational facility, specializing in business, arts, technology and science, is an oasis with a rambling campus, lanes and paths that meander past spacious, well-groomed lawns and groves of shade trees. Bradley University is home to several files dealing with the Earps' 1872 residence in Peoria.

2. Civil Affairs Court was at 28 Adams Street. Criminal Court was between Adams and Jefferson. [Peoria Directory]
3. It is alleged that fire struck the toddling town when a cow owned by one Mrs. O'Leary became extremely agitated. In a fit of pique she wrecked her stall and kicked over a lit kerosene lantern. With the straw ablaze, the entire barn was quickly engulfed as the flames leapt to adjoining wooden structures. Mrs. O'Leary ran for her life and survived; the cow was never seen again. 15,000 buildings and houses were destroyed. [*Oxford Encyclopedia*, p296.]
4. *Daily National Democrat*. January 6, 1872..

CHAPTER 8 ❖ Master of the House
1. Court records and Earp Files, Special Collections, Bradley University, Peoria, Illinois.
2. Also known as "Mother" Sears, she was Peoria's most notorious madam. Located in Ward Six, a respectable area of town, her house stood near the intersection of Steubenville and Kettrelle streets. Sears House was the largest and most popular brothel in town. [Peoria police files]
3. The two pimps were William Randall and James Dougherty, George's uncle and mentor respectively. Why they were there is unknown. [*Daily Transcript*. January 14, 1872.]
4. While researching the Illinois branch of his family tree, one Ted Lengendorf was reading copies of the *Peoria Daily Transcript* from 1872 when he noticed the name Wyatt Earp. Curious, he read the article and realized Earp had been arrested in February 1872 during a police raid on a Peoria brothel and charged "as a resident." Not interested in Earp per se, but feeling the item might interest others, he informed the moderator of a website specializing in Earp lore. The item was posted as a matter of interest and the revelation caused some excitement. The excitement would have been greater had subsequent arrests been uncovered at the same time. Interest would also have been greater had it been known that Wyatt was in Peoria with Mattie and Morgan. [See www.oldwesthistory.net]

CHAPTER 9 ❖ Taking Care of Business
1. Earp stumbled in and out of trouble until well into old age. In 1911 he was charged with running a bunko scheme in Los Angeles with two old Tombstone cronies, Walter Scott, the famous "Death Valley Scotty" and Ed Dean. Wyatt gave an alias — William Stapp. He was acquitted. During prohibition he was charged with assault. Engaged in bootlegging, he was driving an ice wagon as a front. Ice blocks concealed the main product. When a customer and he had an argument Wyatt assaulted him with a pair of ice tongs. That arrest netted him ten days in jail, which he served, again under his favorite alias of William Stapp. [*True West*, September 1994, p19.]

2. There were eighteen hotels registered in Peoria in 1872. Only five could be considered respectable. [*Root's City Directory*]
3. Mayor Brotherson and Captain Gill's first crackdown of 1872 resulted in 87 arrests over three nights. [Peoria Public Library]
4. Peoria City Warrant issued February 26, 1872. [Bradley University, Special Collections, Earp File]
5. Guessing the unpublished names is not difficult. Sarah Haspel, Carrie Crow and Mattie Earp leap immediately to the forefront.
6. Bradley University, Peoria Campus, Special Collections, Earp File.
7. Account of the trial proceedings and comments of editor Kent can be read on page 4 of the *Daily Transcript*, February 28, 1872.
8. Earp's address is noted: Earp, Wyatt S. res. Wash. bs 3 a Hamilton. [*Root's Peoria City Directory 1872*, p11, on file in Peoria Public Library.]

Chapter 10 ❖ From Frying Pan to Fire

1. Wyatt's sense of trust was firmly ensconced in his psyche. It would come to the fore again in Tombstone when he was betrayed in a deal he had made in good faith with John Behan concerning the appointment to the Puma County Sheriff's office.
2. Haspel House closed permanently several months later. Madam Haspel re-married within a couple of years and appears to have settled down to a respectable life. [US Census (Peoria) 1876.]
3. *Peoria Daily Transcript*, May 11, 1872.
4. *Peoria Daily Transcript*, April 24, 1872, p4.
5. *Peoria Daily Transcript*, April 24, p4.
6. Phone conversations with office manager. [Peoria County Coroner's office, December 8, 2003.]
7. In 2002, an archivist at UIWC assisted this author in a search for the transcript but found nothing. [University of Illinois, Western Campus.]

Chapter 11 ❖ Peoria Pulls the Welcome Mat

1. The charges were once again "Keeping a house of ill-fame." [Peoria Court Records]
2. Walton's boats plied the Illinois River in circuitous routes from Lacon in the north to Alton in Missouri. The Beardstown Gunboat ran the east side of the river while its sister operated along the western bank. [Various accounts from Illinois newspapers circa 1871–75.]
3. Accounts from various Monmouth, Illinois papers. [Courtesy of Dr. Wm. Urban, Professor of History, Monmouth University.]
4. Courtesy of Roger Jay, a Maryland researcher and author, in a series of emails during 2004.
5. A funeral service for George Randall, age 22, was conducted on September 18, 1872 at Old Christ Church in Peoria. He was buried in the public cemetery. [Peoria Public Library]

CHAPTER 12 ❖ Navigational Error
1. *Daily Transcript*, September 10, 1872, p4, col. 3.
2. When Mattie identified herself on that date in court with the alias, Sarah Earp, she unknowingly sowed the seeds of a controversy that would arise 100 years later and continue among historians for several years. [See Appendix 3: A Question of Identity.]

CHAPTER 13 ❖ Once Again Those Fields of Corn
1. In 1878 Peace was re-named Sterling and named the County Seat. [www. kancoll.org/rice/]
2. Several statements concerning Earp, alleged to have been made by Adelia, are untrue. A memoir, supposedly her reminiscences, is in the Earp Collection of the Colton, California library. It was fabricated by an English hoaxer, but, despite its having been proven totally bogus, there are still those who refer to it for research.
3. Kansas records for 1873 are sketchy. Some are held by the KSHS and a great number are held in private collections and city archives. Access to those records, which are in no particular order, is difficult.
4. Lake was creating a legend of a fighting lawman hero not a sedentary farmer. If he was aware Earp spent that year farming, he would not have wanted to print it. Instead he had him buffalo hunting and arresting the notorious Ben Thompson in Ellsworth. Both were Lake fictions that have since been debunked.
5. Also called Texas longhorn fever and tick fever, it was causing problems for Kansas farmers. Texas longhorns had developed immunity to the disease, but Kansas cattle were contracting the disease in alarming numbers. Kansans lobbied authorities in Topeka. Realizing the way to state prosperity lay in farms, not in transient Texas cattle, Topeka acted quickly. Large areas were designated from which Texas steers were prohibited. Abilene was at the center of the restricted area. Texas ranchers scrambled to find new major railheads from which to ship their cattle to Chicago. Wichita and Dodge City fitted the bill. In 1872 both towns became terminals. [KSHS and www.kancoll.org]
6. Probably Keno Hall where James was the bartender–manager.
7. www.kancoll.org/rice-co-pl.html
8. The Panic of '73, a financial crash of staggering proportions, carried ruin throughout the nation. On October 1,1873 the banking firm of Jay Cooke & Co failed through ill-advised financing of the Northern Pacific Railroad. Panic spread as one failure was followed by another. The entire country was affected. Many war veterans were involved because President Grant, whom they trusted, had been duped (by a son-in-law) into lending his name to the promotion. It was the worst financial disaster in the USA to that point because so much wealth was involved. Thousands of homesteaders, ranchers and farmers lost their lands. [www.kancoll.org]

CHAPTER 14 ❖ **Wichita**

1. Wagon trains had to leave Missouri in early spring to avoid the risk of being trapped in the Rockies by early October snows. The ill-fated Donner party (1846) departed too late and many of the settlers perished in the California mountain canyon now called Donner's Pass.

2. When a town slowed down or a mine folded the boomers struck out for the next fast-growing settlement. The Earp brothers were boomers in every facet of the term. So was Mattie. The first California gold seekers of 1849 were called boomers. They were not called '49ers until the name was given to them by the press.

3. It was officially known as West Wichita, the name it bears today in its capacity as a respectable suburb.

4. Bartholomew, Ed. *Wyatt Earp: The Untold Story*, p95.

5. Lowe was charged with murder but managed to arrange bail pending his trial, which was scheduled for December. The day of the trial, however, Lowe failed to appear. He and his wife, "Rowdy Kate," had sold their establishment and hightailed it west to Denver. A few years later "Rowdy Joe" Lowe, who was drunk, unwisely decided to shoot it out with a city police officer, who was sober. "Rowdy Joe" was never known for exercising good judgment. [Wichita *Eagle* files and Denver Police records]

6. Hurdy-gurdy girls were also extremely popular in the Dawson Creek (Yukon Territory) saloons during Canada's Klondike gold rush of 1897. Many made fortunes. These women, for the most part from Europe and mostly respectable, made a good living ensemble dancing on stage. Between shows they waltzed and danced jigs with patrons for a dollar a dance. [KSHS and BC Archives]

7. Meagher, correctly pronounced Ma'har, was born in Ireland c.1843. He was acting as an interim city marshal on a one-day appointment in Caldwell, Kansas when he was killed on December 17, 1881. [KSHS Caldwell Records]

8. Letter to E.B. Allen, Mayor of Wichita, dated April 10, 1871. He did not elaborate on the "existing emergencies." [KSHS Wichita Records]

9. In January, Meagher married Miss Jennie Fitzpatrick, a resident of Leavenworth, Kansas. [*Wichita Eagle*, Thursday, January 9, 1873.]

10. Meagher's methods of enforcement closely resemble those of John S. Ingram, a Canadian lawman who, with his fists and a no-nonsense attitude, tamed Winnipeg, Calgary, and Rossland, BC.

11. "Hurrahing" was riding at breakneck speed back and forth along the main street while firing pistols wildly into the air. It was usually a group endeavor.

12. Madams were fined $20. The girls paid $10. In winter the fines were halved. Girls who were sick or otherwise idled would not be fined. In 1875 fines remained year around at winter rates (no reasons given). Two

dollars remained with the court as costs with the rest going to the city. The fines in reality were left-handed business licenses, but were seen as upholding Kansas state laws prohibiting brothels and prostitution. [Wichita City Records and Police Court Records]

13. Meagher returned in 1876, won the election and served two more years. [Wichita City Records: 1876–8.]

CHAPTER 15 ❖ The House at 12 Douglas Avenue

1. Hattie eventually married a Tombstone rancher but later divorced him, went to California and disappeared from history. Thomas was killed by Apache renegades near Tombstone (c. 1887) while driving a wagon for a mining outfit. [Courtesy G. Boyer files.]
2. Wichita old-timers invariably described Wood as a two-bit card sharp, a tinhorn gambler, a sadistic lout, a laborer and a shiftless, lazy, no-good bum. [Wrampe, Ann. *Wichita Township's Soiled Doves.*]
3. Wichita Public Records, 1875 census.
4. Georgie Wood and Laura Smith appear in court records under their own names, indicating they were not working for Bessie. They apparently later came under Bessie's protection because after 1875, when Wyatt joined the police force, no further fines were collected from any of the women at 12 Douglas Avenue.
5. Kate Elder was born in Budapest, Hungary, Nov. 7, 1850 and died in Prescott, Arizona on Nov. 2, 1940. [Boyer, Glenn G. Who Was Big Nose Kate? *Wyatt Earp: Family, Friends & Foes.* Vol. 1. 1997.]
6. By 1885 Kate had resumed contact with siblings and nieces.
7. In the spring of 1875 a special Ford County census lists a Kate Elder, age 24, from Iowa, working as a sporting woman in Tom Sherman's Dance Hall in Dodge City. This was, in all likelihood, "Big Nose Kate."
8. The portrayal of Kate in Patricia Jahn's pseudo-biography *The Frontier World of Doc Holliday* has little value as a biography of either Holliday or Kate, but has merit in details of frontier conditions. The best account of Kate and Doc is in Karen Holliday Turner's *Doc Holliday: A Family Portrait.*
9. A step above Police Court and one step below District Court.
10. This was George Wood's house. [1875 Wichita Census]
11. The charge probably could have been tossed out on a technicality then and there. The brothel had not been set up on June 3, but had been operating, at the very least, since the previous October.
12. The total bail of $1,000 was equivalent to $8,500 in present day dollar value. [Friedman's Inflation Calculator and www.westegg.com]
13. Although charged, Mattie Earp was never fined as a madam. Bessie was twice fined as a madam, but not until March 1876. [Wichita Court Records]
14. See Appendix 4: Madam of Mystery.

CHAPTER 16 ❖ The Trial of Madam Mattie

1. William Baldwin was appointed to the position of City Attorney in 1872 but stayed only a few months before returning to private practice as a defense lawyer. He was later appointed to the position of Probate Judge. [Wichita City files, 1871–77.]

2. This was one of Judge William Campbell's first major cases following his appointment to the 13th Judicial District in 1873. Born in Lincoln County, Kentucky in 1845, he had been admitted to the bar in 1866 and had moved to Kansas in 1869 and married Kate Barnes of Estel County, KS. They had seven children during a long and happy marriage. He engaged in private practice until his elevation to the bench, a position he held until 1882 when he returned to private practice in Wichita. He practiced there until he retired. In 1933, at the venerable age of 88, he granted an interview to the Wichita *Eagle* in which he compared the times of the present day to those of his early days in Kansas. [*Wichita Eagle* files, 1933.]

3. Records of District Court Clerk, Sedgewick County, Kansas. September 1874 file.

CHAPTER 17 ❖ Oh, It Was a Very Good Year

1. One wonders if Mrs. Blackman may not have, quite unknowingly, supplied the name for the mysterious Mattie Bradford. It seems too similar not to arouse some suspicion.

2. Wrampe, Ann. *Wichita Township Soiled Doves*, pp 6–7.

3. Eva Earp remains unidentified but Minnie Earp is believed to have been, and probably was, Minnie Martin, wife of one William "Hurricane Bill" Martin, a local outlaw of some note. At the time Bill was serving seven years hard time in the Kansas State Penitentiary for horse theft. He whiled away his spare hours writing misspelled letters to various editors in which he decried the terrible miscarriage of justice that had befallen his innocent self. His tales of woe were often printed (mainly as comic relief) but no one ever believed him. [Ibid and the Wichita *Eagle*, *passim* 1874–6.]

4. Census of Sedgwick County, March 1, 1875, City of Wichita, p151.

5. One of the many Internet sites involved with Earp lore states Wyatt married a prostitute while in Wichita. No name is given nor is a record of the marriage cited. Obviously the writer was unaware that Wyatt was already married to a prostitute (Mattie) when he arrived in Wichita. [www.sparticus.schoolnet.uk]

6. A highly fictionalized (even comical) version of how Wyatt Earp was hired as a Wichita lawman is to be found in *Wyatt Earp, Frontier Marshal*. [Lake, Stuart. *Wyatt Earp, Frontier Marshal*, chapter 1X, pp 95–102.]

7. Bartholomew, Ed. *Wyatt Earp: The Untold Story*, p95.

8. Earp single handedly subdued a noted fugitive, W.W. Compton, after a running gunfight through the city's streets and alleys. He later retrieved

a horse and buggy Compton had stolen earlier in Coffey County. Compton received hard time in jail and Wyatt received plaudits. [*Wichita Weekly Beacon*, May 12, 1875.]

9. Miller & Snell. *Why the West Was Wild*, pp 145–6.

10. Meagher's livery business had failed, so he contested the 1876 election to the marshal's office. Smith was the incumbent but Meagher was the voters' choice and he won handily. Smith later remarked publicly that Meagher knew some of his policemen friends were defrauding the city treasury. Whether Meagher knew of any fraud is unproven, but Smith's allegations concerning policemen as culprits had some basis considering Wyatt's later predicament.

11. Wichita Court Records. Case Docket #347, April 1876.

12. "Bucking the tiger" was the phrase that recognized the odds favored the dealer. The "tiger," though traditionally friendly to the dealer, was known to turn on occasion and maul him severely.

13. Whether this included the women using Earp as an alias then in Wichita, just Wyatt, or Wyatt and Mattie, remains unknown. James, after all, was gainfully employed.

14. The Vagrancy Act could not be considered according to a notation penned by A.W. Oliver and C.M. Garrison at the bottom of the letter. The act was so generic it was often used as a "catch-all" law, but Topeka authorities refused to allow it to be invoked in this matter. [Memo regarding Letter from the Police Court to Town Council, dated May 10, 1876.]

15. The Woods moved to Caldwell and were heard from no more after 1878. [Wrampe, Ann. *Wichita Township Soiled Doves*, p24.]

16. With the closing of Bessie's house, Wichita's favorite playpen reverted to a house at 33 Water Street reputedly operated by a madam calling herself Dixie Lee. The evidence indicates, however, that Dixie Lee did not arrive in Wichita until 1878. This is unfortunate for western history researchers and writers as a rivalry between Madams Bessie and Mattie Earp and Madam Dixie Lee would have likely proven extremely interesting. [Author's files]

CHAPTER 18 ❖ Dodge City and the Gambling Circuit

1. Dodge City had remarkably few killings during the ten years between 1876 and 1885. Only 16 such deaths are recorded, an average of 1.6 per year. 1878 was the worst with five fatal shootings. One was George Hoyt whom Wyatt Earp may, or may not, have shot from the saddle on July 26. Lake claimed Wyatt shot Hoyt, but no proof exists to support the claim. [KSHS, Dodge City Death Statistics.]

2. Mean daytime temperature for Dodge City in July 1876 was 87°F. [KSHS]

3. Luke Short was among the most successful of the western gamblers. He died a fairly wealthy man, in bed, at age 39, on September 8, 1893. Ede-

ma, commonly called dropsy, claimed him. The affliction had troubled him all his life.

4. Short killed Charlie Storms, a professional gunfighter, outside the Oriental Saloon in Tombstone on February 21,1881. He killed James Courtwright, an ex-marshal turned protection racketeer, with a lucky shot in Fort Worth, Texas on February 8, 1887. [Masterson, "Famous Gunfighters of the Western Frontier." *Human Life*, vol.1V, April 1907, p 10. See also: Cunningham, Eugene. *Triggernometry*, pp 215–16.]

5. When Masterson was commissioned to write several articles about western lawmen for *Human Life* he mentioned Wyatt only when necessary and, while always complimentary, adulation was lacking. Still the two seemed the best of friends before Bat went to New York and for many years after. Masterson died a decade prior to the debut of *Frontier Marshal*, but one wonders what might have been his comments on Lake's book and his assertion that the two men had met as buffalo hunters and that Wyatt had hired Bat. He might also have had some comments about Lake's claim that Bat had been Wyatt's deputy in Dodge City. That claim would have come as surprising news to Masterson who had been a Dodge City (and Ford County) lawman long before Earp appeared in that town.

6. Dozens of famed gunfighters served as lawmen in Dodge City, among them Morgan Earp, Bill Tilghman, "Mysterious Dave" Mather and Jim, Ed and Bat Masterson. All were tough; none would hesitate to club a miscreant into submission in order to make a point, and all were willing to kill if necessary. Mather was especially willing to kill, as he exhibited no qualms or regrets when he killed a fellow policeman. [KSHS]

7. An exception to this plan was in 1877 when Earp is not recorded on the police payroll. [KSHS, Dodge City Records.]

8. "Doc" Holliday, who was later to become Wyatt's best friend, was also in Deadwood during that winter, but obviously his path did not cross with that of the Earps as he never mentioned knowing the Earps' until he met Wyatt in Texas in the spring of 1878. [Tanner, Karen Holliday. *Doc Holliday: A Family Portrait*.]

9. Boyer files and in conversations at Tucson in 2005.

10. One of Morgan's present-day biographers, Kenneth Vail, has uncovered some evidence that Morgan had been to Deadwood twice. [An email to author in 2005.]

11. Pulp magazines with such titles as *The Frontier*, *Texas Rangers*, *Gunfighters & Outlaws* and even *Ranch Romances* adorned newsstands. All fictional, but exciting reading, they sold from 10¢ to 25¢. Today these magazines can be bought from collectors for upwards of $10 to $25. [Author's files.]

12. By 1876 Deadwood had already been well tamed by the town's first sheriff, Seth Bullock, a Canadian entrepreneur turned lawman. Bullock (born

near Windsor, Ontario, Canada, July 23, 1849) eventually became a leading rancher and holder of vast acreage. He built the town's grandest hotel, The Hotel Bullock. He was later elected as a Montana State Representative, became a fast friend of Teddy Roosevelt and when Roosevelt became president became one of his most trusted advisors. He served also as a US Marshal in later years and was a decorated veteran of the Spanish–American War. Bullock died in South Dakota, September 23, 1919.

13. For reasons never explained, Earp consistently referred to her as Kate Fisher when he was relating his adventures to Stuart Lake in 1927. Kate had never used Fisher as an alias at any time during the period she knew the Earps. [Lake, Stuart. *Wyatt Earp, Frontier Marshal*, pp 197, 198, 202, 223, 238, and 265.]

14. In a letter to a niece, written many years later, Kate said she had introduced the couple to "Doc" in 1875, but this could not be as Wyatt and Mattie were still in Wichita. By then Kate was probably having memory losses due to advanced age. It is, however, a proven fact that "Doc" was practicing dentistry in Dodge City in 1878 so the year of introduction was most likely 1877 when all four were in Fort Griffin.

15. In Tombstone, in 1881, Holliday challenged John Ringo over an ongoing dispute. Had not one of the Earps stopped them, there is little doubt either Holliday or Ringo would have died that afternoon. At another time he came close to gunning down an unarmed Ike Clanton in a hotel dining room. This time Morgan Earp got between him and Ike, giving Clanton the chance to hurry out.

16. Tanner. Karen. *Doc Holliday: A Family Portrait*, p 96.

17. Tanner, Karen. *Doc Holliday: A Family Portrait*. Passim.

18. These were letters to Lillian Lane Raffert, daughter of Kate's sister, Rosalia Haroney, written between 1938 and 1940. They were viewed by the author in 2005. [Boyer Collection, Tucson, Arizona.]

19. Kate seems to have forgotten that in Arizona Doc's TB had gone into remission and there were no coughing spells. Still, he carried his bottle at all times. [Boyer files, viewed in 2002.]

20. Tanner, Karen. *Doc Holliday: A Family Portrait*, p169 quoting Cummings, Mary Katherine [Big Nose Kate], *The O.K. Corral Fight at Tombstone: A Footnote by Kate Elder*, p81.

21. Shanssey owned a saloon in Fort Griffin but he did not make the introductions, and Wyatt was not pursuing Rudabaugh. Wyatt was not a lawman at the time but was in town for the winter dealing faro. *[Frontier Marshal.* p192.]

22. Italics added by author.

23. Kate's intense dislike of Wyatt and her resentment toward Mattie had begun in Wichita when Wyatt brushed her aside upon Mattie's arrival. The two women, though they worked together, were never more than cool towards each other. Kate could never understand how Wyatt could

reject her for Mattie, whom she considered an ill-bred farm girl. Kate and Mattie eventually reconciled (in Globe) but resentment lingered to the point where Kate would never again refer to Mattie other than "his wife" or "Wyatt's wife."

24 See www.larned.net/rogmyers/rogmyers/html and click on The Earp Files. Details of Earp's 1877 summer are well documented within. [Author]

25. Though Front Street was not long it was easy enough to remain lost in the crowd that milled in and out of the numerous saloons and dance halls. An astute woman could be in the thick of the action every night and never be seen.

26. An 1887 map of Dodge City indicates the intersection of Spruce and First as only 600 yards (about three blocks) from Front Street. [KSHS]

27. Frank Waters, in *The Earp Brothers of Tombstone,* quotes Allie Earp as stating that Wyatt had become a deacon in the church. Considering Wyatt's activities this seems far-fetched and suggests the likelihood of it being another of Water's fictions. It should be viewed with extreme skepticism.

28. *The Gazette*. Dodge City Section, August 27, 1878.

29. Bartholomew cannot be considered an unequivocal expert on the Earps as he was too biased against Wyatt to be objective. Although he researched areas that included Mattie, he attached no importance to her. During his enquiries into Wyatt's Wichita days he missed the connection between Wyatt and Sally Earp. In fairness, he did not know Wyatt had a wife and, as most of the women in Bessie's house were using Earp as surnames, he obviously considered Sally Earp just an alias for yet another of Bessie's girls. He had no idea she was Mrs. Wyatt Earp.

30. Lawmen of the era protected their own favored ladies of the night as well as family members engaged in the sporting life. The Earp boys were no exception.

31. Alice Chambers and Kate Howe, two of Dodge City's more famous night ladies, fought in the middle of Front Street one afternoon in a dispute over who would claim a handsome drover as her *amour de jour*. They clawed, screamed and rolled about in the dust for quite some time before a lawman separated them and hauled them before the presiding magistrate who levied fines against both and sent them to their respective houses with a warning to improve their public behavior. [*Dodge City Times*, March 24, 1877.]

32. In 2002 I received a copy of a letter written many years ago by Mrs. Merritt Beeson, (curator of a Dodge City museum dedicated to Wyatt Earp memorabilia) to Mrs. Mabel Cason (Josephine Earp's biographer). The letter indicates Wyatt's mistress was Lily "Dutch Lil" Beck, a woman of the town. No police or court records list Beck as ever having been arrested in Dodge City, not surprising with Wyatt as her protector. She left Dodge City about 1880 and information from Morris, Illinois shows

a woman called "Dutch Lil" Beck was a madam there from 1882 until about 1912. Similarities indicate they were the same woman.

33. One story that continuously makes the rounds has Kate being arrested for public drunkenness and fined $1.50. There is no court record or newspaper account of the incident, arrest or fine.

34. The popular story that Doc had been locked up in a hotel room by the town marshal and that Kate had set a distracting fire to a building at the far end of town, had stolen two horses and then freed Doc is not true, but is part of the Holliday legend. The story was originated by Wyatt Earp and embellished by Stuart Lake. [*Frontier Marshal*, pp 197–8.]

35. Dodge City *Times*. June 27, 1878.

36. He may have decided there was too much competition. Another dentist, longer established, spread rumors about Doc that may have driven some business from him.

37. Between 1870 and 1879 thousands of migrants and overlanders passed through Dodge City on their way to California and Oregon, nearly all in search of farmland. Many found it in Ford County and went no further. As those settlers prospered they gained in political power and forced changes in the way Kansas looked at Texas longhorns and their drovers in general, and spline fever in particular. [www.kancoll.org/agriculture/]

38. In fact, the drives did not end until 1886. If an omen was necessary for authenticity it could have been the massive blizzard that swept the state the previous winter.

39. Sixty-six years later *Polonaise* again hit the top 40 charts when Perry Como popularized it as *Til the End of Time*. [CBC Radio news item. "North American Hits of 1879," September 18, 2003.]

40. Kansas State Historical Society, Dodge City Records.

41. Earp's version of his encounter with Allison is reminiscent of his alleged 1873 arrest of notorious gunfighter Ben Thompson in Ellsworth, Kansas. Neither account stands up to serious investigation.

42. No relation to the Ed Kennedy who was arrested with Wyatt at Fort Smith in 1871.

43. Kennedy was later released for lack of evidence. Rumors that his wealthy father (a Texas cattleman) had bought off the authorities were rampant. [www.oldwesthistory.com]

44. Revolvers in the 1870s and 1880s were made of iron and were very heavy. The lightest pistol weighed two pounds, five ounces. A Walker Colt was four pounds, nine ounces. Either would cause a considerable dent to one's head. [Sources: *Gun Digest* and similar publications.]

CHAPTER 19 ❖ Tombstone

1. The Sampling Room was located at 434 Allen Street.
2. When White was shot by "Curly Bill" Brocius (real name reportedly

John Graham) Virgil continued under the new city marshal, Ben Sippy. Virgil was later elevated to city marshal when Sippy was fired. Brocius disappeared March 24, 1882. It is generally conceded Wyatt Earp had shot him that day. [Boyer, GG. *Wyatt Earp, Family Friends & Foes*, Vol. 1V. See also "Curly Bill Has Been Killed At Last." *Real West*, June 1984.]

3. Morgan could not resist the lure of Tombstone. He resigned in March after three months on the Butte police force. [Chaput, Don. *The Earp Papers: In a Brother's Image*, p37.]

4. Wyatt worked much of his life for Wells Fargo, mostly in the capacity of detective. [Author's files]

5. The story that Wyatt earned his space from the Oriental owners as a reward for his forcible eviction of an undesirable gambler is all part of the legend. Rickabaugh hired him for a far more pragmatic reason: he needed his gun.

6. "The Gamblers' War in Tombstone" and "Short vs. Storms." [*Wild West*, October 2004, pp 38 & 30 respectively.]

7. For a short, interesting biography of Leslie, see_*Silver, Sex and Six Guns: Tombstone Saga of the Life of Buckskin Frank Leslie.* [Douglas D. Martin. Tombstone Epitaph Printing (1962).]

8. The Reno gang chose to ignore the warnings. One cold December night, while in custody awaiting trial, Frank, William and Simeon Reno and gang member Charles Anderson were forcibly removed from the New Albany jail. They were immediately hanged from a railway trestle. The rest of the gang quickly dispersed and were heard from no more. [Library files. *The Indianapolis Star*, Indianapolis, Indiana, December 1868.]

9. Morgan was often called Seth, his middle name, when he was young and many in his family continued its use in later years. [Author's files]

10. A well-known authority on Tombstone (who shall remain nameless because of friendship) once wrote that Kate arrived in Tombstone in 1879 and opened the town's first brothel in a huge tent. People still believe the tale. In fact, by the time Kate did see Tombstone (1880) there were dozens of such places already up and running. Kate hated the town from first sight and left within days.

11. Tombstone's Asian population (routinely referred to in Tombstone newspapers as Celestials) endured great malicious prejudice. They were miners, laborers, laundry operators, storeowners, and practitioners of Oriental medicine, but these hardworking men and women were generally portrayed as pimps, drug dealers and prostitutes. Their district was portrayed as the epicenter of evil. It is doubtful if Mattie ever set foot in Chinatown for she was no less prejudiced against Orientals than were her peers.

12. Described in the official document of the mortgage later taken on the house as: "The house and lot on Fremont Street situate [*sic*] about one hundred feet (more or less) from the southwest corner of Fremont Street

and westerly from the house and lot of Virgil Earp two lots intervening between the hereby mortgaged and said lot of Virgil Earp" The house was next door to Pete Spence, one of Morgan Earp's alleged slayers. [Document filed and recorded on February 14, 1882 by A.T. Jones, County Recorder.]

13. Nellie Cashman, (b. Ireland 1850; d. Victoria, BC Jan. 4, 1925) was a truly liberated woman in every way. She parlayed a small fortune made in Nevada into a larger fortune in Tombstone; but it was in the goldfields of Canada and Alaska that she became a millionaire, and a legend. She is buried in Ross Bay Cemetery, in Victoria, BC. [BC Archives. See also: Meyers, E.C. *Wild Canadian West*, pp 136–41.]

14. One of her present day relatives feels the condition was a pre-cancerous symptom of cervical or ovarian cancer.

15. Opium, and to a lesser degree heroin, had an international following during the nineteenth century. European royalty and noblemen, Russian tsars and courtiers, Asian rajahs and emperors, prime ministers, presidents, senators, prominent artists, actors and authors, among them Arthur Conan Doyle and Oscar Wilde, were opium users. Doyle's fictional creation, Sherlock Holmes, and Wilde's anti-hero, Dorian Gray, were portrayed as addicts without blame.

CHAPTER 20 ❖ When Dreams Fade and Die

1. Some writers claimed the Earps and Holliday were engaged in stage robbery. This nonsense sold books and magazine articles and also provided a few newspaper stories. [*Seattle Post Intelligencer* printed several such items during 1912–13.]

2. Dealers were well paid depending on locale. In the US southwest $25 a day was minimum. In western Canada and the US northwest $8.00/hour was average, and in BC many preferred to work on percentage. [ASHS & BC Archives]

3. In 1882 Wyatt Earp received $5,000 from US Marshal Crawley Dake for work he did to help quell the Cowboy Raids in Puma County. [Reports of US Examiner Leigh Chalmers re: his enquiry into accounting procedures of funds (approximately $200,000) disbursed by US Marshal Dake from 1879 to 1883. Reports are dated August 13 & September 3,1885. See also: "Lawlessness & Cowboy Depredation in Arizona Territory 1880–81." These documents are located in Washington National Archives.]

4. Wyatt always called her Sadie, never Josie or Josephine. So did the other members of the family.

5. Foolishly, Josephine registered the lot in Behan's name and the house in her name. Behan eventually tired of her and evicted her, no doubt hoping to get the house as well. Behan got the lot but apparently she sold the house to someone who moved it to another location. [Cason Manuscript]

6. During 1929–31, when Stuart Lake and Josephine were fighting over publication of *Frontier Marshal*, he maliciously insinuated Mrs. Young's boarding house was of ill repute and that Josephine had been "the queen of Tombstone's saloon girls." He was wrong about the boarding house. [Author's files]

7. Some, including her present-day relatives, believe Mattie attempted suicide during this period but there is no irrefutable proof. Possibly something in one of the letters to Sarah holds a clue, but at present no one seems to know where those letters are. Until they resurface, if they ever do, there is no way of knowing.

8. Movies that mention Mattie depict her as a drunken strumpet, an embarrassment to the sterling marshal. One notable scene has her arriving in Tombstone in a state of fearsome inebriation, barely able to remain seated in the wagon. She then falls to the street while alighting. In fact her drinking was under control until mid-1887 when she began her total descent.

9. The Private Journal of George Whitwell Parsons. [On file at the Arizona State Historical Society, Tucson.]

10. For a good biography of this legendary gunfighter, see: Gatto, Steve. *John Ringo*. Protar House, Lansing MI. (2002)

11. Spence's real name may have been Elliot L. Ferguson, but this is open to debate.

12. Billy Claiborne was killed on Nov. 18, 1882 by "Buckskin Frank" Leslie outside the Oriental Saloon. Leslie was acquitted. Claiborne is buried in Boot Hill, but even in death he gets no respect; his name on the grave marker is misspelled. [ASHS]

13. Phin spent several years in jail, was eventually released and died in bed in 1902. Ike was killed in 1887 by a range detective. Billy, the bravest Clanton, proved it as he lay dying following the gunfight near the OK Corral.

14. Also in the gang was one Frank Spencer (b. Tennessee, c1857; d. Kamloops, BC, July 1890) who is not to be confused with Pete Spence. Frank Spencer hurriedly left Tombstone in November 1881. He went to Montana where he rode briefly with "Dutch" Henry's rustlers until vigilantes chased the gang into Minnesota. Spencer then fled to Canada and, in 1885, was working on a Kamloops, BC ranch when he killed fellow ranch hand Pete Foster in a dispute over ownership of a bottle of rye whiskey. He escaped to Oregon, but in 1890 foolishly returned to BC. He was arrested, tried for capital murder (1st degree), found guilty and hanged. [Trial transcript, Regina vs. Spencer. BC Supreme Court, Kamloops, BC. See also: Meyers, E.C. *Wild Canadian West*.]

15. The Earp version is basically true. The rustlers were not ambushed. Ordered to surrender, they came up shooting. The second part of the Earps' claim is technically correct. Mexican troops were indeed with them.

[Mexican correspondence to USA authorities. US National Archives.]

16. A light carpet of snow had fallen the previous night. The temperature at noon was still only 40°F (4°C). [ASHS files.]

17. James and Warren did not participate. James, alerted to the impending shootout, had grabbed two pistols and was on his way but arrived after the shooting was over. Warren had gone back to California after the August gunfight at Skeleton Canyon. He returned when Morgan was murdered to help Wyatt hunt those responsible. [Boyer collection, reviewed by author in 2000.]

18. Adding some credence to this theory is the fact that the day prior to the gunfight Morgan Earp journeyed to Tucson to find Holliday, who was attending a fiesta with Kate Elder. Morgan informed him that he would be needed in Tombstone the following day. The two men, and Kate, returned within hours to Tombstone. [Kate's account of the meeting is detailed in a letter, dated March 18, 1940 from Kate to her niece, Lillian Raffert. Boyer collection, Tucson, Arizona.]

19. Indications of Mattie being present at any event were never part of her salience. In keeping with this trait of anonymity there is likewise no mention of her being with the other family members when they gathered at Hatch's Pool Hall the night Morgan was killed.

20. Kate claimed in later years to have witnessed the gunfight from Doc's room, but some basic research (and a little elementary geometry) shows she could have seen nothing at all from the vantage point she described.

21. The Cason Manuscript notes make it clear Josephine was not about to make disclosures about Mattie or that she and Earp were considered married. When she did finally confess the details about Mattie, Mabel Cason decided to withdraw from the project for she had no way of knowing how many other false statements Josephine had made and declared as true. [Notes and letters pertaining to the Cason Manuscript, Boyer collection.]

22. Josephine told her prospective biographers, Mrs. Cason and Mrs. Ackerman, that she had rushed to the scene but, seeing that Wyatt was all right, did not go to him because "the shooting was over and I was too frightened to get closer." More to the truth is that she probably saw Mattie was with Wyatt and the others and discreetly stayed in the crowd. [Cason Manuscript]

23. There were more than just a few citizens who wished the Earps would quietly leave town, but none dared say so aloud. Regardless of how lionized the Earps have been over the years, they were greatly feared in Tombstone.

24. Holliday undoubtedly was under stress, for he began to display an even shorter temper and began drinking more. He needed Kate but was too proud to go to her. He felt that departing Tombstone, even temporarily,

would be construed as fear and that would have violated his Georgian code of honor.

25. Frank Stilwell, a hired gun, held a grudge against the Earps. They had arrested him the previous year on suspicion of stage robbery. At the time he was a deputy sheriff, so Behan was forced to fire him.

26. Will McLaury, a lawyer, has long been suspected of having financed the shooters. He had returned to Tombstone to settle his brothers' estates and left town quickly after Morgan was killed. Wyatt, however, did not run him to ground, although he certainly could have.

27. Wyatt was also worried about Josephine's safety so he sent her to stay with her parents in San Francisco. He assured her he would contact her shortly and would come to her as soon as possible. [Cason Manuscript]

28. Wyatt's concern seems strange. If he was planning on leaving Mattie why was he so worried about her safety? This question has been raised often but there seems to be no answer. Nonetheless, he seems to have still had some feelings for her even at that late date.

29. Howard, a lawyer, would have insisted on the changes, as he would have known the paper was illegal without Mattie's agreement. He was looking out for his own interests. No collateral obtained under such circumstances would be declared valid in a court challenge. Howard knew Mattie well enough to know she would dispute it.

CHAPTER 21 ❖ Farewell to Tombstone

1. It has been related in several stories about the murder that bystander G.A. Berry was struck by the bullet when it passed through Morgan's body, suffering a thigh wound. He was left unattended in the excitement and had bled to death. Not so. G.A. Berry survived and did not die until about 1906. [Boyer, G. in a note to author, June 2000.]

2. No less than three doctors arrived: Goodfellow, Millar and Matthews. Dr. Goodfellow wrote the report on Morgan's death. [The Goodfellow Diary – 1882. Arizona State Historical Society.]

3. Although recovering satisfactorily from his wounds, Virgil was still weak but emphatically insisted on going to Morgan. Some friends carried him to the pool hall.

4. *Tombstone Epitaph*, "The Deadly Bullet," March 20, 1882.

5. Stories that Louisa was visiting friends in a town some miles distant and did not return to Tombstone until the following day are false. She was in her room at the hotel and rushed to be with Morgan. This story probably originated because the *Epitaph* neglected to mention her as being present.

6. Louisa remarried in California to a Gustav H. Peters on December 31, 1884. She died of edema (dropsy) on June 12, 1894, age 37. [California Public Records, Sacramento. Also confirmed in an email message to the author from one of Louisa's Wisconsin relatives researching her story.]

7. Stories that Mattie departed for Colton with Virgil, Allie and Louisa are products of fiction. Her departure with James, Bessie and Hattie is on record. [*Tombstone Epitaph*, March 25, 1882.]
8. An excellent book is available on the vengeance taken against the Clanton gang by Wyatt Earp and his friends. [Boyer, G.G., *Tombstone Vendetta*.]

CHAPTER 22 ❖ The Road to Pinal

1. *Tombstone Epitaph*, March 25, 1882.
2. James and Bessie settled in California. Bessie died in 1887, age 44. James died, age 84, in 1926. [State Records. Sacramento] There is no record of Hattie's ultimate fate.
3. Wyatt attracted shrewish women. Josephine possessed no little abundance of shrewishness herself. The forty years that Josephine and Wyatt shared were often tumultuous, an almost even split between bliss and blitz. Their romance would not likely inspire a latter-day Shakespeare or Keats to write a play or compose an ode to this unlikely pair.
4. Boyer, Glen G. *I Married Wyatt Earp*, p239.
5. Some believe Mattie went back to Tombstone but there is no basis in fact for this assumption. Nothing shows Mattie resumed residence there. Because she was so well known, the return of Wyatt Earp's wife would have been news. One of the two papers, probably both, would certainly have noted her return. Neither mentions her after March 25, 1882.
6. When Kate was almost 90 she told an interviewer (Dr. A.W. Bork) she had managed a hotel when she lived in Globe. It was a hotel in name only. [Appendix 2: The St. Elmo Connection.]
7. The route held other perils as well. The Phoenix–Globe coaches averaged three hold-ups each month. [Globe Historical Society]
8. Boyer, G.G.: *Suppressed Murder of Wyatt Earp*, p45.
9. Wyatt's return to Arizona as early as 1886 was a calculated risk. Ike Clanton had sworn out a warrant charging Wyatt with murder following the gunfight in Tombstone. The warrant would still have been valid.
10. The Gilchriese research pertaining to Mattie Blaylock is often flawed and, therefore, is subject to doubt. He never learned her real name and throughout his writings consistently calls her Matilda. [Author's files]
11. Josephine confirmed she and Wyatt had been in Globe when she told her biographer, Mabel Earp Cason, that Wyatt had chanced upon John Behan on Broad Street. According to Josephine, Wyatt without so much as a word knocked his old enemy out with one punch. The encounter cannot be verified. Behan laid no charges, but even without a formal charge the incident would have warranted mention in the press had a reporter gotten wind of it. Josephine is known to have exaggerated Wyatt's penchant for vengeance but, had Wyatt encountered Behan, he may well have done some such thing. Josephine's story may be fanciful or exaggerated, but should not be discounted out of hand. [Cason Manuscript]

12. Kate eventually took Holliday to her brother Alexander's farm hoping to nurse him back to health. Despite her good efforts she had no success. [Tanner, Karen Holliday. *Doc Holliday: A Family Portrait*, pp 216–222.]
13. Kate spent all of it looking after Doc, as he was so ill he could not work much or even gamble with much success. Before she joined him he had temporary work guarding a mining claim and he also dealt faro for a while at Leadville, but she convinced him to go to her brother's home. From there it was all downhill. (Tanner, Karen Holliday. *Doc Holliday: A Family Portrait*, pp 216–222.]

CHAPTER 23 ❖ **End of the Road**
1. The Silver King resumed production — of copper — in 1912 and a settlement built up around it. Shortly after, its owners closed it forever when their smaller mine, named Silver Queen, began to out produce it. Silver King and some of its buildings still remain, but visitors to the site must first receive permission from its owners, as it is a restricted area.
2. During Pinal's best years no less than forty saloons and dance halls, all operating on a "we never close" basis, flourished. By 1887 only two saloons, and no dance halls, remained. [Arizona Historical Society, Tucson. Pinal file.]
3. Pinal County Record, July 12, 1886.
4. During the early years a camp called Silver King was established near the mine. With a population of about 250 it had three stores, two hotels and several saloons. Eventually, its population relocated in Pinal. [University of Arizona, *Books of the Old West*, p28.]
5. In 1890 the post office closed and the ten people remaining departed, leaving Pinal to the desert. By 1901 the entire town had completely disappeared. Buildings were demolished and the material removed for use in Superior. Eventually not even foundations remained as the desert reclaimed the entire area, including the wheel-rutted main street. [Arizona Historical Society, Pinal file.]
6. Gabriel had held the office continuously from 1878–1882 and again from 1884–1886. He almost did not live long enough to begin the 1888–90 term. In a gunfight at Florence on May 31 he received three bullet wounds, one near fatal. Joe Phy, who had been Gabriel's deputy in 1866, held a grudge against Gabriel who had fired him for drinking on the job. More recently Gabriel had arrested him for felonious assault. Phy ran for sheriff in the March election and resented losing to Gabriel. Drunk and nursing his on-going grudge, Phy cornered Gabriel in the Tunnel Saloon. In the ensuing gunfight eleven shots were fired. Three hit the sheriff, one very near the heart. Phy was hit four times and died in the street. Gabriel was exonerated at the inquest by reason of self-defense. Thanks to his rugged constitution he was back on the job within three weeks and lived until 1898. [ASHS, Pinal file.]

7. Some of those friends have descendants still living in the Superior area. They know stories of Mattie's days in Pinal. They tend to be protective of her memory, but will share their knowledge. It is a matter of finding the right people and asking the right questions.

8. Mabel Earp Cason, a relative of Wyatt, agreed to write Josephine's memoirs, but gave it up when she realized Josephine was hiding facts important to the project. Particularly vexing was Josephine's reluctance to talk about the events in Tombstone. Her refusal to be forthright was the reason Mrs. Cason resigned as Josephine's biographer. Her work to the point where she quit is known as the Cason Manuscript and gives authentic details of Wyatt's life and times. This writer, having read the manuscript, can vouch for its authenticity.

9. There must have been sufficient conviction in Josephine's voice to convince Mrs. Cason of her sincerity. Mrs. Cason had little faith in Josephine's avowals, having long before determined that few of her revelations were completely truthful. In this instance however, Cason wrote in a letter, she detected sincerity and a sense of genuine guilt in Josephine's admission. Josephine had in effect admitted to her biographer that she was to blame for Wyatt's desertion of Mattie. [Cason Manuscript file. Tucson, Arizona.]

10. *Arizona Enterprise*, Globe, Arizona, 1883–88, various issues. ASHS, Tucson.

CHAPTER 24 ❖ **Final Curtain**

1. Frank Beeler left Pinal in 1888 to disappear into the silence of time. Where he went no one knows, for he was not heard from again. There is, however, in a cemetery near Los Angeles the grave of a man named Frank J. Beeler. The gravestone indicates he was born in 1823 and died in 1903. Aside from the dates and name, no other data is given. The Frank Beeler who befriended Mattie was aged 65 so he would have been born in 1823.

2. The following narrative is taken from testimony given at the inquest into Mattie's death. [Appendix 1: Coroner's Inquest Report.]

3. If Globe had a resident dentist he did not advertise. It is more likely a Phoenix dentist visited to set up temporary services from time to time.

4. Toothache remedies were many and varied. Rose attar, salt, soda, cayenne, tarragon and crushed cloves were used, alone or in varying combinations, as poultices or rinses. Even the ineffective bloodletting was still used in some areas. Opium gave relief. Oil of cloves became popular during the last half of the nineteenth century. Its popularity has extended to the present. Mattie would have used one or all of these remedies. [Various drug compendiums.]

5. The situation regarding Mattie's teeth is common knowledge in the Superior area. [Conversations with M. Gonzales and others, 2004.]

6. Beeler's testimony at the inquest shows he was incapable of estimating time. He thought he left Mattie before noon to go to work. It was closer to 1:00 p.m. He was unsure of when he returned from the saloon to fall asleep in her spare room. He testified he thought Tom Flannery arrived as he was leaving for work. Flannery actually arrived between 7:45 and 8:00 p.m. Beeler was also befuddled about the time he returned to find the doctor there. He thought it was "four or five o'clock." The doctor actually arrived about 8:30 p.m. [Appendix 1: Coroner's Inquest Report.]

CHAPTER 25 ❖ "We, the Jury, find…"

1. There was never serious thought given to the possibility of the death being a homicide. However, two questions asked of Frank Beeler suggest Coroner Burson may have considered the possibility of negligence by Beeler in the administration of the laudanum. Beeler adamantly insisted he had counted out exactly fifteen drops into Mattie's cup despite her request for twenty. He admitted adding a small amount of whiskey that was dictated by Mattie. The coroner was obviously satisfied, as the line of questioning was not further pursued. [Appendix 1: Coroner's Inquest Report.]

2. The family faithfully tended the grave from that time forward. When the parents grew old their children accepted the task. Today a young member of the family continues in the role. To the family she has become "Our Mattie" and they defend her memory carefully. [Author's note]

3. *Arizona Enterprise*, County Events Column, July 7, 1888. Arizona Historical Society.

EPILOGUE

1. The late Mabel Earp Cason of Whitmore, California had been sought out by Josephine to write her memoirs. Mrs. Cason agreed and worked diligently, but quit when she realized Josephine was withholding pertinent data, especially about Tombstone. Josephine finally admitted to Mrs. Cason that Wyatt had lived with a woman named Mattie "for 10 or 12 years" but that Mattie had died. [Boyer, Glenn, *Suppressed Murder of Wyatt Earp*, appendix 3, p79.]

2. The yacht was owned by Elias J. "Lucky" Baldwin, a financial adventurer and longtime friend and occasional business associate of Wyatt Earp.

3. Waters inserted Mattie into his book, *The Earp Brothers of Tombstone*, just before it published. This occurred some years after Allie's death. Mattie had, by then, been revealed, but her part in the book is an obvious add-in to the original manuscript known to Allie. [Author's files]

4. The inscription smacks of levity. It reads: To Wyatt S. Earp. As a slight recognition of his many Christian virtues, and steady following in the footsteps of the meek and lowly Jesus. (Signed) Sutton & Colburn. [Boyer, Glenn. *Suppressed Murder of Wyatt Earp*. Photo section between page

271

xxiv and page 1.] The bible is in the possession of the ASHS, Tucson.

5. Merritt Beeson was the son of Chalk Beeson, one of Wyatt's closest Dodge City friends.
6. Marquis died before the research was completed, so he never knew the outcome of his revelations.
7. Virginia "Ginnie" Edwards (b.1880) died in 1935. Adelia Earp Edwards (b.1861) died in 1941.
8. A letter containing such claims, dated in 1967, is in the Boyer collection. [Read by author courtesy of Mr. Boyer in October 2002.]
9. Boyer, Glenn. *Suppressed Murder of Wyatt Earp*, pp 21–4 & 41–3.

POSTSCRIPT

1. The coyotes are the least of the perils. These animals are shy and fearful of humans. Odds are better than 100–1 that a coyote would ever attack as, unlike wolves, they are not pack animals. Still, wild creatures can be unpredictable, so caution is advised.
2. The second marker was secured firmly by chaining it to a railroad tie. The thief simply cut the chain, indicating he had arrived with bolt cutters in hand.

APPENDIX 1 ❖ Coroner's Inquest Report

1. Original document on file at Arizona Historical Society, Tucson, Arizona.
2. Copied from original document including spelling and grammatical errors.

APPENDIX 2 ❖ The St. Elmo Connection

1. This explains why she had seemingly disappeared completely. Researchers and historians had been looking for Kate Elder, Kate Holliday or Kate Fisher and had no knowledge of her having married George Cummings in the interim.
2. Kate became a widow in 1915 when Cummings committed suicide.
3. Kate's choice of words is interesting. One does not buy a lease. Lease means rent. Buy means purchase. Kate's "purchase" was likely the buying of a share in the "hotel." [Author's interpretation]
4. Nineteenth century dictionaries defined hotel as "noun; a large or superior inn." Hotel was also a colloquial euphemism for a brothel. The single bond between the two was that both were buildings with bedrooms. Legitimate hotels were required to be registered and licensed. Houses of ill fame, being illegal, were not encumbered by such documents. Kate's "hotel" falls into the latter category.
5. It was of course a hotel when Globe's Freemasons held meetings there pending construction of their permanent temple. [Globe Historical Society]

6. Five hundred dollars in 1882 was equivalent to almost $8500 in today's value. Kate, who had done very well financially during the years between 1877 and 1881, would not have been hard-pressed to line up such an amount.

Appendix 3 ❖ A Question of Identity

1. Careful search of police files, US Census and Illinois records unearthed nobody named Sarah Earp, in any capacity or social strata, living in Illinois from 1870 to 1876. Neither does Sarah Earp appear within any regional census lists or directories. Sarah Earp simply did not exist beyond being an alias for Mattie.
2. The theorist, as did others, probably drew his information from a book written by Ed Bartholomew. In the book, *Wyatt Earp: The Untold Story*, Bartholomew originated the notion that Mattie and Wyatt had met in Dodge City about 1877. Where he got that idea is not known, as he provided no references for his suggestion.
3. Although unsubstantiated, there is a belief among some Peoria historians that Sarah Haspel eventually left Peoria for Chicago, where she "married" a professional prizefighter. No records in Chicago are available to support this, so it remains another supposition.

Appendix 4 ❖ Madam of Mystery

1. Bartholomew, Ed. *Wyatt Earp: The Untold Story*, pp 94–98.
2. Bartholomew, Ed. *Wyatt Earp: The Untold Story*, p96.
3. Wrampe, Ann. *Wichita Township's Soiled Doves*, pp 6, 24–25.

Appendix 5 ❖ The Etiquette of Ignominy

1. Pearl Younger, daughter of Belle Starr, fits this category. Following an interval as a soiled dove and madam, she married an elderly rancher and lived into old age. Pearl Hart, possibly the west's most inept stagecoach bandit, also falls into this grouping.
2. In large cities the district was sometimes called "the tenderloin," a term coined by an unknown reporter.
3. In 1878 Dodge City, Kansas, forty-eight recorded prostitutes worked Front Street. Those with police protection remained unrecorded and were never arrested. [KSHS files.]
4. "One-horse town" denoting a very small town is a sanitized version of the original term. Old westerners, a risqué lot, referred to a small settlement as a "one-whore town."
5. "Red light district" is an American term. Canada's Old West towns generally identified such areas by location or landmark. In Winnipeg the sporting area was referred to as "the Social Center." In Calgary it was the "Nose Creek area." In Saskatoon it was "The West Side." [Gray, James H. *Red Lights on the Prairies*.]

6. "From the wrong side of the tracks" suggests such a person is unsuited to respectable society. [*Brewer's Dictionary of Phrase & Fable*, p1169.]
7. Thomas J. "Bear River" Smith is credited with inventing the deadline. As city marshal in Abilene, Kansas (1870) he prohibited denizens of the sporting district from entry to the respectable part of town except during certain hours and on Sunday mornings. The street became more romanticized than effective. [KSHS]
8. Pearl Miller operated in Calgary's elite district of Mount Royal for years. She was never bothered. She eventually "got religion" and spent the remainder of her long life encouraging and helping sporting women escape to a better life. [Gray, James H. *Red Lights on the Prairies*, pp 140–174.]

   Chicago Joe, a Helena Montana madam, operated unhampered into the 1920s. Her clients were judges, politicians and state officials. [MHS]

   Mother Thankful Sears of Peoria ran her house in a residential area. She was rarely bothered. [Peoria Police Records]
9. "Keeper of a house of ill fame" was legalese denoting both owners and madams. Many madams were hired so the male owners could remain unknown.

BIBLIOGRAPHY

Bartholomew, Ed. 1963. *Wyatt Earp: 1848–1880. The Untold Story*. Toyahvale, TX: Frontier Book Co.

Boyer, Glenn. 1997. *Suppressed Murder of Wyatt Earp*.* NM: Historical Research Associates.

———. 1997. *I Married Wyatt Earp*.* Tucson, AZ: University of Arizona Press.

———. 1997. *Wyatt Earp: Facts* Vols.1–6.* NM: Historical Research Associates.

Chaput, Don. 1994. *The Earp Papers: In a Brother's Image*.* Encampment, WY: Affiliated Writers of America.

Cunningham, E. 1947. *Triggernometry: A Gallery of Western Gunfighters*. Caldwell, ID. Caxton Printers.

Gatto, Steve. 2002. *Johnny Ringo*.* Lansing, MI: Protar House.

Grainger, Byrd H. 1983. *Arizona's Names: X Marks the Place*. Tucson, AZ: Falconer Pub. Co.

Gray, James H. 1971. *Red Lights on the Prairies*.* Toronto, ON: Macmillan Publishing.

Jahns, Pat. 1957. *The Frontier World of Doc Holliday*. Lincoln, NE: University of Nebraska Press.

Lake, Stuart N. 1931. *Wyatt Earp, Frontier Marshal*.** NY: Houghton Mifflin Company.

Meyers, E.C. 2006. *Wild Canadian West*. Surrey, BC: Hancock House.

Miller, Nyle H. & Joseph W. Snell. 1963. *Why the West was Wild*.* Topeka, KS: Kansas State Historical Society.

Morgan, Lael. 1999. *Good time Girls of the Alaska-Yukon Gold Rush*. Vancouver, BC: Whitecap Books.

O'Connor, Richard. 1960. *Bat Masterson*. London: Four Square Books.

Peterson, Roger T. 1990. *Field Guide to Western Birds*. NY: Houghton Mifflin Company.

Tanner, Karen H. 1998. *Doc Holliday: A Family Portrait*.* Norman, OK: University of Oklahoma Press.

Tuller, Roger H. 2000. *Let No Guilty Man Escape*. Norman, OK: University of Oklahoma Press.

Turner, Alford E. 1980. *The Earps Talk*. College Station, TX: Creative Publishing Ltd.

Waters, Frank. 1960. *The Earp Brothers of Tombstone*. NY: Bramhall House.

———. 1946. *The Colorado*. New York: Rinehart & Company [Rivers of America series].

Wrampe, Ann. 1984. "Wichita Township Soiled Doves." Wichita Public Library local history series.

*   **Recommended reading.**

**   **While much of Frontier Marshal is highly fictionalized it should be read. It gives an accurate account of Wyatt Earp's courage.**

Newspapers and magazines:

Daily Nugget, Tombstone
Wichita Eagle. Kansas
Tombstone Epitaph. Arizona
Tombstone Daily Nugget. Arizona
Times. Dodge City, Kansas.
Ford County Globe. Kansas
Daily Transcript. Peoria, Illinois
Daily National Democrat. Peoria, Illinois
Fort Griffin Echo. Texas
Frontier Echo. Jackboro, Texas.
Black Hills Pioneer. Deadwood, South Dakota.
Arizona Enterprise. Globe. (1883–88)
Pinal County Record. (1885–86)
The Drill. Pinal, Arizona (1880–84)
Weekly Monitor. Fort Scott, Kansas.
True West. 1989–94. Various articles.
Wild West. 2001–2004.
Argosy. 1950–60. Various articles.**
True Magazine. 1955–1960. Various articles.**
Blue Book. 1950–1960. Various articles.**
Human Life. Vol. IV. January, 1907.**
                Vol. IV. April 1907. **

**   **Can be found in larger public libraries in "special collections" sections.**

Other sources, as noted individually, and:

Arizona State Historical Society (ASHS)
Bradley University, Peoria, Illinois
British Columbia Archives
Cason Manuscript (Courtesy of Boyer collection)
Globe Historical Society
Illinois State Vital Statistics (Marriages and Deaths)
Iowa State Historical Society (ISHS)
John Gilchriese collection Kansas State Historical Society (KSHS)
Montana Historical Society (MHS)
Peoria Historical Society
University of Illinois, Western Campus (UIWC)
www.cowtownswest.com
www.kancoll.org
www.westegg.com/inflation

INDEX

Also by E.C. (TED) MEYERS

• •

Totem Tales
Legends from
the Rainforest
E. C. (Ted) Meyers
ISBN 0-88839-468-3
5.5 x 8.5, sc
80 pages

Wild
Canadian
West
E. C. (Ted) Meyers
ISBN 0-88839-469-1
5.5 x 8.5, sc
208 pages

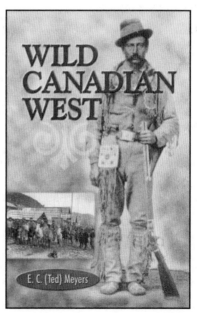

hancock
house

• •

View all HANCOCK HOUSE *titles at* www.hancockhouse.com

More **HANCOCK HOUSE** biography and history titles

Broken Arrow #1
John M. Clearwater
ISBN 978-0-88839-596-2
5.5 x 8.5 • sc • 160 pages

**Captain McNeill
and His Wife
the Nishga Chief**
Robin Percival Smith
ISBN 0-88839-472-1
5.5 x 8.5 • sc • 256 pages

Cold Lead
Mark Dugan
ISBN 0-88839-559-0
5.5 x 8.5 • sc • 176 pages

**Crazy Cooks &
Gold Miners**
Joyce Yardley
ISBN 0-88839-294-X
5.5 x 8.5 • sc • 224 pages

Deadman's Clothes
Dale Davidson
ISBN 0-88839-608-2
5.5 x 8.5 • sc • 144 pages

**Discovery at
Prudhoe Bay: Oil**
John M. Sweet
ISBN 978-0-88839-630-3
5.5 x 8.5 • sc • 304 pages

End of Custer
Dale Schoenberger
ISBN 0-88839-288-5
5.5 x 8.5 • sc • 336 pages

**Frontier Forts & Posts
of the Hudson's Bay
Company**
Kenneth E. Perry
ISBN 0-88839-598-1
8.5 x 11 • sc • 96 pages

Incredible Gang Ranch
Dale Alsager
ISBN 0-88839-211-7
5.5 x 8.5 • sc • 448 pages

Into the Savage Land
Ernest Sipes
ISBN 0-88839-562-0
5.5 x 8.5 • sc • 160 pages

Jailbirds & Stool Pigeons
Norman Davis
ISBN 0-88839-431-4
5.5 x 8.5 • sc • 144 pages

**Lewis & Clark Across
the Northwest**
Cheryll Halsey
ISBN 0-88839-560-4
5.5 x 8.5 • sc • 112 pages

Loggers of the BC Coast
Hans Knapp
ISBN 0-88839-588-4
5.5 x 8.5 • sc • 200 pages

Outposts & Bushplanes
Bruce Lamb
ISBN 0-88839-556-6
5.5 x 8.5 • sc • 208 pages

**Raven and the Moun-
taineer**
Monty Alford
ISBN 0-88839-542-6
5.5 x 8.5 • sc • 152 pages

Ruffles on my Longjohns
Isabel Edwards
ISBN 0-88839-102-1
5.5 x 8.5 • sc • 297 pages

**Songs of the Pacific
Northwest**
Philip J. Thomas
ISBN 978-0-88839-610-5
8.5 x 11 • sc • 208 pages

**Stagecoaches Across the
American West
1850-1920**
John A. Sells
ISBN 978-0-88839-605-1
8.5 x 11 • sc • 336 pages

**Timeless Trails of
the Yukon**
Dolores Cline Brown
ISBN 0-88839-584-5
5.5 x 8.5 • sc • 184 pages

Tomekichi Homma
K.T. Homma, C.G. Isaksson
ISBN 978-0-88839-660-0
5.5 x 8.5 • sc • 72 pages

Vancouver's Bravest
Alex Matches
ISBN 978-0-88839-615-0
8.5 x 11 • sc • 352 pages

**Walter Moberly and the
Northwest Passage
by Rail**
Daphne Sleigh
ISBN 0-88839-510-8
5.5 x 8.5 • sc • 272 pages

**White Water Skippers
of the North**
Nancy Warren Ferrell
ISBN 978-0-88839-616-7
5.5 x 8.5 • sc • 216 pages

Wild Roses
dutchie Rutledge-Mathison
ISBN 0-88839-625-2
8.5 x 11 • hc • 72 pages

Wild Trails, Wild Tales
Bernard McKay
ISBN 0-88839-395-4
5.5 x 8.5 • sc • 176 pages

Warplanes to Alaska
Blake W. Smith
ISBN 0-88839-401-2
8.5 x 11 • hc • 256 pages

**Wings Over the
Wilderness**
Blake W. Smith
ISBN 978-0-88839-595-7
8.5 x 11 • sc • 296 pages

Yukon Riverboat Days
Joyce Yardley
ISBN 0-88839-386-5
5.5 x 8.5 • sc • 176 pages

Yukoners: True Tales
H. Gordon-Cooper
ISBN 0-88839-232-X
5.5 x 8.5 • sc • 144 pages

hancock house

www.hancockhouse.com